PERFECT CITIES

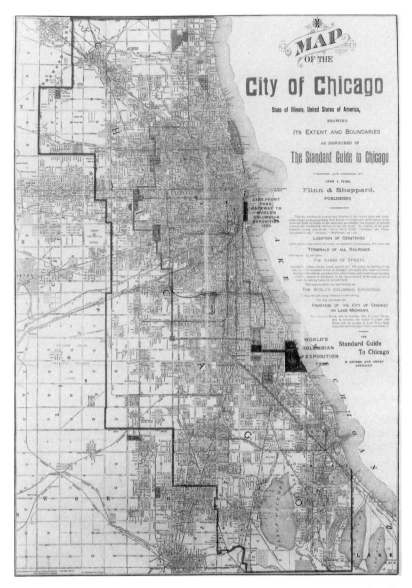

Chicago. The map of Chicago from almost any period is immediately distinguishable as a two-dimensional painting of geometric shapes upon geometric shapes abutting the gradual curve of Lake Michigan. (Rand McNally, 1893, Library of Congress)

JAMES GILBERT

PERFECT CITIES

Chicago's Utopias of 1893

THE UNIVERSITY OF CHICAGO PRESS / Chicago and London

JAMES GILBERT is professor of history at the University of Maryland.

The University of Chicago Press, Chicago 60637
The University of Chicago Press, Ltd., London

© 1991 by The University of Chicago
All rights reserved. Published 1991
Printed in the United States of America
00 99 98 97 96 95 94 93 92 91   5 4 3 2 1

Library of Congress Cataloging-in-Publication Data

Gilbert, James Burkhart.
    Perfect cities : Chicago's utopias of 1893 / James B. Gilbert.
        p. cm.
    Includes index.
    ISBN 0-226-29317-3
    1. Chicago (Ill.)—Popular culture—History—19th century.
    2. Chicago (Ill.)—Description—1875–1950. 3. Chicago (Ill.)—
    Social life and customs. 4. Utopias. I. Title.
    F545.G43 1991
977.3′11041—dc20   90-48235
                                                                    CIP

Contents

6

7

Illustrations

T HE SEATS THAT CARRIED the boy toward the city were hard, made of woven straw, the kind you work your fingertips into to pass the time. Everywhere there was grime, a silvery powder in the light and on the flecked dirty floor, but when you touched it, it turned your fingertips gray. The windows, especially, were wreathed in great smears of the dust, giving the impression of a hovering, dirty fog. Perhaps this, carried in the air, was what I smelled. Or it could have been the ozone sparking out from the electric overwires of the train.

This was how I traveled to Chicago as a young boy, coming in from an outlying town on the outskirts, on the prairie. For awhile, our house looked across to a tract of prairie—or what I imagined it to be—a slightly derelict-looking, vacant lot of tall grasses and abundant rabbits set in a patchwork of green lawns and coming construction. That, I imagine, is what the edge of Chicago has always looked like: a road that ends nowhere; a preposterous and arrogant expansion of streets hanging distantly onto a central grid (I lived about 200th Street South); a feeling of permanent transition, with the city seeping into the thick black soil, emerging from the water table. All of these were reminders of a faint link to the city, a map with ostentatious fringes laid flat on the land. Something possible for the future. I always said I came from Chicago, but actually I came from a suburb just beyond Chicago's southeast edge.

Riding into the city on the Illinois Central, peering at the old green sign with the stenciled letters "888 miles to New Orleans" at our train station, was to a young boy's imagination a voyage into the future, into the possibilities of adulthood, into antic- ipation of more immediate excitement, of making connections with the real, and for me exotic, world. (As if to emphasize the contrast, our tiny town center was constructed to look like an English village: safe, serene, and far from the city.)

Of course, I was not the only one who made this trip. My father took the train daily to his law office on LaSalle Street. My mother went every Friday, it seemed, to Marshall Field's for lunch in the Walnut Room or to hear the symphony at Orchestra Hall. This pattern of my going into the city persisted at least until the town of Park Forest sprang up not far from us on an old golf course and filled up with William Whyte's organization men and women and their shopping centers and parking lots. Or was it, perhaps, that my adolescence just accidentally coincided with the destruction of old habits and the demise of an old-fashioned city, with the rise of sub- urbia as a way of life? In any case, that was when I stopped going downtown.

To a young boy of seven or eight, peering out at the emerging city as we slowly passed through the stations and reached, finally, the large downtown streets of the presidents, there were three high points. One was Pullman, visible and puzzling through the grimy windows, with its dark red-brick clock tower. I knew about and had slept on thickly starched sheets in rolling Pullman cars on overnight trips, but the area meant little to me other than a name. Next came the museums—the Field Museum and the Museum of Science and Industry, with their magical enticing wonders. And, finally, the sud- den glimpse of the city that emerged when we rounded a bend in the tracks, swelling, it seemed, out of the lake, or perhaps dropped down from some dizzy height onto the horizon. The mysterious, distant bluish city of skyscrapers. Did I really observe this from the train? Is this a compound of all of my entries and visions and imaginations— of everyone's—entering the city? Is this what Chicago really looked like?

Emerging out of the Randolph Street Station buried under the streets, my most vivid memory is a passageway of smells—a popcorn stand, a florist, and then the acrid odor of pollution—exhaled by the city in motion. Then came the confusing streets, with theaters whose illuminations, in the shadowy skyscraper daylight, colored the dark streets. Or the blinding, bright sunshine of Michigan Avenue if I turned the corner in the other direction. There are also my memories of an immense department store like Marshall Field's. These begin with the discreet plunk of paging bells, then the utter confusion and embarrassments of the smells and sounds from the ground floor notions and make-up counters, and the somber, wood-clad refuge of the men's store. And last, there is a distant memory of my father's law office, of his books and black leather chairs and sofas. And, on one occasion, lunch at the Attic Club.

But most of all, I remember the Railroad Fair located at Burnham Park on the lakefront. This curious, dated, somehow incongruous exhibit in the summer of 1948 was, and is, for me a centerpiece of my recollection of the city. I went again and again, perhaps because it was, literally, an imaginary continuation of my trip into Chicago and beyond, and a dream of a permanent journey away from childhood and home. Perhaps it was because I too, like the designers of the unfortunate fair, could not help looking backward to a time when trains symbolized excitement, movement, and, of course, my Chicago. But what a pathetic, small, anticlimax of a fair it was, with its dusty Indian Villages, its reconstructed French Quarter from New Orleans, West Coast vacation "wonderlands," its ultra-modern Pullman cars, Elsie the cow (because she traveled by rail), and its show, "Wheels A'Rollin'." This pageant, fair brochures proudly proclaimed, was the most spectacular outdoor performance since the world's fairs of New York and Chicago in the 1930s. It celebrated an American history that unfolded along an ever-expanding horizon of iron rails. Each tableau ended with trains crossing the stage to fill the backdrop of Lake Michigan.[1]

"Small boys ought to be taken," said a woman to the *Chicago Tribune* during that summer. And so I was. But this artificial fair possessed none of the glitter of the jewel of the Columbian Exposition or even the 1933 Century of Progress. Nor was Chicago, despite appearances in the early 1950s, as grand as it seemed from my diminutive perspective. What I idealized was, although I didn't know it, passing quickly away. There is undoubtedly some irony in attending a fair that proclaimed its parentage among the great celebrations of the past but which, in a sense, was really trapped by the past; it celebrated the city for what it had been. If this was appropriate for me, perhaps it was the first glimmer of the historian's vision, which is to be as enthusiastic about, even to confuse, the past with the present and the future. This habit of mind must have been an instinct.

I hadn't thought of these things for years until midway through the research for this book when I suddenly recognized that the elements of my interest corresponded to certain very vivid clusters in my memory of trips to Chicago. This is fortunate in a way. Not because it allows me to confess that writing history always dips into autobiography, but because what I remember of Chicago is a shadow, a suggestion, an echo of what had been created in the 1890s and still remained during my childhood. Those things I remember are, or were (since many are now gone), imbedded as shards in a past that, like a great mound of silt, gradually accumulates, covers, and hides that amazing period.

And, of course, there are unanswered questions that occur to me. Did my father ever know the founder of his law firm, John P. Wilson, who was counsel to the Chicago World's Fair and an intimate of the major figures in this book? What was the other Chicago like, the North Shore world, where the great founding families of the city had retreated in the twentieth century and where I once paid a visit, wide-eyed, to a huge house commanding a bluff over Lake Michigan? Why did my father hide us from this? Did we live on the South Side of the city to be close to deep family ties in Southern Illinois, or to avoid Chicago's aristocracy?

One last memory—about the act of remembering. Around the time my family purchased a television set, I recognized a familiar face on the evening Chicago news. A man was parading with a sign in front of Louis Sullivan's Garrick Theater, scheduled, as I learned, for demolition. It was Hugh Duncan, a neighbor, a secretive, mysterious sort of person (to a boy), who had scattered cornices and capitals and old terra cotta pieces from wrecked Louis Sullivan buildings around the unmowed grass of his front yard.

I don't recall what I thought then of this event, except that the impression of seeing it is still strong. Now, of course, I know that he was one of a small but continuing band of Chicagoans dedicated to saving the visible memories of the city in its heyday. Of course, not all memories have been preserved in this collective effort, for there

Wheels A'Rollin' Pageant at the 1949 Chicago Railroad Fair. The reenactment of railroad history (in this case the meeting at Promontory Point) played against the lake backdrop and was a constant reminder of Chicago's central role in this story. (Photo by Dr. Frank E. Rice, Chicago Historical Society)

are and were many, many Chicagos that had nothing to do with this outdoor museum of architecture that Duncan loved. But it was a part of Chicago, at least, that was coming into existence during the moment that I have chosen to explore in this book. For such acts, any historian and lover of the city must be grateful.

There are many people to whom I owe a debt in writing this book. The Woodrow Wilson Center provided nine months of support and colleagues who graciously and patiently heard me spin out the results of my research. I am particularly indebted to Barbara Lanz, Victoria Abado, Charles Neu, John Gillis, Larry Moore, and

Michael Lacey. I am especially grateful to my research assistant, Michael Gelb, for his enthusiasm and ingenuity. The University of Maryland provided funds for research trips to New Haven and Chicago. There, I met nothing but pleasant support and aid from the library at the Yale Divinity School and, in Chicago, at the Moody Bible Institute, the Chicago Public Library, the Newberry Library, the Chicago Historical Society, the Pullman Historical Association, the Harvey Public Library, and the Thornton Township Historical Society. Professor Listen Leydendecker helped me contact Mr. Phillip Miller who very kindly gave me permission to look at the papers of Harriet Sanger Pullman.

My colleagues in Washington and elsewhere also have provided insights and support. I am especially grateful to David Nassaw, Ruth Jordan, John Judis, Jack Wilson, Donald Scott, Roy Rosenzweig, Dan Bluestone, Peter Kuznick, Nelson Lichtenstein, Jackson Lears, Michael Kazin, James Banner, John Greven, Miles Bradbury, Ed Lurie, and Harold Livesay. The Hagley Museum in Delaware invited me to present an early version of this work as did the University of Maryland Conference on modern religion. Friends in Australia where I spent four months on a Fulbright listened to my ideas on Chicago and proved that historians everywhere tend to be the same: intelligent, critical, and gracious. I particularly want to thank Shane White, David Goodman, Richard Waterhouse, Neville Meaney, and Graham White. Doug Mitchell of the University of Chicago has been a good friend, critic, and editor throughout. Finally, I am indebted to the close and imaginative reading of my manuscript by Robert Wiebe and Michael Ebner.

One

ITINERARIES

T HE YEAR 1893 was a time of immense and lasting change. The precarious economic boom of the previous years tripped into a deep depression. Unemployment, strikes, business collapse, and political realignment changed America profoundly. From the tangled roots of economic misfortune and social struggle emerged the beginnings of Progressivism (or modern liberalism) and the foundations of the corporate restructuring of the American economy. Sometime around this date, the Victorian moral economy and polity gave way to the brusque assault of the modern world.

In the history of the imagination, 1893 was also a remarkable time, and nowhere more so than in Chicago. That year perhaps a tenth of the American population packed its bags and caught the train for a pilgrimage to two Chicagos: the shining white city of the World's Columbian Exposition on Lake Michigan, and the smoky gray city which hosted it. Their voyage made this the most significant tourist event in American history at a point when tourism itself was only a recent possibility for many people, and still an improbability for most.

The background of this occasion had a dramatic history. Three years earlier, Chicago business leaders had wrested the quadricentennial celebration of Columbus's first voyage to the New World away from New York City. Create for us a commemorative festival of America, the United States Congress had demanded, and the architects responded with plans that fulfilled their own private dreams of an ideal city and an ideal-

1

ized Chicago. Invoking the approval of history, and the authority of civilization and culture, the builders immodestly proposed to sum up all of human progress in their monuments and displays and their ecumenical conferences on the state of human knowledge. What they accomplished was a good deal less than this but, nonetheless, enormously fascinating.

The choice of Chicago to represent the ideal American city was viewed by New Yorker and European skeptics as preposterous. How could a city with so little history, with no firm foundation of time nor mortar of tradition beneath the structures of its toplofty skyscrapers and commercial establishments, claim to speak for civilization? And how could a city that boasted having the most cosmopolitan population in America pretend to be American at all? But in a curious way, that was the point. Chicago was the quintessential American city because it was unique—the newest and the most foreign. In the lexicon of nineteenth-century imagination, that made it the most representative of modern urban places: to many Americans, urban was synonymous with strange.

Despite its magnitude and importance during that eventful summer in Chicago, the World's Columbian Exposition at Jackson Park was only one site among many where visitors could encounter a specially planned, regulated, and carefully designed urban environment. Thousands made side trips to the famous company town and works at nearby Pullman, just a few miles south of the Fairgrounds, where the railway cars that conveyed them in splendor to the city were assembled. Many more explored skyscrapers and department stores. Almost a tenth of the tourist population entered tents or theaters to hear Dwight Moody describe his strategy to loosen an evangelical whirlwind in the city. Chicago's parks and wealthy avenues attracted others. The city itself, or rather selected parts of it, became stopping points along an extended itinerary of monuments to various experiments in planning for a perfect city.

It is my intention in this book to explore, something in the manner of a historical tourist, parts of Chicago visited by millions of Americans during 1893. I do so with two qualifications. Like the middle-class visitors to the city in the 1890s, I will not venture into the vast city of the men and women and children who actually built this urban environment and who remained behind once the Fair was destroyed in the conflagration of 1894. This is not a book about work or workers but rather about leisure and especially about the imagination. And imagination, in the late nineteenth century, labored diligently to deny much of the reality of Chicago or, at least, place it within special confines. Furthermore, I realize that in translating the literary and visual evidence of this period into contemporary language, I am perpetrating a certain distortion. I am sure, however, that my subjects would recognize this as analogous to their own efforts to describe and circumscribe the city. For they were engaged in reorienting their vision of society in a way that made everything that had gone before fair game for imitation and quotation. The plasticity of their vision even extended into the future, which they hoped to fashion in their own image.

If, as I have suggested, the tourist environments of Chicago in 1893 were not intended for all Americans (just as many zones were to be avoided), who were the objects of this attention and planning? Who was the audience? Why were these idealized patterns of urban life so narrow and exclusive? What problem motivated so many men and women to speculate upon the ideal arrangement of the city? The answers can be suggested by examining the elites who designed these environments and the burgeoning middle-class groups who were their clientele. The problem both groups confronted was, in simplest terms, diversity and cultural confusion—just as Henry Adams, in his complicated way, suggested it was in his autobiography. How, in the new urban environment, could middle-class and elite Chicagoans comprehend the kaleidoscopic changes in behavior and culture that colored everything they saw around them? As the visible clutch of tradition was replaced by the invisible hand of the marketplace, how could elite and middle-class Americans—all believers in morality, traditions, and propriety—control this environment, yet find space to participate in what was so obviously new and exciting? What was their relationship to commercial popular culture? For the visitor to Chicago in 1893, the specially fabricated environments of the city are about having urban culture both ways—about becoming a spectator in both worlds. For the men who designed these environments, it was a brilliant effort, even if ultimately flawed, to impose a grandiose but limiting format upon the multiplying diverse cultures in the city.

To inquire about the ambiguous position of the middle class toward emerging city cultures in the nineteenth century means relinquishing an old and unhelpful cliché, which is that middle-class Americans have contributed little else to popular culture than censorship boards and sneering disapproval. The full story must include these testimonials to intolerance, but, of course, there is much more. The middle classes of Chicago, and elsewhere in America, participated in and helped to create modern popular culture. Naturally, they tried to do so on their own terms. An exploration of some of these terms is the subject of this book.

Without some limitations, this could be an enormous undertaking. But because the subject of my book is concerned with the project of imagining a total urban environment, I will not explore some specific institutions such as department stores, parks, or other such limited places. They are important, but they will not reveal the story in the way I intend to relate it. Instead, I will concentrate on four total urban environments: the imagined city of the guidebook literature to Chicago and the Fair in the 1890s, the World's Fair itself, the paternalistic experiment at Pullman, and the World's Fair campaign by Dwight Moody with the evangelical city founded by his benefactor Turlington W. Harvey.

In this book I have used a number of words that require definition here. I will confine my discussion of these first principles to the section that follows in hopes that the reader will remember something of my position on these very difficult and complex propositions and so as not to complicate the story of the four Chicagos that I plan to visit.

The first of these is a controversial but necessary term: the *middle class*, the central actors of this unfolding drama. They were the audience, the group in whose name much of the cultural reform of the city was undertaken. In very general terms, I use "middle class" to designate a large and growing group of nonmanual workers, businessmen, and professionals attached to the expanding service, retail, professional, and entertainment portions of the economy. In 1893, this group could be considered the second "new" middle class on a historical continuum that runs from the early nineteenth century to the present. Curiously, wherever one freezes the action in this history seems to produce an image of both change and continuity; in other words, an emerging middle class. That is perhaps one of the most obvious defining characteristics of this group.

Historians have thus far identified three distinctive periods in the development of this group: a formative period, a new middle-class era, and a modern (contemporary) middle class. In some respects, these periods are not only distinct but also continuous. In the early era the middle class began to form in the Eastern United States. Between the 1830s and the 1860s, owners and operators of small factories and retail establishments and shopkeepers and artisans and farmers developed an awareness of their special position in society. They invested considerable energy in newly intense and self-conscious family structures. This new family structure aggressively took upon itself a wide variety of social tasks and responsibilities, among the most important of which was its self-perpetuation. Besides family, evangelical religions and reform also played an important role in defining middle-class life-styles, particularly in the Northeast and upstate New York, from which many of the first two generations of Chicagoans emigrated.[1]

While middle-class self-awareness expressed itself in family and religious institutions in this early period, more secular voluntary associations gradually began to soak up middle-class energies from the 1830s onward. From the beginning, these institutions displayed the social and moral aspirations of their members in terms of an ascetic, religious view of the world. Eventually, these associations began to change, to segment and to divide, reflecting new divisions in the middle class itself. Between 1850 and 1880 a host of new organizations grew up, embodying the ambitions for a new civic culture based upon such institutions as the Lyceum, the YMCA, the Sabbatarian movements, and, of course, prohibition.

Although these middle-class organizations announced a universal public spirit and disinterested social purposes—a generalized American identity even—there grew up alongside them after the Civil War specialized associations preoccupied with protecting and expanding professions. The general result, by the turn of the century, was fragmentation and specialization and a revised middle-class self-awareness and culture predicated on universal standards and exclusive organization.[2]

Robert Wiebe, in his remarkably durable *The Search for Order*, identified two interrelated changes in the late nineteenth century. The first was the rise of the new middle class, distinguished by new organizational skills developed to apply to new urban problems and opportunities. These vocational opportunities brought professionals into a wide variety of businesses and professions. The second was an accompanying reaction to cities which defined these rapidly changing environments in terms of disorder and uncontrolled change. Taken together, the rising status of experts and bureaucratic specialization in the context of a definition of the city as a frontier of strangers spelled out the dangers of modern society and the opportunities for experts and professionals to solve social problems.[3]

This new culture of professionalism was perhaps most distinct and obvious in the new universities that appeared in the latter part of the nineteenth century. But, in fact, expertise, specialization, and redefinitions of social and work relationships occurred on a very wide scale.[4] Even at the lower end of this new middle class, the growth of new forms of white-collar work inside government bureaucracies and businesses called for different forms of behavior from men and women who became salespeople, clerks, and typists.[5]

Perhaps inevitably, such widespread shifts resulted in new forms of class awareness as distinctions between white-collar and blue-collar work and life-styles emerged more strongly. By the end of the nineteenth century, in terms of work, family organization, ideology, and consumption patterns, a distinct and growing middle-class life was readily apparent.[6]

Two characteristics of this history of the new middle class strongly impinge upon the story of Chicago in 1893. There were substantial continuities from the formative period, when strong religious commitments and familial traits prevailed. Identity then was defined in a layered sense of belonging that radiated outward from the individual to the family to society, and emphasized security and stability. This fit handsomely—the small-scale enterprise and localism of American cities in the early nineteenth century—but it also remained an expectation for many of the cultural reformers of 1893. Young men who grew up in the 1830s and 1840s and who rose to the leadership of Chicago society often retained the aspirations of their childhood experience.

The second point is that this initial structure was almost immediately challenged when new sorts of groups entered the middle
class and new environments became their habitats.[7] However one
defines it, at the turn of the century this new middle class included
a far more heterogeneous group of Americans than its predecessor.
It was far larger. At its lower end, white-collar workers were often
stuck in low-paying jobs with no apparent mobility—especially in
the case of women. And it occupied a relatively more important
place in the newly emerging industrial cities of the East and Midwest. But while its members were inventing new vocations and acting in different ways, they did not entirely cast off older notions of
behavior, propriety, and culture—thus the troubled, even divided
consciousness of self at the turn of the century.[8]

In the Chicago of the 1890s, a great many men and women
entered the middle class through the doors of new professions and
careers, but many entered a room that they still hoped to furnish
with old, familiar objects, with the knickknacks of Victorian morality and propriety. That is why the commercial culture of the city—
its theaters, dance halls, and saloons—seemed to be a particular
threat to traditional notions of respectable culture. These institutions of public resort contradicted the values of evangelical culture.
And respectable culture may well have been one of the critical
marks of middle-class self-awareness. Urban popular culture appeared to emerge from the strange and subtle customs of immigrants or working men and women or somehow, simply, to be conjured up by the urban environment itself. Theodore Dreiser, who
began his literary career as a reporter in the early 1890s in Chicago,
expressed this confusion perfectly in his novel *Jennie Gerhardt*.
Writing about the impact of modern means of communication and
transport, he described one of his characters: "Lester Kane was the
natural product of these untoward conditions. His was a naturally
observing mind, Rabelaisian in its strength and tendencies, but confused by the multiplicity of things, the vastness of the panorama of
life, the glitter of its details, the unsubstantial nature of its forms, the
uncertainty of their justification."[9]

This is not a new response to the city, as the long history of
urban guidebooks, advice books, and self-help organizations suggests.[10] Horatio Alger's boy heroes faced a similar bewilderment,

and his dual guidebooks about New York (around the city and up the social ladder) emphasize and neutralize the strangeness of urban culture to aspiring rural youths who were an important element of the American population moving into the cities in the late nineteenth century.

So the new middle classes constituted a vast, sharply aware audience for whom the city was an abode but not quite a home. They, as much as the foreign immigrants who crowded its tenements, were its newcomers; they, too, were the creators of the modern city. What they achieved in this new environment is testimony to their importance and to the revolutionary potential of the new instruments of culture that were arising around them.

The years from 1870 to 1900, and within this time from 1880 to 1890, witnessed a remarkable expansion of new middle-class occupations. In this period, the total number of workers in America more than doubled, from 12 million to 29 million. But there were striking differences in the rates of expansion within this large aggregate that reveal the importance of middle-class positions (see table below).

Broken down further, these broad totals reveal some significant changes, in particular in employment related to the expansion of modern communications and popular culture. The most spectacular growth occurred in three areas: salesmen and saleswomen,

Selected Changes in Occupation Growth, 1870–1900

Occupation	1870	1900	Increase (%)
Agricultural pursuits	5,900,000	10,300,00	174
Manufacturing and mechanical	2,677,000	7,085,000	264
Professional	371,000	1,258,000	339
Trades and transportation	1,224,000	4,766,000	383
Domestic and service	2,263,000	5,580,000	256

Source: United States Census, *Occupations at the 12th Census* [1900].[11]

commercial travelers, and actors and showmen. Steep rises in the number of journalists, artists, bookbinders, printers, hotel owners, musicians, photographers, and architects testify to the creation of a large infrastructure of urban commercial culture.

Furthermore, rapid increases in other forms of service industries related to retailing, banking, transport, and distribution of goods offered greatly expanded opportunities, particularly in major population centers, for men and women moving into these rapidly changing cities. At the same time, some of the older, traditional middle-class professions grew much more slowly. These include teachers (an exception was in college education), government workers, and ministers (see table below).[12]

There are also significant changes in the relationship of immigration to emerging patterns of work in the city. As might be expected, the national origins of the labor force differed dramatically within various occupations. The foreign-born were especially concentrated in manufacturing and low-level service industries,

Some Comparative Growth Rates in Professions, 1870–1900

Profession	Growth (%)
Salesmen and saleswomen	Over 1,000[a]
Commercial travelers	1,280
Actors and showmen	1,076
Architects	893
Bankers and brokers	690
Journalists	568
Hostlers	370
Teachers	353
Professionals (aggregate)	338
Ministers and other clergy	287
All workers	232
Government officials	213

[a] The census in 1870 combined clerks and salespeople; therefore, I have estimated this figure. It may, in fact, be far higher.

whereas native-born are clustered in the professions. This tendency is underscored by an exception—that only the British-born showed a substantial representation among those immigrants who did figure in these more traditional middle-class categories. Another conclusion that can be drawn from these figures is that cities, above all, were the centers of new manufacturing and middle-class positions. A higher percentage of both professional and manufacturing opportunities were concentrated in large cities. The city, as we will see shortly in a further description of Chicago, was becoming a particularly attractive place for both middle- and working-class workers. Inevitably, these groups shared city space in terms of work, housing, and recreation.[13] It should not be surprising, therefore, that questions about culture should be a major concern in the institution building of major cities such as Chicago in the late nineteenth century, and a primary consideration for those who tried to visualize the shape of emerging urban life.

Urban culture, in terms of the new professions and class mobility it extended, inevitably became a source of uneasiness as well as opportunity. Because it offered such visible and apparently easy social mobility, employment in the reproduction and sale of culture and information in the late nineteenth century attracted a significant percentage of aspiring men and women who were themselves foreign-born or came from families with immigrant parents. The cultural impact of such persons from immigrant stock was found, therefore, far beyond the confines of the saloon where they might readily be expected—and dismissed by middle-class urbanites. Instead, immigrants were also represented in large numbers among journalists, musicians, publishers, and hotel and amusement entrepreneurs.[14]

A second term I shall employ throughout the book is *elite*. During the latter half of the nineteenth century, this group emerged and sharply differentiated itself from the middle class to create and command the business and institutional life of the nation. Coming as most did from the common stock of basically Protestant, evangelical culture and sharing a similar geographic beginning point in New England, upstate New York, and the mid-Atlantic states, this group also experienced the rough mobility of American life. In fact, its experience was far more extreme than those who remained in the middle class. While they shared fundamental cultural practices and beliefs with members of the middle class, they also, quickly, invented differences, sometimes in the most extravagant fashion, for example, by building immense castles as houses, by importing the trappings of European high culture, and by creating a kind of social exclusivity that advertised itself as the reward of station.

This group was of but not in the middle class. While it maintained a similar outlook and shared certain common experiences and fundamental assumptions about religion and character, it was in the process of redefining itself in terms of its new power and accomplishments—by its success. As will be explained in Chapter 2, this impetus generated a group of men and women steeped in a common tradition with the middle class, but who turned this heritage to unique purposes.

Like the word *middle class*, the word *culture* has many meanings and connotations. In the very broadest sense, culture should be defined as the signs, symbols, language, institutions, and behaviors by which one defines oneself and communicates with others inside a given set of boundaries. In this general sense, society is frozen culture and culture is liquid society. But the concept of culture must be subdivided and modified to be applied. Just to list various uses of the word is to begin to glimpse the complexity of the idealized cities created for Chicago in 1893. In this period, we can speak of local (regional) culture, ethnic cultures, popular culture, mass culture, commercial culture, middle-class culture, and elite culture. Each of these modifications suggests that within a larger, shared culture there existed important distinctions, opposition, and potential conflicts. To define the boundaries of various subcultures and focus more precisely on specific groups narrows the definition of culture but makes certain of its functions clearer.

In this book I am particularly concerned with two fairly narrow definitions of culture: commercial culture and popular culture. Increasingly during the 1890s, these two notions can be said to refer to aspects of the same phenomenon. Popular culture in this period certainly included noncommercial and nonurban segments. And elite culture employed commercial formats. But the predominant growth of popular culture and commercial culture, and the substitution of one for the other, marks this as a revolutionary time. Underlying the whole process was the growing importance of new means of cultural production: changes in journalism, photographic reproduction, various forms of amusement centers and parks, theaters, department stores, music and dance halls that several classes and groups in the city frequented. These new commercial institutions made it possible not only to focus local attention on certain new trends and ideas; they began to lay the foundation for a national popular culture. And they ultimately changed the aesthetics—the theatrics—of American culture.

Defining popular culture in this way probably raises more questions than it settles. If this era experienced a long season of revolutionary changes in the means of producing and reproducing culture, it was almost inevitably also a time when controversies over commercial culture sharpened. To understand these disputes, we must ask several questions that also puzzled a generation of Chicagoans. What are the sources of popular culture? Can it be identified with any particular social or ethnic group? Does the identification of popular culture with the city mean that a great many Americans were correct to associate it with immigration and urbanity? Can any social or economic group self-consciously control the instruments and the ideas of popular culture, or is it the result of struggle and/or negotiation? Finally, how do groups that initially find popular culture threatening or immoral make their peace with it?

These are not easy questions to answer unambiguously. There certainly existed a struggle at this time over who should control cultural expression. Some groups in American cities clearly hoped to transform the culture of the new majority living there and revive an older cultural etiquette. Many of these reformers were Protestants who hoped that, in the process of Americanization, immigrants might be convinced to become prohibitionists, political conservatives, and consumers and practitioners of established proprieties. This ambition had a second slightly different version—that American-born men and women streaming into the cities might find there a replica of the social order they had left behind in small towns. Social gospel minister Washington Gladden discussed this problem brilliantly in his *Applied Christianity* in 1886. Describing the dramatic growth in popular entertainments, he formulated a question that went—and still goes—to the heart of the debate: "Does the Church leave the religious wants of the community to be provided for under the law of supply and demand?"[15] Gladden was right: the free market culture—commercial culture—was a critical issue, and he, like many others, hoped to sanitize it by injecting uplifting intellectual and moral content into the new institutions and forms of urban culture.

But just as clearly, there were some in American cities, even among its social elites, who were dissatisfied with this strategy of denomination and redirection. They recognized the vitality of the various forms of popular culture arising in the city. Of course, many were troubled by this development, but they felt its vigor, and they hoped to devise some way to tap that energy or to make it possible to consume this new popular culture in another and more properly middle-class context. Some were persuaded that this is where profits could be made.

In either case, concern about the shape and impact of popular culture at the turn of the century inevitably raised questions about quality, value, power, and profit. Just as surely, the attitude of commentators and social reformers was influenced by the source and aura of popular culture. This became an issue in part because of the rapidly shifting demographics of the late nineteenth-century city. At the end of the century, immigrant and working-class urbanites had developed important and strong and sometimes innovative manners and mores. The rapid commercialization of some of these new customs (their seductiveness, even) promised to spread them to other sectors of the population.[16] Popular culture of ethnic origin could not be ignored; it was a crucial part of the new cityscape.

Popular culture also became snarled in strategies of social control. This old and continuous tactic of class dominion goes back into the 1820s when the urban middle class first tried to convert the cities to their evangelical values. The attempt to control or dominate leisure through civic improvements such as parks, museums, schools, and civic clubs constituted an element in the program of "positive environmentalists" to reshape urban culture. These social conservatives developed a program of traditionalist morality to counter what they identified as an almost subversive growth of popular culture. In this sense, then, the city itself had long been a battleground in the struggle for hegemony.[17]

While the motive of social control should not be underestimated, America's new urban middle classes and elites had to compromise. In the shared terrain of the city, the new middle classes needed, as much as moral stamina, a guide to the institutions growing up around them. They had to be warned away from some places and steered toward others. Ironically, they, not foreign-born workers, responded to efforts to preserve and sustain middle-class propriety in the city. For all the efforts of elites to create institutions that would maintain cultural power over the immigrant working classes, they were probably most effective in propagandizing the middle classes. Perhaps this is because of cultural affinity: the two groups already shared a Protestant culture. Yet efforts at hegemony had an ironic outcome because the creation of respectable institutions of popular culture built bridges between groups in the city no matter what their religious origin or moral and aesthetic interests. There was really no way to prevent such interchanges and adaptations, no way to maintain a rigid separation between the ideas of respectability and commercialized amusements. Indeed, popular commercial culture as it emerged at the turn of the century may well have been a welcome introduction to the diversity and a suppression of the confusion encountered by the new middle classes in the city. For all of these reasons, popular culture was a wobbly, uncontrollable vehicle not easily driven, even by the most powerful and determined men.

This is particularly obvious in the case of fairs and other monumental urban events. In another context, Jean-Christophe Agnew has shrewdly argued that fairs and marketplaces were linked to the rise of the Elizabethan theater. The theater, in other words, provided an experimental commentary on the new and strange social and economic relations visible particularly in the contemporary marketplace.[18] Michail Bakhtin, in his remarkable discussion of *Rabelais and His World*, also focused upon the fair as a place of liberation from restraints, where the marketplace liberated and democratized the experiences of those who entered it. In such democratic places, popular genres penetrate higher culture and speech itself is released from norms, hierarchies, and prohibitions. The result, in the Renaissance age he describes, was innovation and temporary freedom from the pressures and duties of social hierarchy.[19]

By considering the fair—and specifically the World's Columbian Exposition of 1893—both as a moment in the history of fairs and spectacles, and as an experiment in creating an idealized city, it is easy to see the traces of this marketplace liberation and freedom. At the same time, however, the Chicago World's Fair was self-contradictory and exceptional, for it disguised and distanced itself from the effects of the marketplace, and hence from the very notion of the marketplace itself. It proposed an ideal city in which popular culture was controlled and limited. If the format of the Chicago Columbian Exposition was a carefully calculated balance between the neoclassical White City and the commercial Midway there remained a serious problem. Trying to create a controlled fair (a contradiction in terms, perhaps) and a careful cultural environment did not always work. Inevitably, the audience asserted its own priorities and interests. Even in the carefully staged events of the late nineteenth century, which attempted to glorify conservative culture, there was more than a little influence running the other way. This meant that there were two Chicago fairs coexisting in Jackson Park: the first celebrated control and high culture; the second fantasy, liberation, and ethnicity. It was the audience itself which had to integrate these conflicting experiences.

In a sense, I am arguing that the carefully calculated exhibitions of popular culture constructed in Chicago in 1893 reveal the most important characteristics of what we now call postmodern—a term thought to explain the contemporary eclectic mood in culture. If by postmodern we mean the definition of culture in terms of pastiche, collage, juxtaposition, of the breakdown of distinctions between elite and popular culture (of the hegemony of the commercial aesthetic), then this contemporary process can certainly be found in the 1890s in the wondrous incongruities of Chicago. Even then, the growing penetration of the commercial marketplace into every aspect of culture was obvious. The result was a substitution of commercial for aesthetic or moral considerations. And if this naked monster of profit making haunted the dreams of Chicago's elite master builders, they were no more able to control commercial culture then than are today's critics of marketplace excesses.[20] Popular culture, therefore, must be seen as the ambiguous instrument of freedom and chaos, innovation and destruction. It both unites and divides, creating new demarcations of what is public and private, what is accepted and what is not. In Chicago in 1893 it was both the problem and the opportunity that summoned up the grandiloquent dreams of a generation.

The greatest upsurge in commercial culture during the late nineteenth century took place most markedly in American cities. No place during this period more revolutionized the American cultural landscape. Yet we must describe the city carefully, because what we mean by the word today does not invoke the images that surrounded it in the late nineteenth century. In the first place, by *city* in the late nineteenth century we mean, above all, vitality. America's cities then (and especially in the decade preceding 1890) were growing dramatically. Many of them, particularly in the new Middle West, doubled in population every decade or so. While similarly enormous populations simultaneously crowded into Central and Western European urban conglomerations during the same period, this movement was no more pronounced than in the United States and especially in the rim of cities around the Great Lakes and the Ohio and Mississippi rivers (see table below).[21]

Population Growth: Selected American Cities

	1880	1890
New York (Manhattan)	1,206,299	1,515,301
Philadelphia	847,170	1,046,964
Boston	362,839	448,477
Baltimore	332,313	434,489
Chicago	503,185	1,090,850
Milwaukee	115,587	205,468
St. Louis	350,518	451,770
Detroit	116,340	205,876
Minneapolis	46,887	164,738

Source: *World Almanac, 1886, 1891* (New York: New York World Telegram, 1886, 1891), pp. 32, 244.

The city meant vitality and growth, but it also signified centralization and specialization. The focus of economic and social activities in the late nineteenth century was as concentrated or as broad as the limitations of transport would allow. As economic and cultural activity centered in growing downtowns with retail and bureaucratic and cultural institutions located in the same general area, increasingly efficient transport allowed for some population dispersal and urban specialization. Industries engaged in manufacturing, slaughtering, and heavy transport were clustered as were those in retailing and business and banking. Outlying sections of the city, while not homogeneous suburbs, had, to some degree, the atmosphere of small towns. Thus, the city both exploded and imploded, driven simultaneously by centrifugal and centripetal forces.

Looked at as the center of a metropolitan area, the city represented the apex of diversity that tapered off into homogeneity at its extreme edges. For the great inland American cities, set onto vast tracts of wealthy farmland, this sameness at the periphery gave the impression of a cultural uniformity of Protestant values.

The city, however, was an enterprise of originality, containing and representing the new cultural, ethnic, and social variety that was sweeping the nation into the twentieth century. But a problem with immense implications for the late nineteenth century was how to discover just where the fundamental city was located within the large, new urban conglomerations. What was essential in defining a city?[22] No wonder, then, that Utopian reformers, from Edward Bellamy to the planners of the City Beautiful Movement in the first decade of the twentieth century, stressed a city center defined by aesthetic unity. To establish this focal point would not exactly transform the city itself, but at least it might unify the vision, perspective, and expectations of its citizens. The part could thus stand in place of the whole. Chicago could "mean" the skyline or the civic center or even the Columbian Fair.

There is much to be learned by word choices, and the vocabulary of late nineteenth-century urban observers developed for this situation is fascinating. Was the city diverse or disunited? they asked. Referring to the same phenomena, these much used words were actually poles apart, with clusters of opposing connotations.

Diverse meant something positive, implying richness, fullness, and variety; disunited was a negative clash of the same elements. Of course, the city could be—and was—both.

This double vision was not unique to the 1890s for it had been clearly reflected in the Victorian cult of sentimentality and sincerity. Guidebooks and behavior manuals of the mid-century endeavored to present usable guides to social customs in the new cities of the Northeast. Among strangers in the new world of the city, sentimental and sincere behavior was, undoubtedly, a surer guide to understanding one's acquaintances than mere manners and formality. Indeed, fear of dishonest and dissembling men, who exploited surface impressions, summed up an earlier generation's anxieties about the problems of conduct in the city.[23]

Certainly the most obvious feature of the late nineteenth-century city was its cultural heterogeneity and diversity. To be further removed from nature was to be more obviously dependent upon cultural institutions. City dwellers interacted through transitory contacts, through representative organizations, as anonymous individuals, and as audiences in communities of choice. By definition the city meant density, diverse populations, and heterogeneity as well as new institutions and expectations.[24]

This divided landscape exposed a cultural diversity that became the very essence of the American city and a powerful force in shaping modern urban institutions such as the department store, the metropolitan press, the ball park, and vaudeville theaters, each one of which had to cater to different audience or consumer segments. Not surprisingly, the popular culture that emerged by the late nineteenth century represented by these institutions promised a kind of consumer democracy as well as a deadening sameness. This popular commercial culture became a common denominator of Americanism and pretended a powerful egalitarianism. As Gunther Barth has written, "Modern city culture sought to assure the future of the ordinary person."[25]

Such democratic leveling did not go uncontested or uncriticized. The response of late Victorian elites and established middle classes sometimes defined rapid change or the new institutions of popular culture as chaotic. There is no doubt that the monumentality and eclecticism of their architecture intentionally gripped urban designs with the steadying hand of tradition. This grand style had its greatest efflorescence in the giganticized classicism of the Chicago World's Fair in the midst of a city that was exploding with new cultural forms.[26] But there is another explanation for this imposition of classical form on the most dynamic city in the nation. The Victorians, who used history as an embellishment, as a functional part of their urban aesthetic, did so because they rejected designs whose meanings seemed to imply an unregulated commercialism and functionalism. As James Schmeichen has written: "The face of the Victorian city is testimony to the fact that cash-box utilitarianism and want of character were looked on as social losses."[27]

Schmiechen also points to the late nineteenth-century belief in "associational functionalism" which promised that good behavior would result from exposure to good ideas; hence, the potency of classicism. Whatever its practical validity, this assumption inspired others besides traditionalists who waxed eloquent on the belief that environment could play a serious role in creating a democratic, well-adjusted citizenry. The very essence of architect Louis Sullivan's diatribe against the eclecticism of the World's Fair drew upon this (shared) notion that architecture was inevitably a moral and political enterprise—that built environments reflected and shaped behavior.

Yet, just at the critical moment of the late nineteenth century, when the visual city had become an important object of cultural and political reform, some of its most prosperous and important citizens had already abandoned it. This was to be expected, because the same forces that made it possible to focus city life also made decentralization an option. Diverse populations could be concentrated in the center city while specialized enclaves hung back at the periphery in suburbs. Sometimes these suburbs were quickly incorporated into the expanding city; sometimes they demanded a more permanent and exclusive existence. But as the modern city was born in the mid-nineteenth century, so was the modern suburb.

From the very beginning, then, the phenomenon that is so striking about our own age (the centerless city) was implicit in building railway lines out of (or into) the downtown. Until at least the 1920s, and possibly later, the predominant, most important element of growth focused upon the center city. But the suburbs existed almost from the beginning. For example, as railroads spread out around such cities as Boston, and later Chicago, suburban cities sprang up. Many, of course, were pulled into the city by the voracious expansion of its boundaries. Yet this expansion often stopped abruptly, especially after the 1890s when independent towns decided to resist becoming part of their neighboring political agglomerations.[28]

Chicago's suburbs developed gradually. Beginning as attachments to the city, some evolved into middle- and upper-class havens. After 1865, spawned by railroad connections, suburbs came to resemble their twentieth-century counterparts, although they still sometimes lacked the homogeneity of post World War II tract communities. In the United States, the late nineteenth century was a time for an energetic expansion and development of suburbs, particularly in Chicago. Beginning with Frederick Law Olmsted's planned community of Riverside in 1868, Chicago saw the establishment of a variety of suburbs devoted to different purposes. Some were small-scale replicas of Chicago in their industry and diversity; others intentionally limited their economic activities and population.[29]

Inevitably in this middle period in the modern development of cities and suburbs, when both were claiming a new definition and function in the 1890s, new professions such as urban and social planning developed around the ideal of intentionally redesigning the city. Many late nineteenth-century Utopias derived from earlier conceptions of the idealized European city, a place of religious vision and harmony. But in this transitional period, when the City Beautiful planners and less orthodox thinkers such as Frank Lloyd Wright were beginning to reconceptualize the city, they moved away from the timeless conception of the city as the vision of a small community on a hill, to explore idealized and orderly urban forms through a new kind of geometry of expansion. The ideal city could be large and growing, diverse and specialized, so long as it grew according to comprehensible, planned lines.[30]

The modern attempt to plan the ideal city began at a time when the real city was both contracting and expanding, spawning miniature versions of itself and sowing the seeds of the suburban challenge to the idea of a central urban focus. It is no wonder that this roiling and contradictory movement should also give rise to the beginnings of American urban sociology, and in particular at the University of Chicago in the 1890s. There, in the gray stone city, pioneer intellectuals worked diligently to make their observations into the basis of a new conception of the city and society itself. For them, two key ideas defined the range of experience in the city. The first was the breakdown of various forms of inherited cultures (the family, ethnic and religious cultures). The second was the dual process of acculturation which implied a movement out of the city through concentric rings of residences, further and further from the center and, simultaneously, into a more pronounced identification with American culture—at least in its middle-class guise.[31] Their theories echoed and replicated one version of the process of urbanization and suburbanization and cultural reorganization that marked this dynamic period in the city's history. They repeated many of the complaints about city life voiced by reformers and city planners.

One last word is important for my theoretical vocabulary, and that is *tourist*. In some respects, tourism is only a specialized version of the massive internal migrations that characterized America, and especially Chicago, during the late nineteenth century. The unpredictable transition from farm to city or from foreign country to the United States was a common ordeal.[32] And tourism was, in some respects, only a playful version of this experience. It invited the traveler into situations that were intentionally ambiguous, partly familiar and momentarily disorienting.

By the late nineteenth century, travel for pleasure and edification was generally expanding. One sign was the development of the American Express Travelers Cheque in 1891. More important, travel itself changed because middle-class patrons began to replace the much more adventuresome wealthy voyagers of previous eras. For these new tourists, travel was often organized to save "the tourist from negotiating with the native when he gets there." In others words, touring was based upon creating a familiar environment within a strange place, establishing the pleasing illusion of comfort and mild confusion—to have "roughed it" in an alien culture that was rendered unthreatening by the new creature comforts of travel.

Paul Fussel's fine, short essay, "Bourgeois Travel," stresses the same point: in the late nineteenth century, train travel whisked the bourgeoisie off to places designed to satisfy their fantasies: hotels called the Majestic, the Grand, and the Excelsior, and expeditions into the picturesque, in order to fulfill "exotic fantasies and desires—

for escape and the foreign, for the novel."[33] It should be added that in the United States the fantasy often began when entering the plush elegance of a Pullman Palace Car. From beginning to end, the idea of tourism was a structured experience, imposed upon the various realities of the place visited.

Dean MacCannell provides a slightly different but helpful emphasis in his book on tourism. He proposes that tourism is "a kind of collective striving for the transcendence of the modern totality, a way of attempting to overcome the discontinuity of modernity." In other words, the object of tourism is to learn how societies function. Everything, therefore, is structured into a "staged authenticity." Tourism transforms unfamiliar scenery into a model that can best be understood by reference to one's own experience.[34]

The tourist of this era, then, was a person who intentionally placed himself or herself in a strange situation, for pleasure and for instruction. But this could hardly be rewarding if it were a totally disorienting experience. So for those who planned tourist events such as the Columbian Exhibition at Chicago in 1893 or who conducted tours of other Chicago spots, the balance between familiar and unfamiliar was a key to success. And because this experience of tourism was relatively new for so many millions of Americans, the exotic had to be grounded in the obviously conventional. Given the remarkable changes in the American city in these decades, it is no wonder that planning for the ideal city used visible symbols with conspicuous social connotations. The future, in America, had to be made to resemble the past, some accessible past, at least, in which the newly constructed order referred to an approved or familiar social ideal.

Two

CHICAGO

Two Profiles

EVERYTHING ABOUT CHICAGO depends upon perspective. Its very levelness, as if the seams of the earth have been ironed flat, makes it as easy to read as a map. The cardinal points of the compass are obvious, and the grid map fits the horizontals of the topography perfectly. There seems to be no curvature of the earth, and the surface of the lake abuts the lip of the plain without cliffs and without indentations. To locate oneself, there is simply North, South, West, and an edge of the East. No wonder that when the Chicago writer Frank L. Baum drew his fanciful fairy story of the magical city of Oz, he personified the directions themselves.

On this flat expanse, the ever-changing profile of the city is projected. The straight, broad streets and avenues lead off into the horizon, unbroken by curves or hills, as if each emanates from a single perspective. In 1893, at the center, the immense new skyscrapers, great stone flowers, bloomed up toward the light, rising, literally, out of the sucking mud. Further out, there was the patchwork of tall and short buildings and empty lots giving a sense of imminent change and thrust and incompleteness: a tall building here, a group of wood-frame houses, a row of gray-stone town houses, red brick factories, and Chicago's famous two-story tenements. Muffling a cacophony of animal, machine, and human sounds was a heaving cloud of smoke, a sigh of energy exhaled from the growing city. Trailing off at the edges were incomplete streets, ditches, a house here or there, a lamp post, a farm, then the prairie,

1893.✳ GRAND V

Bird's-Eye View of Chicago in 1893. One popular way to portray the city in 1893 was the bird's-eye view. The advantage of this format was the ability to convey a sense of three dimensions. Furthermore, artists could select cer-

CHIGAGO. ✳ 1893.

tain features to emphasize, such as the site of the World's Fair grounds (to the bottom, left). (Library of Congress)

laced with creeks and streams. Some of these places had names, and even a few had residences. Most were plans and hopes that would later become part of the city or its network of suburbs.[1]

At the mercantile-cultural center of the city, the great new department stores brushed against offices and cultural buildings like the Art Institute and Orchestra Hall. Near these institutions were the great castles that lined Prairie Avenue on the Near South Side or the residences of the newly fashionable North Side. Linked by ownership were factories and slaughterhouses, most located on the South Side of the city. On the banks of these extended streams of wealth, power, and privilege perched crowded, precarious little houses and tenements, gathered like impoverished small towns, and filled with vast numbers of immigrants pouring into the city from Europe and from the surrounding farming areas. Streets ran into other streets at right angles, or sometimes plunged through the green edge of a broad park or boulevard, or sometimes ended in a cemetery. Tying it all together were plank and paved roads, a lazy, cess-filled river, new elevated railroads (completed in 1897) making a loop around the center of the city, flinging people in and out of the downtown as if by centrifugal force, and the stations of great railway systems dumping commerce and travelers into the center.

This, in 1890, was the grandest city in the Midwest, the second in the nation, and the seventh in the world. A commercial center of unbounded energy, it erected huge stores, warehouses, mail-order houses. Communities existed within communities: settlement houses, congregations, parishes, neighborhoods, ethnic groups, clubs, reform groups, and, of course, political organizations. Chicago's "drummers," roaming like Methodist circuit riders, plied the countryside with goods. To the great families who organized and profited from the city, its factories and mercantile houses required a kind of sanctity, which they hastened to proclaim with *architecture*. Even the stockyards boasted a memorial gate erected by the great architectural firm of John Root and Daniel Burnham. The thought, perhaps, was to embellish through art what could not be decorated with philosophy or religion.

While the laborers who built these factories and slaughterhouses lived in utilitarian squalor, some of their employers imagined a Utopia, and they called for planners to build suburbs or outlying towns like Riverside, Oak Park, Pullman, and Harvey, and the White City at the World's Fair of 1893 as well as their own mansions. No wonder that the British historian Asa Briggs called Chicago the great "shock city" of the 1890s. He meant that it portended the future, like Los Angeles after it, and Manchester, England, before, where it seemed that any possibility, any change was plausible.[2]

The giddy economy of the early 1890s in Chicago, like other Midwest cities, spun the real estate market to dizzy heights. Then the Panic of 1893 brought an end to a mammoth binge of land speculation and urban incorporation. But before this pause, Chicago's appetite for ingesting its neighboring settlements seemed as insatiable as the schemes of land companies to lure the city into new expansions by throwing up towns and suburbs around its periphery. One of the last and greatest consolidations occurred in 1889 when suburban areas, led by business leaders, ministers, lawyers, and doctors—by the established middle classes—petitioned and won the right to be Chicagoans, to link themselves to Chicago's fire protection, water system, transport, and taxation.[3] Then, after 1889, this wild expansion had pretty much ended, as the suburbs became more obviously middle class and the city more obviously foreign-born. The next layer of contiguous suburbs, including Cicero and Oak Park, resisted incorporation. After the turn of the century few suburbs wanted to become part of the city. Automobiles and roads made sprawl easier to live with and even attractive. A declining faith in economic and residential centralization plus rising middle-class self-consciousness and exclusiveness erected a wall of settlements around the city.[4]

The Chicago that prepared to greet millions of visitors to the World's Fair in 1893 was, itself, only a recent fabrication.[5] Only sixty years old by the 1890s, Chicago had seen a great burst of development after the Civil War, based upon transport, manufacturing, and slaughtering, that made men's fortunes. This growth almost doubled the population every decade in the late nineteenth century so that the city expanded from about a bustling 300,000 in 1870 to a metropolis of almost 1,700,000 in 1900.[6] The fastest growth, however, occurred in the years immediately preceding the World's Fair.

Buoyed by waves of immigration, Chicago's population in 1893 had the typical population characteristics of an American city but in an exaggerated measure. Although about 20 percent of the United States population was foreign-born, almost 41 percent of Chicagoans had been born abroad; an almost equal number had foreign-born parents. Most of this population was German and Irish. But the 1890s was also a period of rapid transition in the national origins of immigrants. By 1900, Chicago had more Poles, Swedes, Czechs, Dutch, Danes, Norwegians, Croations, Slovaks, Lithuanians, and Greeks than any other American city.[7]

Compared with the state of Illinois, Chicago sustained an enormous growth during this period, while rural areas actually declined in population. It was also the only city of considerable size for hundreds of miles. Acting as a magnet, Chicago attracted populations from Pennsylvania, Ohio, New York, Indiana, Wisconsin. As might be expected, the city exhibited curious imbalances in age groupings. It lagged behind the rest of the country in percentages of persons forty-five and older and under six, but was substantially higher in the twenty-one- to forty-five-year range.[8] Inside the city, certain wards showed a considerably higher male population than female, indicating the transitory character of the residences and lower percentage of family formation, while other wards displayed a more even distribution.[9] In effect, there were two sorts of cities co-existing and jointly occupying the same area: one with established patterns of family and residence, and the other highly transitory and in the process of formation. In contrast to the surrounding area, Chicago was, in part at least, a city of immigrants and strangers.

Chicago's population was housed in circumstances that made it very different from Eastern cities. New York, for example, concentrated a significant portion of its population in large dwellings, apartment buildings, and tenements. Philadelphia, on the other hand, was predominantly a city of smaller houses. Chicago, too, had small houses and some larger tenements, but its most characteristic arrangement was the two-family duplex.[10] Unlike Eastern cities, Chicago had a relatively low density of population; that is, there were fewer persons per total land area. Compared to New York and Philadelphia, Chicago's real estate assets and personal property were quite low, indicating, simply, the very newness of the city. Although a commuter city like Boston and New York, it still had fewer commuter trains than either of those cities.[11] With more streets or alleys than any other city, half were paved with wood in 1890.[12] Yet Chicago's slums, according to a report by U. S. Labor Commissioner Carroll Wright in 1894, did compare in terms of crime, crowding, and other indicators of instability and hardship with the older slums of Baltimore, New York, and Philadelphia.

During the 1880s, the industries that grew most rapidly in the city were men's clothing, foundry and machine shops, slaughtering, agricultural implement manufacture, and printing. New middle-class employment in clerking, sales, and the professions increased especially rapidly.[13] As befit its new importance as a manufacturer and emporium, Chicago also became, during this period, a major national center of publishing and entertainment. The growth of Chicago was, in the words of a historian of book publishing, "one of the phenomena of the closing years of the nineteenth century." In the context of the huge growth in reading, particularly fiction reading at the end of the century, this gave the city a major role in the revolution in American popular culture.[14] The city counted fifteen theaters, 250 amusement halls of various sorts, and over 5,000 saloons. This was second only to New York and far larger than Philadelphia, a city with a comparable population. There was, for example, one saloon for every 212 persons (one per 127 in the slums).[15] Compared with Philadelphia, there were twice as many actors and many more commercial travelers and salesmen and saleswomen.[16] Finally, Chicago boasted significant numbers of architects, musicians, literary and scientific people, artists and teachers, bookbinders, and other cultural professions. Despite the irregular growth of the city, its cultural institutions kept pace with its spectacular increase in size.

Many of these categories of cultural employment were distinguished by different percentages of foreign- and native-born. Employment throughout the nation showed marked concentrations of certain ethnic groups in different occupations. There was a disproportion of foreign-born, for example, among certain groups of skilled and unskilled workers including tailors, brewers, launderers, hucksters and peddlers, cabinet makers, and bakers. Native-born workers almost completely dominated the positions of lawyers, telephone and telegraph operators, agricultural laborers, teachers, college professors, stenographers, and typists.[17] Chicago followed this general trend with a disproportionate percentage of professionals who were native-born whites with native-born parents. This was particularly true of lawyers and physicians; however, it was less so for actors, architects, artists, clergymen, and music teachers.[18] In other words, certain cultural industries offered considerable opportunity for foreign-born Chicagoans. Finally, in Chicago, among clerks, salesmen, and typists and stenographers, the foreign-born or native-born with foreign-born parents filled jobs in approximately the same percentage as they constituted the population.[19]

This suggests that the cultural professions and the new middle-class audiences for them represented all population sectors of Chicago. There were, to be sure, exaggerations at the lower and upper ranks of professions. For example, lawyers were much more likely to be American-born, while saloon keepers generally came from immigrant origins. But opportunity and mobility were clearly visible in the middle. This pattern more or less corresponded with wage levels also—with domestics, mining, and manufacturing toward the bottom; with wholesale and retail, and with local government employment toward the middle; and real estate and some clerical workers at the upper end.[20]

Of course, the situation was not static, and, as in other American cities, mobility upward in terms of professions and outward in terms of residence was an important contemporary characteristic of Chicago. Although such things are difficult to measure, there was also considerable mobility between occupation groups, but in many cases this was intergenerational. Thus, it could take generations to move from the farm to a white-collar job or from a small business position to leadership in a large enterprise. Mobility from laborer upward, however, particularly at this period, could be even more difficult, especially because in many cases it involved simultaneous acculturation.[21] The business and cultural leadership at the center of this study experienced a more extreme and special version of social mobility than was characteristic of most other groups in Chicago.

For those Chicagoans who made their way into the middle class or higher, there were two possible accommodations to the city. One could abandon it in favor of the suburbs and minimize one's contact with the city to employment and selected cultural institutions. The

Adams Street. This typical street scene illustrates the ground-level, visually confusing hubbub of downtown Chicago. Faintly seen in the distance is the headquarters of the Fleming Revell publishers of Moody's works (see Chapter 6). (William T. Barnum, ICHI-20919, Chicago Historical Society)

other was no less exclusive, but it engaged the city itself, seeking to transform its institutions and make it a more hospitable place for middle-class and elite residents. For this group especially, the organized city of government, cultural, business, and mercantile institutions was the focus of their activities.

To design acceptable urban life-styles in a context of rapid change, or even just to make peace with the city, Chicago's prominent citizens summoned up ideas from a variety of contexts and put them to work in their designs to refashion the shape of urban culture. In doing so, they hoped to establish a sense of permanence, even a moral direction, a dominating perspective, from which to organize experiences with the various cultures of the city. To accomplish this meant confronting and overcoming the problems of change, disorganization, and diversity.

Both elites and the new middle class explored this unsettled cultural topography. For example, this situation deeply affected nineteenth-century middle-class life in Union Row, an area of Chicago that tried to maintain its integrity against the swift changes in the economy and culture. The diversification of occupations in the period, writes Richard Sennett, "may have produced a feeling of disorganization much like the culture shock of immigration." Mobility upward and fear of downward mobility introduced instability and uncertainty. By the time that the middle class had begun to abandon Union Row, many of the community and other original ties had dissolved, leaving an excessive reliance upon family and church.[22]

This description is reminiscent of the developing sociological theory held by the new urban sociologists at the University of Chicago and by settlement house workers such as Jane Addams. The experience of immigrants in the city, they proposed, broke down traditional culture and made newcomers particularly susceptible to new urban cultural developments: the culture of the city streets. The implication of Sennett's work is that middle-class urbanites experienced something of the same drift. And they, too, caught up in swift cultural and social change, would be susceptible to the newest entertainments and fads.

That this new culture was seen as pernicious and even dangerous was something of a cliché during the late part of the nineteenth century, but it was, nonetheless, a powerful thought. Merchant John V. Farwell (supporter of Dwight Moody and YMCA activist) wrote in 1889 that the new popular literature was betraying young men:

> Yellow covered novels, police expositions of crime, unblushing publications of infidel and atheistic views, are being circulated with enormous rapidity, and are steadily corrupting a rising generation. It is sad and discouraging to see the railroad news agents employed in their dissemination, and I trust that

this volume [*The Secret of Success*] may displace the vile trash too often sold to the young and innocent.[23]

Of course, this was ancient and weary advice, but it captured the worries of a successful generation who believed that they had advanced by hard work and moral commitment. Unfortunately, social mobility did not automatically deepen social sophistication. So this was probably the only message such men believed appropriate to pass on.

Yet the 1890s in Chicago propelled a rapid transition in attitudes toward the city. As suburbanization speeded up, as middle class and elite consciousness increased, and as residential segregation grew, both in the city and between suburbs, the twentieth-century pattern of city development became discernible. The very diversity of the city was a challenge that many Americans found overwhelming, whether it be the confrontation with dissimilar religions or new ethnic groups or simply the challenge of too much choice. As a prominent businessman from Kansas City, Missouri, inquired of Turlington Harvey (another of Dwight Moody's benefactors) in 1887: How did the First Methodist Church of Chicago solve the problem of remaining in the city? A few of the wealthy members of his own congregation, he explained, wanted to sell their downtown church. "They do not like the mixed element—and stranger element; while a large number, . . . think that the Church should be maintained in the heart of the City, especially in view of the fact that this is a City of strangers."[24] This alarm over the city of strangers seemed to provide a link of sympathy and self-interest between Chicago's Protestant elite and members of the new, expanding middle class.

It is no coincidence that in 1892 Chicago's (and America's) greatest architect, Frank Lloyd Wright, separated from the firm of Sullivan and Adler in order to concentrate on designing middle-class housing for suburban Oak Park rather than for a city of strangers. Wright's insistence upon providing a closed environment for the family, protected in a sense against the invasiveness of the city, expressed a sentiment in stone, wood, and glass that drew many middle-class and elite Chicagoans to the suburbs.[25] That was a route that became increasingly practical after the 1890s as railroad and then automobile transportation made the suburbs more attractive. Everett Chamberlin, in a booster's view of Chicago and its suburbs, explained clearly why the suburbs might be such a haven when he wrote of nearby Evanston: "The people are most homogeneous and scarcely an evening passes but is celebrated by some gathering at which the feast of reason and the flow of soul proceed uninterruptedly along."[26]

A different way to approach the city was to repossess it by creating a new urban culture that could stand in the place of what was being lost in the tumult of diversity. As Helen Lefkowitz Horowitz has written, certain members of the native-born elite "assumed responsibility for shaping the cultural opportunities of Chicago as a whole,"[27] and they established a symphony orchestra, libraries, museums, and the University of Chicago, all endowed institutions of enormous cultural importance for the city. The concentration of many of these institutions within the center of the city gave testimony to the interest of philanthropists in adorning the urban environment as defined by its cultural, mercantile, and manufacturing elite.[28]

This movement of cultural and civic boosterism culminated in 1909 with Daniel Burnham's Plan of Chicago. In his testimony to faith in centralization and a multiclass society, the principal architect of the World's Fair suggested embellishment of the city center, broad traffic arteries, and a beltway road and park system around the city. Among those who still believed that it was possible to assert control of the city, Burnham wanted to centralize the mutually reinforcing institutions of business offices, cultural institutions, shops and banks, hotels and theaters, and transportation facilities. With this center and adequate parks and parkways, the life of the "wage-earner and of his family is made healthier and pleasanter" while, at the same time, this newly attractive city would keep "at home the people of means and taste" acting as an attraction to draw in those who "seek to live amid pleasing surroundings."[29]

Perhaps this was a feasible vision for some, but Burnham was finding a virtue among several contradictory urban developments. He also underestimated another kind of reality about the city—its decentralization. By this time, many areas like Chicago's North Side had their own centers with churches, schools, hospitals, clubs,

lodge houses, theaters, coffeehouses, and palm gardens and saloons. Indeed, the city was a place of many subordinate centers, not
just the grand apex of skyscrapers and institutions of high culture.[30]

Simultaneous with the creation of buildings and institutions of
cultural philanthropy in the 1890s in the center city and its prolifer-
ating suburbs, Chicago was also distinguished by a burst of literary
energy that expressed itself especially in poetry and fiction. This
Chicago Renaissance had a foundation in the world of cultural production. The literary resurgence was based upon the great increase
in journalism and publishing and in the establishment of important
cultural journals such as the *Dial* in 1880, the *Chap-Book* in 1894,
and *Poetry* magazine in 1912, and such informal institutions as the
Little Room where intellectuals met after Friday symphony concerts. The embellishment of buildings, museums, and houses and of
elite life within them gave opportunities to the growing group of
architects, artists, and musicians and writers.

Perhaps more noteworthy was the development of the Chicago
novel, led by writers such as Eugene Field, Robert Herrick, Hamlin
Garland, Henry Fuller, and Frank Norris. Existing as a kind of critical appendage to the new genteel institutions of the elite, this first
literary generation of basically realist writers turned their pens to an
ambiguous and contradictory celebration and criticism of their city
and its leading social and economic figures. Their heyday was short.
By the second decade of the twentieth century they were being replaced by a new group of writers including Floyd Dell, Carl
Sandburg, and Edgar Lee Masters, who took a more complex view
of the city and who were more rebellious against it as well as against
the small towns from which they had fled.[31] During the 1890s and
into the first years of the twentieth century, however, the booster
realism of the early writers promoted the conclusion that Chicago
could become a cultural center of extraordinary potential.

At the same time, another sort of renaissance was occurring,
one that often troubled the intellectual and cultural leaders of the
city in a vague but serious way. This was the creation of working-
class and immigrant entertainments. Besides the huge number of
saloons that catered primarily to men, there were new amusements
such as vaudeville, dance halls that became important in the 1890s,
amusement parks, and, eventually, storefront movie theaters. While

these amusements often awakened middle-class censorship movements and were the frequent target of antivice crusades, they were nonetheless the raw material of a vibrant, new popular culture emerging in the city that would eventually, in a more refined form, attract middle-class patrons.[32]

Chicago, then, was a city of extremes and contrasts accentuated by the cultural intervention of an elite group of businessmen and philanthropists. No doubt part of their motivation was the social control of immigrants, of the political energies of the majority of the city's residents, and the regulation of the work environment. Cheap and docile labor was, to be sure, the essence of their fortunes. The labor strikes of the 1870s and the Haymarket Affair of 1886 had crystallized fears and perceptions of the city environment which such a short passage of time could scarcely erode.[33] Yet, there were other motivations, too, that had to do with reclaiming the city for themselves, for making it a place where, in Daniel Burnham's words, at last people of means won't "be so ready to run away and spend their money in other cities."[34]

In attempting to rebuild the city in the image worthy of their imagined status and responsibilities, Chicago's elites envisioned a genteel city. They aimed to impose a moral order that would, like a map, guide the resident to the proper places and into the proper attitudes. While many of the institutions they established were meant to cater only to select groups, other institutions were intended to be more popular and aimed as much at the burgeoning middle classes as at themselves. Indeed, among the first generation of builders, businessmen, and moral leaders of Chicago, the possibility of a permanent social elite was something only for their children and, perhaps, some of their white-collar employees to enjoy.

The appeal of the new cultural institutions existed because the inventors of the great experiments of 1893 in social and cultural planning shared a heritage that was very much like the new middle classes of the city. Certainly elite by accomplishment and presumption, they enjoyed a remarkably similar and nonelite background with many of the younger generation then making its way into banks, merchandising, and bureaucratic work of all sorts. Coming from relatively similar circumstances, they had made their way to the top of Chicago's business and social world by dint of an exceptional self-transformation.

The principal figures in this book—Dwight Moody, Turlington W. Harvey, George Pullman, Daniel Burnham, and Marshall Field, Harlow Higinbotham, John V. Farwell, Potter Palmer, Lyman Gage, and Philip Armour—constituted a very particular generation of Chicagoans acutely aware of the problems of cultural diversity and confusion in the city. Most were born in the 1830s and lived until the first few years of the twentieth century. Their entrepreneurial activities transformed the basic Chicago industries: merchandising, banking, slaughtering, lumbering, and transportation. To a lesser or greater extent, they were also principal figures in the construction of the World's Columbian Exposition, in two of Chicago's most famous suburban Utopias (Pullman and Harvey, Illinois), and in the promotion and financing of Dwight Moody's remarkable World's Fair crusade of that year. In some respects, they were the models for the characters in the new realist novels about the power and ruthlessness and cultural acquisitiveness of big businessmen. Yet they were also the leading philanthropists for a range of institutions from churches, to lay Christian organizations like the YMCA, to civic clubs, and museums and symphony orchestras. This special mixture of religious, innovative business experience, and cultural philanthropy, which was their defining characteristic, resulted in the extraordinary events of 1893.[35]

There was nothing more striking than the similarity of their backgrounds and the profile of their accomplishments. Almost all of these men were born in or around the "burned-over" district of western New York during the years of the hottest conflagration of preaching and religious turmoil in that agitated land of American Protestantism. Most of them descended from long-established New England families who had immigrated to that area. Few of their families at the beginning of the nineteenth century were prominent or important. Their fathers were either small merchants, craftsmen, mechanics of one sort or another, or farmers. Their backgrounds, in other words, perfectly fit the description of the evangelical middle-class formation so characteristic of that era and area (see table p. 38).[36]

   Besides the uprooting experience of moving from upstate New
York and Massachusetts to Chicago, this generation of embers from
the burned-over district shared a similar rise to leadership in Chicago's business, social, and cultural worlds. By 1893 they had moved
to the forefront of Chicago's new and raw elite: a second generation
of institution builders and city boosters but a first generation of
enormous fortunes. Of course, many of the men they worked with
to create the urban Utopias of 1893 did not share this background or
they belonged to a later generation of businessmen. Yet the coherence of experience among the leadership was striking. Coming from
farms or small towns in upstate New York, they generally left home
at an early age to become clerks in stores or small businesses. At least

Name	Birthplace and Residence	Date	Religion
Philip Armour	Stockbridge Madison Ct. (NY)	1830	Congregational
Daniel Burnham	Jefferson Ct. (NY)	1846	Swedenborgian
John V. Farwell	Campbelltown Steuben Ct. (NY)	1825	Methodist
Marshall Field	Conway and Pittsfield (MA)	1835	Presbyterian
Lyman Gage	Steuben Ct. (NY) Rome and Oneida	1836	Methodist
Turlington Harvey	Siloam and Oneida (NY)	1835	Methodist Father an abolitionist
Harlow Higinbotham	Joliet (IL) Family moved from Oneida (NY) in 1834	1838	Methodist
Dwight Moody	Northfield (MA)	1837	Congregational
Potter Palmer	Albany Ct. (NY) Oneida	1830	Methodist
George Pullman	Brocton, Chautauqua Ct. (NY)	1831	Universalist

two of them (Armour and Pullman) joined the Gold Rush in the western United States for a brief period. Pullman, Harvey, and, to some extent, Armour were involved in one variety or another of urban Utopian community building. Philip Armour's Mission and nearby Armour Flats, plus his Armour Institute of Technology, constituted a sort of dispersed community within the city, while Pullman's thoroughly planned and regulated community south of the city and Harvey's Teetotal Town represented more ambitious centralized efforts at social and moral planning.

Not surprisingly, many of these men were involved in one way or another in the retail revolution for which Chicago was justly famous. These include Marshall Field, Potter Palmer, John Farwell, and Harlow Higinbotham who were all, at one time or another, associated with the enterprise that eventually became Marshall Field and Company. Field, Palmer, and Higinbotham, plus Gage, Armour, Pullman, and Harvey worked hard to secure the World's Fair for the city of Chicago, and Gage, Palmer and Higinbotham were all noteworthy in deciding its final form. Pullman, Armour, and Jacob Leiter (formerly a merchandiser) were all instrumental in creating the Field Museum after the Fair. This should come as no surprise, for their experience in merchandising—which was a major purpose of the Fair—gave them invaluable experience in organizing the gigantic display of goods and cultural objects. The Fair was the showcase for these revolutionaries of Chicago's manufacturing and merchandising world, for it allowed them to demonstrate how they would place consumerism in modern urban culture.

The more religiously involved members of this group—Harvey, Moody, Farwell, and Armour—were instrumental in creating many of Chicago's lay-Protestant civic organizations such as the YMCA, the Chicago Relief and Aid Society, and a variety of church organizations and buildings. Farwell and Harvey spent considerable amounts of money and time helping Dwight Moody establish his permanent home of urban evangelism that eventually became the Moody Bible Institute. Whatever their specific commitments, all of these leaders involved themselves in activities that coupled enterprise to religious, civic, and cultural activities.

If the beginnings of Chicago society had initially emerged around several important Protestant church groups before 1871, the fire of that year dispersed these congregations forever. In the re-built city, both secular and lay/religious institutions emerged with greater importance. Particularly by the 1890s, cultural institutions such as the symphony orchestra, the University of Chicago, and civic clubs were emerging as strong competitors to religious societies and charity boards as prestigious institutions.[37] Even among the second generation of elite families, however, religious institutions still maintained a notable station. More important, many of the secular institutions were imbued with spiritual purposes. They were intended to elevate and educate. Thus, what may appear today to be a confusion of motivations was actually a rather broad belief that cultural institutions of all sorts could be directed to the same end: the cultural reformation of Chicago.

The elite that guided these institutions of moral suasion shared the experience of thousands of immigrants to the city in the late nineteenth century except, perhaps, in a more compressed and extreme measure. They discarded the calling of their fathers and even invented new occupations and careers. They endured geographic mobility, moving from small towns or farms to a fast-growing urban area. But there were also large differences. Most Chicagoans of the late nineteenth century were either immigrants to the United States or had foreign-born parents. A great many of these were not Protestant. The new middle class that emerged in this period grew up around the very economic institutions created by the elite group: mercantile, banking, transport, and manufacturing companies. Most of all, however, the new middle class of Chicago rarely shared the intense, evangelical cultural background of the elite.

The evangelical experience that jolted upstate New York in the Great Awakening of the 1830s represented a fundamental reorientation of American Protestantism. Rushing along areas contiguous to the Erie Canal (what Whitney Cross has called the "psychic highway"), the great revival from 1825 to 1837 was a selective virus that particularly infected immigrants from New England.[38] Made more susceptible by the turmoil of the tumultuous city building and population growth of the area during this period, residents were particularly attuned to millennial predictions and consequently to the consuming need to perfect society before the final coming of the Christ.

Stimulated and led by New Measure preaching within the established sects, by such preachers as Charles Grandeson Finney, the shifting congregations and audiences were swept by notions of free will and liberated from Jonathan Edwards's incarceration of American souls in Calvinist theories of original sin. Although Finney's preaching caused serious splits in the established churches and outrage among those who believed that he represented an intolerable infection of Jacksonian democracy within the churches, he managed to attract the attention and financial backing of several important New York merchants, particularly when he moved his crusades into the city.[39]

A handsome, athletic, sociable man, Finney used his ministry to distinguish among various sorts of acceptable and unacceptable forms of popular culture. He supported temperance and rigorous Sabbath observance, but at the same time promoted various fads such as Sylvester Graham's whole grain diet and defended the public display of emotionalism in church services.[40] Like many in the disturbed congregations of the area, he was active in social causes such as abolition.

When millennialism swept through the burned-over district, it was often accompanied by various forms of Utopianism. Indeed, the cross-fertilization between these two expressions of moral and social perfectionism created a confusing hybrid of communitarian experiments such as the Oneida Community, Millerism, and the socialist "phalanxes" of Fourierism. Salvation, for a time in upstate New York, might appear in almost any guise, particularly as the movement evolved into the 1840s.[41]

Besides preaching the millennium, the ministers of the revival emphasized something that no rising young man would want to dispute in the 1830s: that character and society were malleable. This understanding of the transiency of institutions, the possibility, even necessity of change, and the compulsion for rectitude guided the thousands of young men and women who abandoned this area after the 1840s and took up residence in such cities as Chicago. They brought with them what Michael Barkun has called "cognate themes," or the belief in a variety of related experimental and Utopian social panaceas.[42] Evangelicalism and millennialism were thus a crucial background for capitalist, Utopian thinking of the antebellum period and beyond, into the 1890s. They added the ferment of optimism and perfectionism to the intoxicating plans for urban reform.

Because of their background in this environment, the George Pullmans, Philip Armours, Marshall Fields, and Turlington Harveys of Chicago could interpret their enormous success, their establishment of great fortunes and new forms of commercial culture as part of the change that had shaken their families loose from the staid and conservative Protestantism of New England. What they brought to Chicago was a willingness to experiment and change personally, and a belief that this was, and ought to be, sanctified by religious institutions. No wonder, then, that this new outpost of the burned-over district on the shores of Lake Michigan should witness the emergence, by 1893, of some of the greatest cultural and spiritual experiments of the nineteenth century. In this special light, the World's Columbian Exposition at Chicago can be understood as the consummation of an earlier phase of American perfectionism. Only this generation could have created the grand consumer culture on display in Chicago and yet, at the same time, so occupied itself with the moral and social implications of the rising tide of popular culture which it generated on the same fairgrounds.

Perhaps part of the reason for this seeming contradiction was that while this generation excelled in self-confidence and success, it lacked the language and categories to explain its accomplishments. A fondness for values of an earlier, parsimonious agricultural world did little to articulate the consumer culture, with its extravagances of promise and profits that these men had concocted.

This anomaly can clearly be seen in an advice pamphlet written by Harlow Higinbotham and published by the *Saturday Evening Post* in 1900. Recounting the steps to his own success, Higinbotham spent considerable time talking about the role of quick-witted boys, ever ready to seize the opportunity presented by circumstances. Sounding almost like Horatio Alger, he recounted a cautionary tale of a long trip he once took to recover some investments of his retail firm. Persistence and cleverness netted him the sums involved and the praise of his employer. The behavior that worked for him, he assumed, remained valid for the next generation of striving young men. While this might no longer be appropriate, Higinbotham's continuing faith in the small steps to success reveals his belief in the precepts of middle-class culture, despite his rise out of it into Chicago's elite.

In his advice to other retailers, he was also singularly uninteresting, as if being associated with Marshall Field's dramatic innovations had no effect whatsoever on his imagination. For merchants he advised maintaining fresh stock, limiting credit, and advertising judiciously and with some variety. He counseled paternalism and profit sharing, and justified the accumulations by millionaires "for the sake of the small armies of men, women and children depending for the necessities of life upon the safe conduct of the great enterprises managed by these men."[43]

On one point, however, the merchant and president of the World's Fair Board had a remarkable insight. In the world of philanthropy, Higinbotham shrewdly described differences in approaches that various businessmen might take. For manufacturers, he argued (and he well might have meant Pullman and Harvey), it was easy enough to construct an ideal community and provide "halls, churches, libraries, schools, gymnasiums, theatres, and club houses to be used exclusively by the men and women on his pay-roll." The merchant's employees, on the other hand, because they represented all social classes from the club member and fashionable people to lower-ranked clerks, could not be "considered *en masse* in any plan for their advancement which would necessitate their meeting together or sustaining a common social relationship."[44] This multicultural reality which reflected the burgeoning consumer world of the city was perhaps best represented in the World's Fair with its separated appeals to a variety of audiences and tastes.

Despite the self-confidence, even arrogance of this vision, Higinbotham and his generation of Chicago's elite had to share power in forming late nineteenth-century culture with a generation of very different origins and perspectives. This rival group can best be exemplified by Sol Bloom, a Chicagoan who later became a congressman from the Silk Stocking district of New York City. In 1893, Bloom was a crucial participant in the creation of the World's Fair Midway. Born in 1870 in Pekin, Illinois, to Polish-Jewish immigrant parents, he moved with his family at a very young age to San Francisco. While still a teenager, he became treasurer of the Alcazar Theater, owned by Mike De Young, publisher of the *San Francisco Chronicle*.[45] At the age of nineteen, with savings of $80,000, he departed on a world tour. One of his first stops was at the Paris International Exposition where he booked the North African sword swallowers, glass and scorpion eaters, and belly dancers for an American tour.

In 1892, because of his contacts with De Young, who was active in the planning of the Chicago World's Fair, he received a commission to come to Chicago to help work with the Midway concessionaire groups. As he recalled it, he was brought in to "straighten out these temperamental fellows."[46] What actually happened at the Fair and Bloom's position in the administrative structure remains something of a mystery because of his unsubstantiated recollections.[47] Yet his claim to bringing belly dancers to the Fair and his authorship of the classic melody for the "Hootchy Kootch" dance are probably accurate.

The point about these backgrounds is in the contrast. The great entrepreneurs of Chicago never shed their spiritual background forged in the burned-over district or their assumption that culture could be an instrument of God's grace or at least His moral order. Sol Bloom, on the other hand, was an entrepreneur of the popular culture of the city streets. He had, after all, helped to create it. Most significant, he did not carry the moral baggage that judged culture by preexisting standards. The value of culture, for Bloom, was its economic success and popularity. Thus, the marketplace replaced moral affirmation rather than confirming it. In the confrontation between these two ideas and approaches to urban culture, our story begins and ends.

Three

APPROACHES
Discovery from a Distance

Economically, the metropolis may be described as the urban embodiment of the international fair. Its routine is subordinate to the exhibition and sale of goods. But the fair has two sides: business and pleasure; and as business takes on a more abstract form, with greater stress on monetary manipulation, regularity, mechanism, mathematical discipline, the need for compensatory relief becomes greater. The traditional pleasures of the fair—jugglers, acrobats, gamblers, sideshows, sexual license of all sorts—cease to be sporadic: they too become part of the metropolitan routine. The metropolis itself may be described as a World's Fair in continuous operation.

> Lewis Mumford, *The Culture of Cities*[1]

Seen from a distance, Los Angeles is a white city. It gives the effect of an exposition . . . a world's fair . . . placed against the background of the mountains. There is about it the impression of a beautiful mirage, likely to fade into unreality. Its tall buildings rise like the turrets of a fairy world.

> Harry Carr, *Los Angeles: City of Dreams*[2]

C HICAGO IN 1892: the Phoenix City, brushing off the ashes of the Great Fire; the Garden City; the Paris of the New World; the city of "I will." Chicago, with no history

except beginnings, a plain plowed by real estate speculators, an itinerary for the future, the great middle-class city. A city of endless
diversity and change. Chicago in 1892: the most immigrant city in
America, the black city of smoke and grime and violence, the least
American of towns, the "shock city" of the 1890s.[3]

As one guidebook put it in 1892:

> Here was a city which had no traditions but was making
> them, and this was the very thing that every one seemed to
> understand and rejoice in. Chicago was like no other city in the
> world, so said they all. Chicago would outstrip every other
> American city, New York included, and become the first of all
> American, if not European or world, cities. . . . This dream
> many hundreds of thousands of its citizens held dear.[4]

Just as the skyline signified Manhattan to New Yorkers, the train
trip through an accelerating density to the center of the city evoked
Chicago. In the Chicago novel of the 1890s, this became a kind of
stereotype. Robert Herrick's *Gospel of Freedom* (1898) contains a
typical picture:

> The complex quality of this wonderful city is best seen as
> the stranger shoots across the prairie in a railroad train, pene-
> trating layer after layer of the folds. First, in the great distance,
> rises a pall of dull smoke, . . . Then the railroad, describing
> irregular curves, crosses lines of streets built up on embank-
> ments with oily ditches below, and intersected by cross streets
> that disappear into the marsh.[5]

During the 1890s, when such impressions were hardening into
clichés, Chicago seemed on the verge of a successful claim to redefine the American urban experience. This redefinition promised, at
least in a general, perhaps even abstract way, to solve a growing
problem of identity and establish a sanctuary of culture and stability
for middle-class families disoriented by the incredible diversity of
the urban environment. Daniel Burnham, architectural master of
the World's Fair, wrote somewhat later of this vision: "The cream of
our own earnings should be spent here, while the city should become a magnet, drawing to us those who wish to enjoy life. . . .
Then our own people will become home-keepers, and the stranger
will seek our gates."[6]

City of Chicago. Currier and Ives print from 1892. Focused through tradition, this rendering of Chicago stressed bucolic elements of the cityscape. The waterway approach, the oversized sailing ships, and church spires quote the icons of an earlier era. Contemporary guidebook literature rejected this archaic view in favor of an aggressive modernity, busyness, and celebratory architecture and public spaces for the pastoralism of Currier and Ives. (Library of Congress)

What was it like to visit Chicago in 1893—to be a stranger at the gates? The answer depended partly upon how Chicago writers, journalists, businessmen, and intellectuals tried to shape the initial encounter with the city. Their practical unanimity of impressions created a structuring vision, a literature that prejudiced what the tourist expected to experience, leading and guiding and forming his or her impressions in advance, creating an imaginary cityscape in which the disorienting experience of an actual visit could be placed and understood.

Because of their efforts, the great Midwestern metropolis rose like an apparition, the spirit of modern urbanism that beckoned the traveler to imagine what all cities would be like in the future. For a few years in the early 1890s, writers, city planners, tourists, businessmen, and middle-class citizens thought of Chicago as the city of the possible, which, despite its remarkable cultural variety, could be made a place of comfort and familiarity. This optimism was decanted with the opening of the World's Fair in 1893 and imbibed by millions of visitors. One of the city's earlier historians said that "during the six months when the Exposition flourished before peoples' eyes, it roused Chicago to an exalted idea of what a city could be like."[7] But this optimism also reflected the very reasons Chicago won the contest to host the Columbian celebration in the first place. The city itself, as well as the great exhibit at Jackson Park, counted as one of the great tourist attractions of the late nineteenth century.[8]

To a remarkable degree, the impression of Chicago was shaped and presented for visitors—and even Chicagoans themselves—by a new literature appearing in newspaper journalism and in city guidebooks, often written by newspapermen or publishers. With a passing acquaintance with most of the city, these journalists attempted, in the early 1890s, to fashion a cityscape, to create a way of seeing and experiencing urban life that would be acceptable to elites and stimulating to the vast audience of newcomers and tourists to the city. This was all the more effective because, in a world which increasingly defined itself through the published word and reproducible photograph, perception was becoming inseparable from the new journalism of the era.

The explosion of urban journalism into a multitude of forms aspired to make sense out of the daily experience of city dwellers and visitors. Different social groups claimed special access and attention in a multitude of specialized city papers. Foreign language newspapers published news of immigrant groups otherwise ignored by English language presses. In established papers, long descriptions of the social activities of the wealthy vied with newer, human interest stories by reporters who roved the city and recorded its diversity. In Chicago, at the opening of the Fair, there were at least twenty-seven active daily newspapers and scores of less frequent journals aimed at various segments of the public.

This dense, variable, and changing writing about the city and urban experience suggested the utility of a large and important guidebook literature to Chicago, published throughout the city's history, but particularly important and widespread in 1892 and 1893 prior to the Chicago World's Columbian Exposition. As introductory literature, these books helped to shape the expectations of visitors to Chicago, to impress upon their experience a vision of the city that the authors hoped would conform to their own, a booster's concept of what the city could be like. More often than not, it also reflected new styles in newspaper journalism and realistic novels.

One of the pioneering journalists in this developing urban realism found his way to Chicago in 1890. He became the reigning journalist of the next decade. His prose sketches provide a sample of the journalism that served to expose the multiple realities of the city—with a tone of bemused detachment. The young writer was George Ade, an immigrant from Indiana, a reporter for the *Chicago Record,* and innovator of a breezy, familiar prose style quickly recognized as a standard for urban storytelling. During the 1890s, Ade wrote several fascinating sketches that opened a tentative window to his adopted city.[9] His frequent metaphor for the city was "Babel," although he meant this as an endearing term.[10]

Confusion of languages and sensations was only, to Ade, a place to begin. Familiarity and perspective brought a reversal of images and ideas and a recognition that first impressions were often wrong—that was his deeper message. His short pieces were fastidiously cut slices of reality held up for examination at a comfortable distance. And, in his longer novel, *Artie: A Story of the Streets and Town* (1896), he spent considerable time introducing the city to readers through his hero, Artie Blanchard, who was "as good as a guide-book."[11]

In a typical piece of journalism, "From the Office Window," Ade assumed his habitual perspective and, in a few short pages, managed to pack into it a world of impressions about the bewildering life around him as well as a lesson in observation. Ruggles, a young Chicago office clerk, is promoted to an office with a window. But such a window. It overlooked an opposite window that stared at him with the eyes of a blind man: "They were there to see through but no one saw through them." Having established himself and the reader as unseen voyeurs, Ade then plunges into his story.

After several weeks, the clerk notices an elderly woman and a young girl who suddenly appear in the building opposite, both preoccupied most of the day with sewing. Ruggles's curiosity rises when he observes the old woman introduce a black-haired policeman to the young girl. Within a few days, a red-haired policeman also calls on the young girl. Thereafter, the officers alternate visits, although Ruggles imagines that the young girl prefers the red-headed suitor. Suddenly, the small procession ends, and the girl vanishes.

After business takes him elsewhere for a year, Ruggles returns to his office, his window, and his scrutiny. He notices to his relief that the old woman is still visible, sewing relentlessly: "Nothing had happened," he surmises at first. And then he catches sight of the girl ("a little older and not quite so merry faced") rocking a red-haired baby in her arms.

This slight piece, positioning the narrator as outsider, emphasizes his detachment, his vaguely aroused interest, his safe separation through the glass. With his unproven assumptions and his wink at the reader, Ade underscores this point of view and suggests a literary syntax in which to place the most tragic events. Even scandalous incidents in the lives of others could be counted as mere curiosities.

Ade assumed this role of the detached observer in other sketches. In "The Advantage of Being Middle Class" he argues two points: it is acceptable, even exciting, to participate in the popular culture of the city and, despite all appearances, there is nothing at all immoral about this culture. The fortunate middle classes, as he defines them, include all Chicagoans whose income placed them among neither "Society" nor the poverty-stricken. Unlike the wealthy, they can smoke when they wish, eat ice cream, listen to "popular" airs, watch an Italian organ-grinder, and feel quite safe strolling in the park.

In the denouement of this sketch, as before, Ade uses the suggestion of illicit sex to accent his contention about the moral environment of the city. He recounts the story of two men walking in Jackson Park, where they glimpse a young woman, first alone, and then, later, sitting on a park bench with her head on a man's shoulder. As the two men walk by, one of them, shocked by what he thinks he has observed, makes a cutting remark, only to distinguish at the last moment a third small head belonging to a child. The couple was married! As he does elsewhere, Ade hints at danger of the sort that Chicago's middle classes feared; he titillates; and then he retreats with a sly and quick reassurance.[12] "Did you really think . . . ?" he seems to ask.

There was no denying the possibility of danger in George Ade's Chicago; indeed, its potential lay everywhere. Yet he scrupulously maintains a safe distance in such stories. His melodramatic resolutions provide a glimpse of something illicit; he lights a flicker of salaciousness and then quickly extinguishes it with a happy ending, all of which make the city appear real (but safe) for middle-class men and women. Diversity, poverty, danger, inhabit the city, he says, but they can be transformed or evaded.

This is decidedly not Theodore Dreiser's Chicago. Dreiser first moved to Chicago three years before Ade, but his importance as a writer came a decade later and his perspective was revolutionary. Given the same material, in Dreiser's hands, the reader, together with the author, would slip into the young girl's room through the window to learn of her misfortunes, or overhear the couple on the bench whisper that they are not married. But even Dreiser at this moment in the mid-1890s had not yet consummated the integration of urban cultures that made his novel *Sister Carrie* so controversial. That would require a gestation period in the different cosmopolitanism of New York City.[13]

For the time being, Chicago belonged to such writers as Ade and his fellow journalist Finley Peter Dunne. Dunne exploited three great dangers of the city: drink, the immigrant, and dialect (representing foreign culture), converting them via his comic sage, Mr. Dooley, into acceptable satires of politics and pretense. Nothing in the 1890s was more worrisome among Chicago's middle classes than immigrant groups in the city and their habits of drink. Yet Dunne, like Ade, playfully unmasked the exotic in his sketches to reveal a conventional core of opinions.[14] The pleasing jolt of recognizing the familiar was stimulated by the prose itself, written in dialect that required slow scanning or even reading out loud for comprehension. Dunne and Ade drew upon the Chicago of middle-class readers of sentimental novels: *David Copperfield, Ivanhoe, The Scarlet Letter, Uncle Tom's Cabin, Ben Hur*.[15] They presupposed a city in which the miscellany of men and women and the diversity of popular cultures could all be disguised inside a more or less traditional middle-class popular culture.

For a fleeting moment in the late nineteenth century, Chicago writers endorsed a perspective that coincided with a middle-class and elite conception of the possibilities of modern urban culture. Facing what everyone recognized as a wildly speculative future, a city already choked with smoke and industry and swollen with immigrants expressing a Babel of cultures, writers, nevertheless, developed a literary orientation that put the city behind glass, that achieved distance from the threat of moral involvement, that saw the city as an accessible fantasy land of spectacles, parks, and public places as well as private lives. This was the city presented to the tourist in the considerable guidebook literature, written for the Fair years, by Chicago's journalists and publishing entrepreneurs.

To understand why this vision of the city developed as it did, a few preliminary remarks are necessary. For middle-class and elite Chicagoans, the city held several special perils. Among them was a short but brutal labor history, marked by violent strikes and the infamous bombing in Haymarket Square in 1886 and the notorious trial of anarchists charged in the affair. In its short history, the city had endured disturbing cycles of fortunes, with dizzy rises and steep declines, with huge gains and losses in real estate and manufacturing. Its streets and housing were overwhelmed by waves of immigrants: Irish, Germans, Scandinavians, and a generation of farm boys and farm girls from the Midwest.[16] Inevitably, politicians arose to unite these groups into crude and sometimes corrupt alliances. Middle-class people often tolerated this arrangement. They also certainly admired the great retail and manufacturing entrepreneurs who made up Chicago "society" and lived in stone castles along Prairie Avenue or in exclusive splendor on the North Shore. They were increasingly aware of the intriguing freedoms of immigrant cultures, but they strove to find their own place.

Beyond this, Chicago was a city of other diversities and uncertainties: where to live, how to behave in public, how to react to the different cultures increasingly visible in parks and public places, how to pick one's way through the multiplicity of possibilities, how to interpret the city visually (was it a glimmering white city or a smokey black city)? These were questions not easily answered. But in the optimistic moment of the early 1890s there seemed to be a possible answer in the idealization of a new urban experience: safe,

Union Depot in Chicago before 1900. This consolidated railway station was one of the largest and grandest entries into Chicago. The photographer has taken advantage of a quiet time for his portrait. (Photo by Gates, no. 36, Chicago Historical Society)

clean, familiar, and self-confident, on the verge of consciousness, at the edge of the future.

This was one purpose of authors inventing a new type of novel about Chicago and aimed at readers among the new middle classes. To create a middle space for such Chicagoans, writer Henry Fuller, for example, described urban society in terms of elevations. The "cliff dwellers" at the top of society had to be made as familiar to readers as the eye-level dwellings of immigrants. In his novel, called the *Cliff Dwellers*, Fuller describes how one of his characters begins to learn to orient himself in the amazing polyglot culture of Chicago. Speaking of the initiation of this newcomer to the city, he writes:

> Ogden had now gone through a novitiate of five or six weeks. . . . He found that there might be an inner quiet under all this vast and apparently unregulated din: he recalled how, in a cotton factory or a copper foundry, the hands talked among themselves in tones lower than the average, rather than higher. The rumble of drays and the clang of street-car gongs became less disconcerting; the town's swarming hordes presently appeared less slovenly in their dress and less offensive in their manners . . . even their varied physiognomies began to take on a cast less comprehensively cosmopolitan. . . . it soon came to seem possible that all these different elements might be scheduled, classified, brought into a sort of *catalogue raisonné* which should give every feature its proper place—skulls, foreheads, gaits, odors, facial angles.[17]

Fuller's novel, like Ade's essay on the middle class, positioned the reader between two extremes, the disruptive and confusing background of the cosmopolitan city and the dangerous and corrupt heights of the cliff dwellers. The *catalogue raisonné* of the city, as he describes it, imposes structure on each element of the unfamiliar. The novel, as so much of the literature of the nineteenth-century city, served as a kind of guidebook, a book of cues and signposts for urban behavior.

Hamlin Garland, in *Crumbling Idols*, universalizes the Chicago experience:

> Already Chicago claims to have pushed New York from her seat as ruler of our commerce. The whole West and South are in open rebellion against her financial rule. Chicago equals, possibly outnumbers her, in population, and certainly outspeeds her in enterprise. The rise of Chicago as a literary and art center is a question only of time, and of a very short time; for the Columbian Exposition has taught her own capabilities in something higher than business.[18]

He continues with a cryptic remark: Chicago is "more American, notwithstanding its foreign population." True enough, but why? He never quite explains. But what we can presume he meant is a paradox that particularly confounded many of his contemporaries. The city exemplified America because it lacked history and form; it was a liminal, emerging urban area, recalling America's mythic beginning as a place without shape, yet inspired and ordered by its consecrated purpose. As Julian Ralph said, "I have referred to Chicago as a typically American city, and so I still believe it to be, but it is American only in the spirit that dominates it."[19]

The conventions developed by this generation of Chicago writers and journalists were repeated in a huge new literature of guidebooks to the city. Because of the impending World's Fair, publishers of all sorts, from established houses like Rand McNally to small printers, turned out scores of guides to the city and to the Fair. Aimed at a special audience of middle-class tourists, whose stay would probably last a week or more, they proposed agendas for visiting the city. They directly addressed an audience that was curious about the city. But, more important, they invented a cityscape intended as a kind of literary cosmetic to be dabbed upon experience itself. The guidebooks described the city as it should be experienced, not as it was. Their unanimity of interpretation is therefore instructive, if unsurprising.

The diversity of these books was quite remarkable, responding to the rapidly expanding markets and special places where one might purchase such a book, and the purposes to which it might be put. Perhaps the most common place to encounter a Chicago travel guide was at a train station kiosk or on the train itself. For example, Rand McNally sold a cheap handbook to the city and the World's Fair for twenty-five cents. These editions, known as "butcher-boy books," were also available by mail subscription. Other Rand McNally books were more expensive, lavishly illustrated, and copiously narrated, clearly intended for a more affluent and less-rushed audience.[20]

During 1892 and 1893, booksellers throughout the nation made Chicago guidebooks available. Anticipating substantial sales, Chicago booksellers like Laird and Lee placed large numbers of announcements and advertisements in national bookseller journals such as the *Book of News-Dealers* and *Publishers Weekly*.[21] These books were clearly intended for visitors preparing to ride the train to Chicago for the World's Fair.

What were the millions of visitors to the city supposed to see and experience? How did the authors of the guidebooks create and then respond to the expectations of their customers? With what terms did they introduce urban experience? How did the guidebooks attempt to structure that encounter and provide a language of tourism that would both particularize the visit and universalize its moral and, therefore, lasting effects?

To some extent, the strategy of presenting the unfamiliar city had already been established in earlier genres of guidebook and advice literature. This was necessary if only because travel, at least in the form of migration, was the experience of many Americans in the nineteenth century. Advice books, and even the contemporary Horatio Alger literature, described both the perils of wrong choices and self-deceptions, and the advantages of finding one's way into a familiar, socially confident world. To encounter the urban world of strangers required shared assumptions about the meaning of behavior that could only come from sharing perceptions and expectations.[22]

This is equivalent to inventing a "mental map" of the city. Such maps, writes Alan Henrikson, are composed out of orientations and strong impressions "by reference to which a person acquires, codes, stores, recalls, reorganizes, and applies, in thought or action, information about his or her large-scale geographical environment."[23] An urban environment can be known through a generalized symbol— like the accelerating entry into Chicago—to which all other perceptions are subsumed.[24] Henry Fuller must have had something like this in mind when he had a character in the *Cliff Dwellers* exclaim about Chicago that

> the name of the town in its formal, ceremonial use, has a power that no other word in the language quite possesses. It is a shibboleth, as regards its pronunciation, it is a trumpet call as regards its effect. It has all the electrifying and amplifying

power of a college yell. "Chicago is Chicago," he said. "It is the belief of all of us. It is inevitable; nothing can stop us now."[25]

If, very often, the initial, unifying symbol of Chicago was a compressed, visual image of the train trip rushing from the empty plains into an unexpected metropolis, this vision replicated certain aspects of the enterprise of tourism itself, with a curious flourish. The trip to Chicago was not a voyage into the past, or the familiar, or even into the exotic. Instead, guidebooks presented it as travel through the present into the future. Chicago guidebook author Carroll Ryan deliberately positioned the reader so he could visualize the contrast between an ordinary tour and the very special encounter with this city of the future: "Looking down on it [Chicago] from the dizzy summit of the Masonic Temple, strange thoughts must fill the mind of him who has traveled far, who has seen the ruins of empires, empires in decay, and this new empire of the west rising with a civilization greater, more intense, more free, more universal than all that preceded it."[26] Rather than being alien or foreign, Chicago represented a generalized American urban experience. Its uniqueness lay only in how clearly it suggested the outlines of the future. The travel books leading the visitor into the city worked diligently to establish and monitor this impression.[27]

One has only to consider an alternative way of approaching the city to envision how destructive and upsetting an unguided tour could be. Sherwood Anderson, in his novel *Poor White*, stresses this confusion in his description of Hugh McVey's entry into Chicago:

> It was evening when he came into the roaring, clanging place. . . . When he got into the big dark station Hugh saw thousands of people rushing about like disturbed insects. . . .
>
> Hugh looked at the people who were whirled along past him and shivered with the nameless fear of multitudes, common to country boys in the city.[28]

Looking at the guidebook literature to Chicago in the early 1890s, we can discover an aspect of the vocabulary that journalists invented to exploit just this sort of anticipated bewilderment.

Publication of guidebooks and histories of Chicago proliferated in the early 1890s, in anticipation of a huge tourist boom for the

World's Fair.[29] Most of them, like those by Trumbell White and William Igleheart, extravagantly generalized about the city. Chicago "is so essentially the most American of the great towns of the United States," they suggested, "that many other cities are foreign compared with it." Thus, it was entirely appropriate that the Columbian exhibit be held in "this marvelous city," this apotheosis of prosperity.[30] Journalist and guidebook author Julian Ralph concluded that Chicago itself would be "the main exhibit at the Columbian Exposition."[31]

Despite virtual unanimity of the guidebooks about the pleasures of visiting Chicago and the value of experiencing the city of the future, there were gaping holes in the story, whole sections of the city missing, and curious interpretations of unpleasant features of the city that the authors felt obliged to mention. Certain parts of the city and one's inevitable brushes with them were either cautiously interpreted or ignored in the truncated geography of the carefully controlled visit. For example, almost every guidebook boasted of Chicago's ethnic diversity. Its huge population of first-generation immigrants far exceeded (as claimed) the percentage living in New York. German-born residents outnumbered American-born, with the Irish a close third. In addition, Chicago had large populations of Scandinavians and Eastern Europeans. Almost every guidebook rhapsodized over this ethnic diversity, but having sung a few notes of appreciation they direct the reader through an itinerary that avoided any direct contact with such populations. By contrast, other parts of the city were examined more scrupulously.[32]

Diversity—confined to a literary preview—introduced another similar point made by most of the guidebooks: growth of population and industry—seen abstractly—symbolized the coming grandeur of Chicago. This future seemed near. The decades around the World's Fair claimed the most spectacular increases in the city's history. The population had more than doubled from 1880 to 1890. Huge new industries sprang up, and with them an extraordinary real estate speculation boom that peaked in 1893. The city surged up and out, building its envied steel-frame skyscrapers at the center and grabbing huge chunks of land at the periphery in 1889 upon which to plant factories and residential neighborhoods. Railroads, manufactures, city transport, department stores, and apartment buildings struggled to keep up with the pace of growth. On a smaller scale, suburbs spawned at the edges of the city tried to reproduce its evolution.[33]

Coexisting with the showy improvements was the shadowy side of the city almost invisible in the guides—the city of misery, poverty, corruption, and scandal, and the commonplace world of work, routine, and ordinary people. In its short history, Chicago had also developed dismal slums; its saloons sprang up everywhere; and its evil resorts became legendary. Its air pollution, dust, and smoke earned it the nickname of the "Black City." The guidebooks did not quite deny such realities; rather, they played them as a dim discord resolved in a hymn to progress.

Some of the early guidebooks of Chicago, written in the 1870s and 1880s, contrast with this later tourist literature because they concentrate so little on such extravagant visions. Few of these early publications addressed a general middle-class audience. As likely as not, their clientele were businessmen and salesmen. Two early works, for example, address the reader as "stranger." The 1874 *Stranger's Guide to the City of Chicago* is filled with advertisements for local manufactures. It catalogs business establishments and civic and official institutions, ending with a street directory. An 1868 guide to Chicago, subtitled a *Stranger's Hand-Book*, follows this same format.

Frank Glossop's somewhat later 1880 guide to Chicago manifests a more confused, even contradictory purpose, as if caught in a puzzling transition between genres. It addresses two classes of tourists: rich and modest. It lists civic institutions, genteel saloons, and theaters, and gives hints about travel. But its order of presentation is almost random. There is no attempt, in other words, to structure the experience of a visit. Finally, Marquis's *Hand-Book of Chicago*, published in 1885, claims to offer the first comprehensive vision of the great metropolis. It includes snatches of history, descriptions of buildings and institutions, clubs and societies. But it suddenly inflates in the middle, swelling up with extensive information about Chicago merchants, lawyers, and real estate brokers, and leading hotels. Clearly, it too is intended for the out-of-town businessman.[34]

Harold Vynne's *Chicago by Day and Night*, published in 1892, typifies a very different sort of male-oriented guidebook. Derivative of a well-developed genre of New York City "by gaslight" books, this mildly salacious exploration of Chicago's night life was both cautionary and explicit, warning the visitor to stay away from scandalous resorts whose addresses and activities it detailed. Vynne, an author for the satirical New York publication, *Town Topics*, also published melodramatic novels whose trademark was to linger over descriptions of seductions, attempted rapes, and other scandalous behavior.[35]

Well grounded in nineteenth-century culture, several of the early business guides mentioned, as a possible leisure-time activity, the custom of cemetery visitation. But in Albert Marquis's later Chicago guidebook, the author invokes this practice as a metaphor to indicate a coming transformation of values. In a section discussing the convention of visiting "cities of the dead," Marquis notes without comment that the city had begun to intrude upon these places. Chicago, with her "industries of bustle of her wonderful and broadening life," threatened to tear up such sites. The modern city was encroaching upon the defunct nineteenth century and its customs.[36]

Most 1890s guidebooks addressed a new audience with a broader purpose than travelers who purchased the earlier business manuals. Their clientele was more obviously middle-class tourists, so mention of commercial establishments focused on the architectural splendors of downtown or shopping. Tourists were also expected to include women. Aimed at the novice visitor, these books endeavored to dispel fears of travel into an unknown environment and yet, of course, to persuade the tourist to rely upon the guide. Almost inevitably, this strategy generated a curiously ambiguous picture of Chicago: the city represented (briefly) as an overwhelming and confusing diversity versus the city that unfolds as a clearly marked, easily followed itinerary of experiences. The only guidebook not to do this chose an alphabetical arrangement of buildings, hotels, streets, and sites; that is, it lacked any guiding principle of experience. But this book was addressed to policemen or other officials who knew the city.[37]

Something of the changing tourist experience is also implied by the length of time deemed appropriate for a visit. During the World's Fair of 1893, two weeks seemed to be the proper minimum. But even a tourist's visit just to the city was expected to be leisurely. And, no doubt, most tourists were presumed to have the means to afford such an extended sojourn.

Based on estimates of hotel prices and food, cab fares and sundries, a modest stay could cost about $30 a week, plus train tickets. Sample fares in 1892 from various points in the United States in second class, one way were: San Francisco, $45.00; Dallas $20.25; New York, $17.00; and St. Louis $6.00. Not prohibitively expensive, even for the late nineteenth century, such amounts nevertheless excluded a great many working-class people or farmers who had neither savings nor spare time to embark upon such a trip.[38]

Looking more closely at the guidebooks of the 1890s, it becomes obvious that the initial address to the reader had already developed into a series of conventions. There were three popular opening formats introducing Chicago, although each only varied the same larger theme. Each opening introduced a city defined at first by its overwhelming variety and unfamiliarity. Charles Powers's gossipy *Heart of Chicago* immediately announces a characteristic theme of a clash of cultures and nationalities. While thoroughly American, the city, he noted, maintained a quota from every "race on earth." On its busy streets could be found "the dusky Arab, the exquisite Frenchman, fair-haired Norwegians, dark-eyed Spaniards, Georgians from Central Asia, Señors from South America, and the squatty Laplander from his ice-bound home."[39]

Robert Musket's intriguing *Chicago, Yesterday and To-day*, expresses a similar sense of awe at diversity. He, too, frames his remarks with a literary strategy—albeit not one of ethnic stereotypes. He chooses a kind of cinematic portrait of a day on the streets. Beginning with a general description of the street system, he pauses at State Street in the business center. "Standing on this thoroughfare," he says, "one sees every nation represented and hears every civilized tongue spoken (and some uncivilized), and as the day wears on, the throng increases, until at six o'clock it presents one of the most animated scenes possible to behold." Building to a rapid climax of confusing impressions, he watches as workingmen and women, rich and poor, black and white, learned and unlearned clamor into public transportation. He then breaks off to another section where he describes Chicago's extensive park system. The juxtaposition makes it clear that the cultural mixing is not threatening to the tourist. Nor is the author actually advising the tourist to assume a daylong vigil on State Street. Finally, just around the corner are broad boulevards and gorgeous parks: while cultures rub elbows downtown, he implies, there are still retreats from this confusion.[40]

A fascinating variation on this theme can be found in *Gody's Illustrated Souvenir Guide to the Chicago World's Fair and New York*. The author addresses ethnic diversity in three different venues: in New York, on the Midway at the Chicago World's Fair, and in the city of Chicago. In each case, diversity anchors the segment, providing a starting-up point for the descriptions that follow. In each example, the reader's attention is drawn swiftly away from multiplicity and confusion to focus on buildings, institutions, and organizations. But there is one anomaly. The author writes that New York is the most cosmopolitan of American cities, founded upon a history of great ethnic richness and diversity. And yet, in two tables, he presents figures that clearly demonstrate Chicago's predominance in foreign-born citizens (71–45 percent). What then makes New York more cosmopolitan? The author emphasizes the traditional and historic immigrant districts that shape the culture of that city. Chicago, by contrast, appears too young to have developed such traditions—or any tradition.[41]

A second opening upon the confusion of cultures depicted institutional diversity, not ethnic variety. For example, Edwin Stine's *What Everybody Wants to Know about Chicago* begins with extravagant descriptions of space and intimidating lists of public and private cultural and civic institutions. Everything is described by cost, size, number, multiplicity. The author lists institutions, places of amusement, societies, clubs, businesses. He enumerates, among other things, 497 churches, 301 newspapers and publications, 3,569 saloons, 31 theaters, 62 societies; art galleries, hotels, music teachers, and photographic studios.

Here the design invites tourists to employ the guidebook for direction through this extravagant menu of possibilities. Initially presenting an inventory of the cultural choices available to middle-class visitors, Stine proceeds to sort them out, to validate special places and institutions. He recommends hotels, proper ways to bestow charity (avoid beggars!), where to shop, how to recognize gamblers, how to take public transportation. Stine maintains a reassuring tone, as did almost all the guidebooks, even about incidents like the Haymarket Affair—a riot resulting from labor's fight for the eight-hour day—which had given the city a violent and intolerant reputation. After only six years the Haymarket had become little more than a tourist curiosity in the pages of his book.[42]

A third variant of the multiplicity theme characterized those guidebooks that chose to narrate the exciting physical entry of the tourist into Chicago. Beginning in the train station (of which there were several), they recount the hurly-burly of the arrival scene. Freighted with baggage, assailed by cab drivers, porters, and hackers of all descriptions, wondering about public transportation, and, most of all, confounded by a list of almost 1,500 hotels and rooming houses, the bewildered traveler is led through the steps necessary to arrive at accommodations. Such guidebooks explained city-enforced cab rates, described porter companies, and listed prices of hotels. In these examples, the format was self-contradictory: it elaborated upon the very confusion it sought to dispel. Reading the guidebook would allow the tourist to avoid the pitfalls the guidebook enumerated and to master the confusion of arrival. Rand McNally's *Handy Guide* published in 1893 contained an early section on cabs, baggage removal, hotels, and restaurants, for example.[43] Hill's *Guide to Chicago* even went so far as to include pictures of the various models of horse and carriage available for rental plus their fees.[44]

A very different but popular guidebook opening upon Chicago emphasized historical distance. A number of guides recounted, with differing detail, the city's singular past, yet with a similar purpose. Almost unanimously, they all agreed upon one point: the past, as any reader might expect to see it narrated, did not exist. In fact, in several books, the past so abruptly dissolved into the present, and the present into the future, that it disappeared altogether.

As a preamble for a trip around the city, this curiously truncated, even absent history reinforced the power of Chicago's image as the realized future. Represented through metaphors of rebirth and renewal, the Phoenix-like city, rising from the ashes of the Great Fire of 1871 or from the labor confrontation at Haymarket, is liberated from the past to occupy an expanse of limitless possibilities. Like a nineteenth-century Los Angeles, it conjured up images of an artificial urbanity, a cultural arrangement imposed upon an amenable site, a city to be created and recreated according to the cultural fantasies of the moment.

Most guidebooks limited their discussion to four or five historical topics, usually including the Indian occupation of the area, the French era, the foundation of the city in 1833, the Great Fire of 1871, and the Haymarket Affair of 1886. Not all tourist manuals introduce each incident, but the Great Fire is never missing. Yet, in each case, the absence of a full historical record becomes cause to celebrate the Americanness of the city, its futureness.

This curious distortion of history could take many forms. John Flinn, in *Chicago: The Marvelous City*, begins with a frontispiece of a female figure reviving, and the caption, "Chicago Has Arisen—Solace in Tribulation." Not even in the Arabian Nights with its glorious colors of "Oriental fancy," he boasts, "is there a tale which surpasses in wonder the plain, unvarnished history of Chicago."[45]

In Bancroft's *Book of the Fair*, the history of Chicago appears incomparable. Search history, the author challenges the reader, and he will never find a city of "such phenomenal development." Thus, the city's past renewal reaches into and defines its future. As Robert Musket expressed it: "This is an age of wonders and this is a city of wonders." The time was not distant when Chicago would be "the metropolis of America."[46] Put bluntly by Carroll Ryan, Chicago "in its particularities is a city of the future. A twentieth century city it should be called, when compared with other cities of Europe and America."[47]

The figurative mooring of this wondrous phenomenon of self-renewal was almost always the allegorically treated Great Fire of 1871. Despite the terrible loss of property, the city rebuilt, on a grander scale, almost immediately, with builders (as legend has it) beginning new constructions before the ashes had cooled. The history of Chicago published by the newspaper, the *Inter Ocean*, repeated what had become by then a cliché: "Taken as a whole, the fire was the most wonderful advertisement that ever any city had, and the prompt action . . . in rebuilding the city so suddenly destroyed turned it into a favorable advertisement." Chicago stood for energy, determination, business acumen in the future, not the past.[48]

This foresight in planning for the future in the midst of clearing away the rubble of ruin (and of history) only accentuated the conviction that new urban forms could be constructed beyond the debilitating reach of tradition, that could cast off the problems of past and present. The dreams of those who imagined a new sort of city could be fulfilled here. This notion seemed to be the essence of the presentation of Chicago to tourists. As a city belonging to the future, renewing itself out of every crisis and change, Chicago had little reason to stress the darker and bleaker side of the contemporary urban world. By displacing the troubles of the past as well as the contemporary reality of the "black city" to their peripheral vision, guidebooks could focus on their essential message: visible through the great confusion of cultures and consumer possibilities in the city was a safe, accessible, futuristic Utopia available to middle-class patrons of the genre. Using such words as "spacious," "expansive," "growth," and "height" gave the inviting impression of welcome and accommodation.[49] As Moses Handy put it in his *Official Directory* of the World's Fair, Chicago had arisen "from dire disaster of the most destructive conflagration ever known"[50] to become one of the greatest cities of the world.

To Daniel Burnham, the absence of historic architecture (because of the fire) in Chicago was really a blessing: "[T]here are no buildings possessing either historical or picturesque value which must be sacrificed in order to carry out plans necessary to provide circulation for a growing metropolis." By the same measure, this absence of historical reference may have stimulated the architect's desire to impose an eclectic design on the World's Fair that emphasized historical references from the neoclassicism at the central Court of Honor to the historic allusions required of each state exhibition.[51]

What this vision of Chicago might reveal about middle-class attitudes to the city cannot be concluded until a few other curiosities about the guidebooks are explored. In almost no case do they provide an itinerary for actual movement through the city, in the manner of a modern guidebook. Those that do stand out. For example, Rand McNally's very extensive handbook, besides confronting the reader with sobering lists of cultural possibilities, proposes two sorts of visits: one male and one female. For men there are amusements,

Devastation after the Chicago Fire of 1871. Visions of destruction were also promises for the future. The history of the city by 1893 could be construed

by its boosters as a paradox in which the past represented only the opportunity for new beginnings. (Library of Congress)

from Italian opera to rambles through the local Hell's Kitchen. Dubious vaudeville shows abound, along with places for "cosmopolitan taste" and dives. For women there are descriptions of department stores, shopping "bazaars," and parks.[52] By placing these possibilities side-by-side with no lurid suggestiveness (as in Vynne's work), the guidebook merely imposed more regularity on the urban experience and expanded the safe places for men and women to visit.

A rival in comprehensiveness was Louis Schick's *Chicago and Its Environs*, published in 1893. Schick carefully explains railroad transport to Chicago, then the arrival and search for hotels, and cabs. He furnishes a cursory description of the city and its institutions. But the most interesting part included several walks around the city. Richly detailed, each of these tours could stand by itself as a literary representation of a slice of the city—making a visit hardly necessary. The author pauses to describe people along the way in considerable detail: the self-important salesmen at the Palmer House, pawnbrokers and "gay young darkees" south of Congress Street in the "Levee" section, boulevards with the castles of the wealthy gentry of the city. This is strongly reminiscent of George Ade's distanced portrait of urban diversity.

But from the tone it is unclear if the visitor was really being invited to make these tours or merely to visualize the results. A stop in front of the Palmer House exemplifies this ambiguity: "As we reach the stately entrance of the Palmer House we notice in various attitudes about the pillars supporting the entrance, types of the throng that go to make up hotel life, with, mayhaps, a city man or two, posing for a brief spell, as a guest of the hotel, in a hope to duly impress some passer-by who does not know him."[53] This is not a neutral description but an idiosyncratic impression, a snatch of journalistic observation, providing the novice with perceptions he or she could scarcely expect to acquire even with a visit. But it does yield a literary understanding. This technique is repeated throughout the "Street Scenes" section, making it clear that the author is injecting himself between the reader and the experience and, at the same time, furnishing only the sketchiest of indications of how actually to walk in the tracks he covers.

Much of the remaining material in the guidebooks is listed by separate category, thus maintaining the impression of diversity in

Chicago institutions, yet providing some means to choose among them. Sights to see are inventoried in various orders, but almost any list would include the stockyards, the boulevards of the wealthy, parks, the commercial center with its grand new buildings, various suburbs such as Pullman and Evanston, cemeteries, the Haymarket, the World's Fairgrounds, and selected governmental buildings and agencies. The arrangment or, rather, lack of order in these sections yields further evidence that this genre does not so much guide the tourist about the city as promote a general picture of Chicago as an urban place to be contemplated as much as visited.

In sum, the Chicago guidebooks self-consciously introduced two sorts of confusion and multiplicity: cultural diversity based upon immigrant variety, and cultural diversity based upon extraordinarily plentiful consumer choices in hotels, restaurants, and social and cultural institutions for middle-class patrons. Rather than thrust the visitor into the thick of such experiences, however, the guidebooks kept him or her at arm's length, only cautiously entering the city at all. The vast underside of Chicago appeared only in sections on diversity, if ever. And enumeration of endless lists of cultural institutions only bolstered the impression that the city contained limitless possibilities for leisure and edification. Except for catalogs of charities or social services, these two worlds were kept apart. By maintaining careful separations—what Lewis Mumford has called a "segregated vision"—the guidebooks avoided the integrated, more dangerous, and controversial moral realism and intensity that Theodore Dreiser later explored in his books and that Jane Addams's Hull-House social workers experienced in their daily work with slum dwellers.

Given its aloofness from history, experience, and moral intensity, this guidebook picture of Chicago easily became the contemplation of possibility, change, and rebirth. The urban experience, like its changing institutions and buildings, could be shaped to fit the aims, the fantasies of middle-class and elite consumers who had a stake in refashioning it to meet their expectations. Reassured by viewing the city through the filtered glass of the guidebooks, middle-class visitors could convince themselves that Chicago really might be that habitable future of American urban life which eluded other cities. Its institutions, built and natural environments, and culture

Chicago Skyline in the Late 1880s. The skyline, from this perspective, was not a jagged silhouette of peaks and valleys formed by skyscrapers but more

70

or less a solid thicket of large buildings. (ICHI-21795, Chicago Historical
Society)

could be constructed in any desirable shape, or destroyed and abandoned. They were, therefore, all the more prepared to accept the artificial and temporary displays at the Fair as a representation of a real future—as a metaphor for Chicago itself.

Guidebook literature resolved the tension that David Lowenthal writes of so astutely as existing between tradition and innovation in the late Victorian age. If, as he says, the past at the turn of the century is often conceived of through "retroactive reconstruction," so too we can see in this literature the future "reconstructed" in the constant rebuilding and refashioning of the cityscape of Chicago and the Fair.[54]

A brief comparison with contemporary New York City guidebooks underscores this impression of an orientation from the perspective of the future in Chicago publications. Gotham's tour books look similar to the Chicago manuals; they possess many of the same divisions and categories. Yet there are important distinctions. History, as such, is sometimes as little noted, but descriptions of buildings, boulevards, and sites are often defined by their historical significance. New York has more of a sense of solidity and permanence. Parts of the city are described in memorable, almost expected terms; landmarks are designated, and quarters of the city portrayed, sometimes with the anticipation that travelers know beforehand what they might encounter.

Physically, New York is frequently introduced by means of a walk up Broadway. Although it would still be easy to lose one's way, given the incomplete directions, this remains an established itinerary. Finally, there is the underlying sensation of sophistication and cosmopolitanism. New York proclaims itself first in the present, not in the future.[55]

What does the peculiar vision of the Chicago guidebooks suggest, finally, about the fictionalized first encounter of middle-class Americans with the multiplicity and diversity of the archetypal modern city invented for them by Chicago's journalists? This is a literature written by self-appointed urban experts addressing themselves to a middle-class audience assumed to be unfamiliar with travel or ignorant of urban places. Choosing to stress confusion, competition, diversity, bewilderment, and cosmopolitanism is, therefore, highly suggestive. It is as if to say that the real city of Chicago is a place of confusion and contradiction to be wary of. But reality is transformed by the game of fiction; the guidebook genre allows only a fleeting impression, an initial hint of danger. The city then conjured up for the tourist becomes, in its own way, more real, immediate, and important even if it is simultaneously a dreamy model for the future, a place where hints of things to come may be glimpsed, where possibility defines itself as probable. This city possesses no experience of history except in the denial of the meaning of history. It is, consequently, a site of the future, a model, a Utopia. Whether visitors actually imposed this vision upon their experience is difficult to know: it is certainly possible, and it was certainly intended.

By why? What was to be gained by this twist of imagination? There is one conclusion, above others, that suggests several intriguing possibilities. It appears that this is in part a project of middle-class popular culture, the envisioned transformation of the urban world into a commodity that could be consumed or discarded—or, even more, changed into something to be created and manufactured to suit the life-styles of those who might use it. Challenged by the diversities of urban culture, clutching only fading dreams of a Victorian moral order, such visions promised to secure living space for the middle class and elite of the city and, simultaneously, a place for the city in a growing, optimistic, capitalistic society. Chicago, for the moment, seemed perfectly suited for such a possibility. Ironically, however, the very effort suggests how far away Chicago was from what the guidebook writers and their readers hoped it might be. In this respect, the guidebook genre represented part of middle-class popular culture designed to span a gap over reality and discover a place for itself in a new urban cultural world.

Four

FIRST CITY

Form and Fantasy

MR. AND MRS. ELVIN JOHNSON, from Sheboygan, Wisconsin, and their two daughters, dressed in their Sunday best, approached the gates of the Fair. Beyond the entry rose the huge buildings of the White City. A hubbub of noise and dust settled over them as they stopped while Mrs. Johnson handed over their tickets. There was no doubt about their first destination: the Wisconsin pavilion, located in the Midwest section of the state exhibits. Along the way they saw several members of the Columbian Guard, dressed in light-blue sackcloth uniforms edged in red and black with pictures, on their chests, of a blazing sun with an eagle's head at the center. The family had agreed: if anyone got lost in the crowd, he or she would ask one of the guards for directions to the Wisconsin exhibit. They would go there first, to orient themselves and see if anyone else from Sheboygan was on the grounds that day.

When they reached the impressive building, Mr. Johnson proudly signed the registry with his name, his wife's, and those of their two daughters. After his name he wrote, "here seven days," in case anyone wanted to find them, and included the name of their hotel. He flipped through the first part of the enormous book of almost 600 pages. It was only early August, and almost half the spaces were filled, with 7,000 names. Mr. Johnson was doubly impressed. There were a lot of visitors from Wisconsin, and they all seemed to stop here.[1] As George Ade wrote for the *Chicago Record*, the state buildings were "in reality large Exposition club houses, where the visitor from each state may find a resting-place and meet his neighbor from home."[2] The Johnsons certainly confirmed this impression.

Another visitor, Theodore Dreiser from St. Louis on assignment from *The Republic* paper, escorted a group of twenty-four Missouri schoolteachers, acting as "literary chaperon" to the Fair for a week. Each day, when the group entered the grounds from the nearby Varsity Hotel, they made the Missouri state exhibit their meeting place. Dreiser was amused by the ladies, daring enough to explore even the risqué parts of the Midway, and fascinated by the Venetian gondolas and evening electric illuminations. But as Dreiser reassured his St. Louis readers, even on that polyglot avenue no one could mistake the identity of his group. A Turkish Jew observing them, he wrote, asked if they might be representatives of a religious group. Another lady, however, immediately recognized them as teachers. As Dreiser implied, it was safe enough for the gentle sex to visit the Fair without any misunderstanding.[3]

When he could break away, Dreiser fetched his father from the North Side and escorted him to see the great exhibition on the lakefront. Together, they followed a different route, meandering through the White City; they rode the Ferris Wheel, saw the recreations of the *Nina* and the *Pinta*, and ended up at the huge German Village on the Midway. Dreiser wrote that it was as "ordentlich as ever a German would wish," and his immigrant father seemed to appreciate this.[4]

Frances Macbeth Glessner left her Prairie Avenue mansion frequently during the summer of 1893 with a party of friends or family for the Fairgrounds. Even before the grand opening, she toured the area. In April, she recalled,

"Mr. [Daniel] Burnham gave us permission to drive in. We took the same man and carriage we took a few weeks ago—and drove for two hours. We went inside the Iowa building which is decorated with corn.

We drove through the Midway Plaisance—and home by the elevated road. John [her husband] left cards for Mr. [Frederick Law] Olmsted and Mr. Burnham.[5]

Frequently during these trips, she and John lunched with Burnham or Olmsted; sometimes the party remained for the evening to watch the illuminations. Often they attended a celebration for a state or national pavilion opening as honored guests. It was a hectic summer of entertaining visiting friends and even Spanish royalty. Frances and her friends attended the classical concerts given by Theodore Thomas and his symphony orchestra on the grounds. On June 18, she recorded her reactions to a different sort of entertainment: "Mrs. O [Olmsted] and I went to the Street in Cairo, in the theater we saw a disgusting dance."[6]

Like every other visit to the Fair, these itineraries were as distinct as the people who undertook them. Different groups used the Fairgrounds for different purposes. For the Glessners and the George Pullmans, the Fair was an extension of their social and cultural lives, and the officials at the exhibit offices were their personal friends. A visit might well include a stop at the administration building to see Burnham or Harlow Higinbotham (president of the Fair), or Olmsted. It might begin with the exercise of a special privilege or courtesy extended by these powerful friends. For the thousands of visitors hailing from other cities in America, the trip meant a major undertaking, from the ride to Chicago and renting hotel rooms to the actual visit. Once inside this grand, artificial city (surrounded by a vast and real city outside its gates), such visitors naturally gravitated toward the familiar, the exhibit of their state or, in the case of foreign travelers, their national exhibit. To accommodate this practice, these pavilions provided retiring rooms, bathrooms, local newspapers, mail services, and, of course, a registry of guests. Just like fashionable Chicago society, such men and women searched out a familiar focal point in the midst of the strange world around them.

For day guests like Dreiser's father, who was one of Chicago's huge number of foreign-born, the Fairgrounds featured another sort of familiar orientation. Two of the largest exhibits of the Midway, the German and Irish Villages, accommodated the two biggest foreign-born population groups in Chicago: Germans and Irish. These imaginative recreations of home, stressing cultural symbols, food, and folk art offered nostalgia as a point of orientation. This was surely not the Ireland or Germany that immigrants had abandoned but a romanticized version, defined by sentimentality. Unlike the foreign exhibits that displayed contemporary British or German society, these ersatz communities were touristic dioramas, a pageantry of verisimilitude, without the sharp bitter edge of memories of their departure or contemporary problems.

All of these orientations exemplify what James Duncan has called the "contrived landscape" of tourism, designed to blend the familiar with the strange in a fashion that is unthreatening and, therefore, instructive (for learning is difficult if experience is disorienting).[7] These beginning points represented, in effect, an extension of familiar places into an exhibition that was meant to represent a great, glorious, and unfamiliar future. It also reproduced the strategy of the Chicago guidebook literature in introducing the city to strangers.

Looking back, after the great White City and the Midway disappeared, and long after Chicago reneged upon its promise of greatness, historians have tended to see the Fair as a symbol charged with portentous meanings. Their sometimes extravagant claims have stressed the place of the White City as the achievement of the hegemonic powers of corporate capitalism or imperialism. Or, conversely, they have described it as the palpable failure of a conservative and outdated architectural vision. This is certainly not what Daniel Burnham, director of works of the Exposition, had in mind in 1891 when he said: "Gentlemen, 1893 will be the third great debate in our country's history [after 1776 and 1861]!"[8] Clearly, he hoped the exhibit would be a transitional point in urban history, in making the city a monumental place for elites and middle classes to live. For Burnham, the "debate" asked the question, Would Chicagoans create a city according to the cultural ideals he tried to define at the Fair?

In a sense, Burnham's hopes were not entirely misplaced. The Chicago Columbian Exposition did represent a high point of optimism about urban culture. In the sweep of its pretensions, the Fair encompassed a total vision that has hardly since been possible. It also represented a remarkable, if precarious, balance of urban forces. In the history of commercial expositions, Chicago represents something of midpoint. Beginning with the London Exposition of 1851, when the two cultures of the city were separated by unbridge-

German Village on the Midway. This exhibit evoked memories of the *Gasthaus*, while the German exhibition near the White City displayed that country's industrial and consumer products. (Chicago Historical Society)

able gulfs—with engineering, science, consumer products, and art gathered in the Crystal Palace, and popular amusements and entertainments strewn, helter-skelter, throughout the rest of the city. With time and more exhibitions, popular culture encroached upon the fair until, at Chicago, it established itself as a separate but equal appendage of high culture and science. Further developments erased the physical boundaries between the two centers and two cultures until, after World War II, with Disneyland in Anaheim, California, and (the evangelical) Heritage Park in Lynchburg, Virginia, the two became indistinguishable.

To understand Burnham's challenge, it is necessary first to take a short excursion through interpretations of the Fair. Historians have generally concentrated upon assessing the meaning of the White City, following the lead of Burnham and the planners of the Fair and the guidebook journalists who directed attention to the grandiose dreams of high culture. Their reactions have also been shaped by architect Louis Sullivan—by his words denouncing the architecture of the Fair as a pastry chef's Beaux Arts layer cake. Offended by the minor place given to his own innovative designs, Sullivan's words were vindictive and memorable: "The damage wrought by the World's Fair," he wrote, "will last for half a century from its date if not longer. It has penetrated deep into the constitution of the American mind, effecting there lesions significant of dementia."[9] Sullivan's use of the disease metaphor was as unforgiving as his hopes for architecture were grand. And when he connected words like *democratic* to his own buildings and architectural theories, he suggested a separation of styles and purposes that has since become a cliché about Chicago culture. Since the Fair, the city has often been pictured as divided into reactionary and progressive tendencies, with realist writers and builders like Dreiser and Sandburg and Sullivan in one camp and reactionaries like Burnham in the opposing group.[10] Other historians have dismissed Sullivan's dire predictions, either suggesting that the architect's own enterprise was less unique than he described it, or by calling attention to the positive impact of the White City.[11]

Despite their disagreement, these assessments generally evaluate only half of the Fair—that which is generally conceded to be architecture—leaving out a consideration of the Midway. Two recent works redress this balance. Alan Trachtenberg uses the symbol of the White City to mark the triumph of hegemonic culture over the city and, in some sense, over the pleasures represented on the Midway. The rigidly fashioned cultural experiences in the White City pavilions represented the political triumph of a Chicago elite

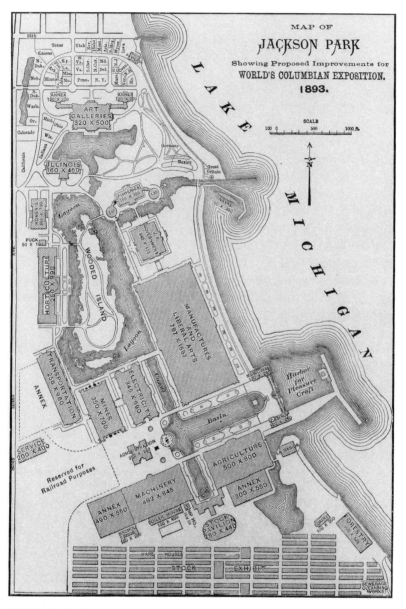

World's Columbian Exposition Map, 1893. Like many guidebook maps, this example from Rand McNally's *Handy Guide to Chicago* resembled in its orientation and scale the map of Chicago itself and did not indicate the location of the Midway. (It actually extended in a perpendicular band to the left of the Woman's Building.) (Library of Congress)

over workers, women, blacks, and immigrants. It was a rebuke to the real city of Chicago and a triumph of order and incorporation.[12]

Robert Rydell imposes a more severe application of hegemony theory to the Fair. In his important work, *All the World's a Fair*, he pays particular attention to the anthropology exhibit and to the design, layout, and meaning of the Midway, which he sees as a kind of popular culture version of anthropology. Both the scientific exhibition, he notes, as well as the section devoted to popular delights were structured by the same notions of racism and cultural superiority. Each, he writes, attempted to assert the cultural hegemony of American elites and to legitimize racial exploitation "at home and the creation of an empire abroad."[13] This meant the demonstration of racial inferiority of Third World societies—something he argues, that was subtly imposed by the arrangement of displays, extending from the most westernized nations at the beginning of the Midway (closest to the White City) to the least "civilized" societies like the Dahomey Village at the far end.

Certainly it is true that the Fair exhibited racism in its displays, but whether the elite which planned it was trying to impose racism on an unwilling audience is another matter entirely. Chicago's business elite which guided the Fair was deeply concerned about the nature of popular culture in the city and went to some lengths to try to regulate and control it, again with the Midway as the focus of its efforts. Whether they even half succeeded, however, is something that requires much more careful examination.

John F. Kasson inverts the standard assessment of the Fair. Although his book concentrates on the development of Coney Island in New York City, he stresses the historic importance of the Chicago Exposition, particularly the Midway. The great White City, he writes, failed in its cultural mission, but the Midway succeeded in spawning new fairs and events. Following its example, these featured a variety of entertainments and a mixture of social classes typical of such new public places as Coney Island.[14]

While Kasson certainly integrates the Fair with the culture of the city, he pays little attention to the White City other than to see it as a failed effort to impose cultural order. Russell Lewis redresses this imbalance and focuses on the White City, but not on the neoclassical exteriors so much as the implied consumer transactions that occurred within. The model for these huge warehouses of goods, he writes, was undoubtedly the department store. Indeed, the Fair represented the "idea of the department store applied to a city scale." Given Chicago's innovations in merchandising and the crucial role of department store magnates in the planning and execution of the Exposition, this restores a major purpose of the White City—its commercial mission.[15]

If Daniel Burnham and subsequent commentators on the Fair are right—that it represented a turning point in the history of American culture—then we must measure carefully the meaning of his prediction. This can only be done by refocusing the problem upon the meaning of the experience of visiting the Fair, with an eye to the ways the Fair was intended to work—and actually worked—and with some attention paid to its place as a representation of the city itself. Perhaps there is no surer guide to this place than the suggestive words of Lewis Mumford who wrote that the "metropolis itself may be described as a World's Fair in continuous operation."[16] What he implies here is perhaps more than he intended, but it is a truth worth underscoring in the case of Chicago. The Fair, with its remarkable contradictions and diversities, was implicitly a metaphor for the city itself. In some fashion or another, almost every element of the city was represented within the exhibition which by its very nature took these elements and distanced and distorted them. While an exploration of fantasies or exoticism of modern science and technology, of anthropology, and of high culture, the Fair was also a distorted mirror of Chicago itself.

The men and women who organized and controlled the Exposition had a bold plan to design a complete vision of the modern American city—one that would include all of its elements in balance. It would compare and contrast two basic cultural ideals, one represented by the White City with its planned high culture, and the other by the Midway's popular culture and unregulated commercialism. In establishing this contest, the administration intended the White City to predominate, to overwhelm, to convince.

The Fair leadership included some of Chicago's most prominent business leaders. Although there were two councils that directed the Fair, one local and the other a national commission, the majority of relevant decisions were taken by the Chicago board of directors. Businessmen Marshall Field, George Pullman, Philip Armour, N. K. Fairbanks, and others were active in the early promotion of the Fair, but they tended to step aside for other men who actually joined the board of directors once the Fair was secured for Chicago.[17]

The committee that actually presided over the planning and functioning of the Fair was headed by Harlow Higinbotham of Marshall Field's department store, with other important figures such as Potter Palmer, who was in the hotel business, and his wife, Bertha Honore Palmer (president of the Board of Lady Mangers). Indeed, the top management of the Fair, as might be expected, was dominated by the retail and service industries and railroad executives who all might be expected either to benefit directly from the Exhibition or have some expertise in merchandising. At the same time, this group was a key part of Chicago's cultural philanthropic leadership. In this sense, the culture of the Fair was continuous with the new cultural institutions endowed by these same men of fortune. (Perhaps the most instructive example of this continuity was the endowment by Marshall Field and others such as George Pullman to preserve the Fine Arts Building from the Fair as a permanent institution for the city after the Fair was over.)[18]

The key man in designing the Fair was Daniel Burnham, the Exposition's chief of works. The much-maligned butt of latter-day attacks by Sullivan, Frank Lloyd Wright, and other modernist architects, Burnham was responsible for many decisions that shaped the design of the Fair. Although this command was, for a time, shared with John Root, partner in his architectural firm, after Root's death in 1891 most of the major decisions fell to Burnham.[19]

Burnham, together with Root, had participated in Chicago's skyscraper development in the 1880s, but his tastes ran to what might be called the civic colossal, a style that borrowed classical motifs to embellish and dignify public spaces. In the Fair, he set the skyscraper's steel framework (invented to support towering walls) to a different purpose—the underpinnings of architectural fantasy. Commentators at the time recognized that the innovative spread

The Lagoon and Palace of Mechanic Arts in the White City. The extraordinary busyness of the facades and statuary of the Fair made the exteriors a pastiche of quotations from European monuments, buildings, churches, and public buildings. (Library of Congress)

foundation (rather than sinking piles) would allow large horizontal spaces.[20]

The decorative aesthetic of Burnham's was foreshadowed by the design for the imposing gateway to the Chicago stockyards which he and Root conceived—a diversion that disguised the slaughterhouse that lay inside. Although the massive shed-like interiors of the White City were clearly functional in their form of design (like contemporary railroad stations), Burnham wanted the exteriors to be as pliable, temporary, and unified as sand castles. Given the plasticity of

Sol Bloom. Dapper Sol Bloom in 1928 is pictured here with Annie Mathews, registrar of New York County. (Library of Congress)

staff, the jute and plaster material used as an exterior covering, this was not only possible but practical. As chief artistic designer of the Fair, Francis D. Millet wrote staff permitted the architects "an architectural spree."[21]

One of Burnham's (and the Fair's) most important decisions was to locate the Midway in its own section on the actual Fairgrounds. Originally placed under the direction of F. W. Putnam, head of the anthropological exhibit and a scientist from Harvard University, the Midway soon outgrew its serious beginnings as a Street of All Nations, evolving into an amusement park with ethnic displays intermixed with entertainments more likely to be associated with carnivals or traditional fairs. As this happened, Burnham decided to hire a more appropriate man to organize the section. His choice was a young Jewish entrepreneur and impresario, Sol Bloom, from San Francisco. Well connected through his friend John Van Demeter, a California representative on the Fair's national council, Bloom applied his experience in theater to the Midway.

Hired by Burnham (Bloom commented that keeping Putnam as head of the Midway was like making "Albert Einstein manager of the Ringling Brothers and Barnum and Baily Circus"), he imposed a very different vision on the Midway. As he later recounted, he did not agree with Putnam's racial theories of Darwinian natural selection:

> I came to realize that a tall, skinny chap from Arabia with a talent for swallowing swords expressed a culture which to me was on a higher plane than the one demonstrated by a group of earnest Swiss peasants who passed their day making cheese and milk chocolate. . . . and I could not pretend to deny that God's handiwork seemed more clearly shown in the music of even a second-rate band than in all the products of the world's mills and factories here on display.[22]

In a sense, Bloom and Burnham represent polar opposites of the Fair, just as the White City and the Midway, although clearly Bloom was the lesser figure. But, like such opposites, there was a strong attraction, a relationship between both concepts of the exhibition that linked them in ways that reflect upon the wider connections between urban cultures in Chicago.

If Burnham recognized a variety of cultures in his plaster city on the Jackson lagoon, he still hoped to maintain grades and levels of value distinguished by architectural styles and placement of buildings. He insisted, above all, that the central Court of Honor remain a built architectural world imposed upon the environment and not one that would reflect and integrate natural landmarks such as Lake Michigan.[23] Around the Grand Basin were constructed, in "dignified" style, the Administration, Arts, Mines, Electricity, Agriculture, and Manufactures buildings. Then, beyond, in a less formal fashion were the Horticulture, Transportation, and Fisheries buildings. Still less formal and unified were the state and foreign buildings. And further away from the center were the buildings of the Midway.

There were subtle distinctions implied by this arrangement. The "city" center consisted of administration, commercial exhibits, the liberal arts, and the arts. Slightly beyond this lay the enterprises that supported the city—industry and agriculture. On the very edge of the White City, commanding the exit (or entrance) to the Midway, was the Woman's Building (with an appended Children's Building). To the north were the state pavilions, arranged in geographic (and political) regions. Then came the foreign exhibits along the lakefront and, finally, the Midway running perpendicular to the main exhibit grounds.

Although Burnham fancied that the Exhibition moved from order in the White City to chaos on the Midway, there was one underlying force of imagination that linked all of the buildings of the site. This was the unifying notion of form and fantasy: each building was designed to evoke an emotion appropriate to the function of the structure. The consumer and scientific revolutions in the interior displays of new goods and inventions in the White City were gathered together for presentation inside an environment of classical quotations. Calling upon a different version of this strategy, Burnham requested state pavilions to summon up memories or stereotypes of the regions they represented: Spanish styles for California, plantation models for the South, and New England styles for that region. So, too, the designs of the Midway exhibits were intended to appeal to the expectations of the audience wandering through its streets.[24] Despite the very different exteriors of the buildings, they were all constructed upon the same principal of fantasy and function—their function as imagined representations of exotic culture dictated their shapes.

While most of the structures of the Fairgrounds linked the arts together, embellishing exteriors with statuary or paintings (in the Midway it could be argued that sign advertisements replaced the more self-conscious art of the White City), this was most overtly accomplished around the Court of Honor. Artistic embellishment adorned the neoclassic buildings of this area and spilled over onto walkways, bridges, and other public places.

Francis Millet, the chief designer of embellishments for the Fair, was immensely optimistic about the consequences of his task. Speaking of the Fair, he wrote:

> There each building has the complement of its architecture in sculpture and in painting. There first in this country, on a reasonably large scale at least, have the allied arts worked together and in harmonious proportions. The immediate fruits of this union, even if it be but temporary, are incalculable; of the final result there can be no doubt. It means the dawn of a real art in this country.[25]

There was much comment on the unity of the artists as well as the arts at the Fair, on the spirit of comradery in pursuit of the same aesthetic and moral ends. As Burnham noted after a preliminary visit to the barren lagoon where the Fair would be built: "The men left the banquet hall that night united like soldiers in a campaign, and Pettiness or Jealousy never raised their heads in the comments of the designers of the fair afterwards."[26] Perhaps this is also what the distinguished intellectuals celebrated in their self-contratulatory banquet in New York on March 25, 1893. There Burnham was feted by William Dean Howells, Charles Eliot Norton, Daniel Coit Gilman, Edwin Godkin, Frederick Law Olmsted, Marshall Field, Lyman Gage, Oliver La Farge, Augustus Saint-Gaudens, and others. As poet Richard Watson Gilder commemorated the meeting:

The White City. View of the central lagoon and the MacMonnies Columbian Fountain with Lake Michigan visible in the background. (Library of Congress)

> Say not, "Greece is no more!"
> Through the clear morn
> On light winds borne
> Her white-winged soul sinks on the New World's breast
> Ah, happy West—
> Greece flowers anew, and all her temples soar![27]

Perhaps it was Greece that Burnham had in mind, or Renaissance patronage, or even Victorian moral order when he contravened the tradition of holding competitive contests to select designs for the principal buildings. Instead, Burnham invited leading architects in Chicago and elsewhere to design specific buildings. This assured some degree of order and a certain level of expectation. But, most important, it reflected the notion and principle that there were existing aesthetic standards, plausible design motifs that could be agreed upon and realized. There would be no ignorant clash of architectural competitors, no commercialism; no marketplace decisions would shape the White City. Rather, Burnham's Utopia rested upon a gentleman's agreement about the best standards of architecture, above and beyond the clash of the competitive cultures of the city. As the chief of works himself said, "The avowed and distinct purpose expressed in the memorial was the congregation of the best artistic talents in the country, without regard to residence."[28] This was precisely what William Dean Howells lauded in the design of the Fair. It was not done for money or for competition but by merit.[29]

Sometimes this firm control of the configuration of the grounds could be suffocating. As George Ferris (builder of the Midway ferris wheel) wrote in June to a colleague:

> In accordance with my view of it, Burnham nor anyone else has any right to dictate whether we shall have a closed or open fence, any more than from an artistic stand point. We must have a closed fence at least eight feet high and it must be made in such a way that it will not detract from the appearance of other concession and grounds generally.[30]

In fact, however, this contretemps only underscores the difference between the guiding principles of the White City and the competitive Midway.

The White City architectural contrivances of staff spoke volumes about Burnham's concept of the city, although his later work in the City Beautiful movement made these ideas even more apparent. In these later designs, particularly his Plan for Chicago proposed in 1909, the architect clarified some of his most cherished ideas about the city. The most important concept was unity itself, the creation of a plan that would impact the entire surface of the city. A key to that unity was the vital center of the city radiating out into residential and productive sections.[31] Luckily, Burnham wrote, there were few buildings in Chicago of architectural value that had to be preserved. Redesign of the city would therefore be easy. Yet Burnham did not intend this advantage as an opening for modernism. Instead, with his referential designs, he hoped to create a new history for the city by borrowing patterns from history, in effect placing it in a European continuity, as a summation of progress.

Behind this plan lay another concept that informs both the later Chicago Plan and the World's Fair design. Burnham's conception was purposely aimed at preserving the city as a cultural center for middle and upper classes. If successful, this would diminish the need of the wealthy to spend time in Paris, Vienna, or the Riviera. As he wrote, completion of the whole plan, including extensive parks and boulevards, would create a kind of civic unity: "In establishing a complete park and parkway system, the life of the wage-earner and of his family is made healthier and pleasanter, while the greater attractiveness thus produced keeps at home the people of means and taste, and acts as a magnet to draw those who seek to live amid pleasing surroundings."[32]

In effect, Burnham had anticipated a major urban problem just as it was beginning to develop: the abandonment of the city by its wealthier citizens. To him, it was still possible to make the urban area a center of established and controlled culture, to create, in other words, a multilayered, multiclass city in which a variety of people would share the same cultural institutions. This was the basic premise also of the Columbian Exposition. Except that in the Chicago Plan and other urban designs by Burnham created after 1893, he neglected to make room for the Midway. That was a fatal mistake, for, as much as anything, the Midway represented another vital form of urban popular culture. Without it, the White City was less than half a city.

Another firm hand visible in designing the Fairgrounds and its public spaces was the great landscape artist, Frederick Law Olmsted. Olmsted found his task very difficult because of contending demands by architects and concessionaries, and by a terrain and climate that he found inhospitable. Chicago's climate, he said was "severe," and the physical environment of Jackson Park foreboding and unpleasant. If a search had been conducted "for the least park-like ground with the city, nothing better meeting the requirement could have been found."[33]

Despite his great contribution, Olmsted was frustrated. He wanted to preserve the centrally located Wooded Island area of the park as a restful natural retreat but had to compromise in allowing a Japanese garden and temple to be located there. If they could have been placed elsewhere, he wrote, "I am sure that the Exposition would have made a much more agreeable general impression on visitors of cultivated sensibility to the influence of scenery." Furthermore, he wished for the buildings in the Court of Honor to stand by themselves, uncluttered by smaller structures or concessions. Again he compromised, with the result that such additions "intercepted vistas and disturbed spaces intended to serve for the relief of the eye."[34] Finally, he had hoped to create just a few entrances to the grounds so that visitors entering would focus on a particular point, the Administration Building. But there were complications when the Illinois Central Railroad failed to put its station where he wished; hence, visitors were allowed to enter the grounds from multiple portals.

If there was a cultural theory that articulated Burnham and Olmsted's urban vision, it is probably best contained in the writings of William Dean Howells, Christian socialist, realist novelist, and (by then) proper Bostonian. Howells in a visit to the Fair saw precisely what Henry Adams meant in his contradictory description of the Fair. Adams wrote that "the first expression of American thought as a unity defied philosophy. . . . since Noah's ark, no such Babel of loose and ill-joined, such vague and ill-defined and unrelated thoughts and half-thoughts and experimental outcries as the Exposition, had ever ruffled the surface of the Lakes."[35]

What Adams beheld—the two Fairs conjoined—Howells also recognized. As he recounted after his first night on the grounds, "Last night we went for our first sight of the fair, and we are simply in rapture and despair! Nothing like it was ever dreamed of."[36] If the Fairgrounds ran from unity to disorder, from culture to competition, Howells clearly favored what Burnham had intended for him to prefer. What attracted Howells to the White City was its comprehensive planning and its freedom from commercialism. The Midway, on the other hand, represented the epitome of the commercial, competitive life, where every exhibit had an entrance fee and every entertainment its price. Howells could conclude that the White City was unblemished by commercialism only by referring to the exteriors of buildings, for inside the grand plaster buildings were thousands of commercial exhibits. At least this was a consumerism that refused to flaunt its price tags.

This was precisely the dichotomy (of culture versus commercialism) that Howells maintained in his Utopian writings, *A Traveler from Altruria*. The splendid planned cities of Altruria mirrored the Chicago White City, while contemporary American cities (he referred to the nation as Egoria—meaning ego, elsewhere) exhibited the confusion and chaos of competitive capitalism. Expose a cross section of such a city and you would reveal a stirring Darwinian tangled bank,

> the filthy drains that belched into the common sewers, trapped and retrapped to keep the poison gases down; you see the sewers that rolled their loathsome tides beneath the streets, amidst a tangle of gas pipes, wires, electric motor wires and grip-cables; all without a plan, but make shifts, expedients, devices to repair and evade the fundamental mistake of having any such cities at all.[37]

If this was a kind of metaphor for the culture represented by the Midway, Howells quite confidently, in his novel, predicted that the working classes, even more than the more "cultivated" people, would welcome a new city based upon the principles of a moralized architecture and city planning and a rejection of the lower sorts of culture.

In establishing the relationship between the White City and the Midway Plaisance, the planners of the Fair recognized precisely this sort of thinking. In his president's report, Harlow Higinbotham wrote at length about the Midway and its relationship to the Exposition. Much objection, he noted, had originally been raised to the original plan for the Midway Plaisance "on the ground that it was undignified and no proper part of a great international exposition." This would have been true, he continued, if it had been dispersed throughout the whole exhibit area, "but located as it was, separate from the Exposition proper, so that those who were not disposed to visit the sights to be seen there did not have them forced upon them, the Plaisance was a feature from the absence of which the Exposition would have suffered greatly."[38]

The Midway offered "an admirable location for picturesque displays characteristic of the customs of foreign and remote nations" as well as amusements and refreshments. By confining this section, it was also possible to control it, he added, so that proper decorum would be maintained.[39] In addition, he noted that the Midway changed and evolved in concept through time as different concessions were permitted and different displays constructed.

If this theory of control and cultural order was the premise upon which the White City and the Midway were balanced, then one can only conclude that the planners of the Fair instinctively understood a complexity that their theory of opposites and choices would not allow. In their public pronouncements they refused to concede equal claims for space by different urban cultures and classes; more important, they overlooked the dependency of both visions of the city upon each other. For just as commercialism and consumerism lay at the very heart of the White City that so ostentatiously disguised their existence in its artistic exteriors, so in the chaotic competitiveness of the Midway lay a kind of order imposed by the marketplace itself, which transformed each exhibit from the curious and unique into the accessibly exotic.

Indeed, the Fair planners had created a vision of the city as a kind of negotiated culture in which nothing was, precisely, what it seemed. That, no doubt is what Randolph Bourne, who understood such matters, had in mind in 1916 when he remarked that "there is no distinctively American culture. It is apparently our lot rather to be a federation of cultures."[40] Although the idea of federation would surely have sat uncomfortably in the minds of the latter-day Victorians who hoped for a victory of culture over competition, the success of the Fair in Chicago, in effect, depended upon the failure of the White City to exclude other cultures.

The actual operation of the Fair reveals the interchange between the two artificial polarities of culture at the Exposition and the efforts (often unsuccessful) of the board of directors to control and shape the experience of visitors. The administrative structure of the Fair was complex. There were Standing Committees, an Executive Committee of Standing Committees, a Board of Directors and the director general, and a Council of Administration. The minutes of these bodies reveal several important and interesting functions of the administration beyond simply the appropriation of money for construction and the approval of plans for buildings and exhibitions.

Considerable time and effort was applied to shaping the relationship of the White City to the Midway and maintaining control of the cultural ambiance of the Exposition. The council was the decision-making body of last resort that approved or rejected displays. Inevitably, a great many varieties of requests reached them, and many of these had to do with what could be called the legitimizing function of the Exposition. To receive a concession or display permit meant to achieve a kind of recognition of the validity of enterprise. To be rejected was, therefore, a stunning blow. The council also heard complaints about problems on the Midway, particularly concerning scandalous or risqué entertainments, and they drew the line of propriety. Finally, the council granted monopolies to various enterprises; for example, official guidebooks and photographic books. All of these decisions had an impact on the experience of the visitor by shaping what would be exhibited, and even by limiting the visual and print records of the Fair available on the grounds as souvenirs.

As an enterprise that validated cultural expressions, the Fair administration could be ruthless in what it accepted and rejected. For example, the Council of Administration on August 29, 1892, rejected the offer of Mr. Richard Allen Dawson of the Colored Man's Association to construct free of charge a grandstand for dignitaries for dedicatory ceremonies. Behind this decision lay the fear of obligation, that African-Americans might demand some future representation on the Fairgrounds.[41] Later the same year, the council rejected a request for a display of statistics revealing the progress of the "colored Race since emancipation," undoubtedly for the same reasons.[42]

Other groups applied for anointment by the council: homeopathic doctors, the Cigar Makers International Union requesting the sale of only union-made cigars at concessions, religious groups seeking the use of Fair facilities for services, women's groups for proselytizing for women's rights. The new University of Chicago was granted the right to hold an extension course on art at the Fair, to be taught by the sculptor Lorado Taft. The council carefully chose among these groups, excluding unions and blacks while allow-

ing religious groups and selected ethnic groups to hold special ceremonies or meetings on the grounds.

During the year of the Fair, the council was increasingly called
to make decisions about the Midway. In part this came because of
the constantly shifting nature of the concessions and the almost
continuous changes occurring on the strip. As the concession agreements with Midway firms clearly demonstrate, one desire of the
administration is very clear. The Fair leadership wanted what it
deemed authentic experiences. The agreement with the Egypt-Chicago Exposition Company of October 1891 instructed that the company "will supply said street with everything necessary to give a true
and life-like representation of said street with its inhabitants." So it
was also in the agreement with the Elia-Souharin Sadullah & Co. of
Constantinople. All dancing and costumes were to be approved by
the ways and means committee. All objects for sale must be of Turkish origin. And the company was to "furnish their employees, natives of Turkey, such sleeping accommodations as they are accustomed to in their own country, and to supply them with such food as
they usually eat."[43] In July, there were attempts to close the Specta-
torium located at the north exterior of the Midway—because of fire
hazards. But it well may be that since it lay just outside the grounds
it, as well as other amusements beyond the purview of the Fair, were
competing with displays inside.

Increasingly, also, the council had to consider complaints of
lewd behavior by dancers and performers on the Midway. From the
beginning, as Higinbotham reported, the administration rejected
some concessions out of fear for the "dignity of the Exposition."[44]
Yet, from almost the first day of the Fair, complaints mounted about
the Midway. In early June, the Council of Administration proposed
to "investigate the performances and customs of the various concessionaires, and, if thought advisable, stop all such performances if
the complaints are justifiable." If a performance contravened Chicago's standards of propriety, then authenticity would have to be
relinquished.

In July, the council ordered the James J. Corbett (boxing) show
closed as being "not of such a character that the same can be approved by the World's Columbian Exposition."[45] In early August,
the director general was asked to investigate "sundry indecent and

immoral features" on the Midway. On August 24, 1893, the dances at the "Persian Palace" were shut "on account of its immoral and indescent [sic] character," although the Persian government sued in court to have its concession reopened.[46]

Beyond watchman of morality, the administration also played the role of guarantor of monopoly concessions. While the council granted a variety of monopolies for Fair distribution, the most interesting have to do with photography and guidebooks, for these two publications would have the most obvious impact in shaping the experience of the visitors. With no free photography allowed on the grounds (other than official shots), there was no way to personalize the memory of the World's Fair visit, no way to individualize the experience through idiosyncratic angles or poses. A prohibitive $2 fee was placed on all hand cameras taken into the grounds. Even then, a booklet, the "Kodak Code" distributed with permission, listed the places where the "best" pictures could be taken. Principal photographic publications had official origins. Indeed, the book *Official Views of the World's Columbian Exposition*, by C. D. Arnold and Harlow Davidson Higinbotham (son of the exposition president), carefully pictured most Exposition scenes as uncrowded, monumental, and leisurely. Those people present were generally formally dressed; women often carried black parasols, and everyone wore hats. Although there were larger crowds shown at concessions—and more children—it is clear that the intent of the book was to capture the picturesque, the leisurely impression, the exteriors of splendid unitary architecture of the White City.[47] Indeed, following the last section of scenes from the Midway, the authors inserted one last photograph: the Court of Honor, as if to freeze the final memory of the Fair in the White City.

By choosing an official guidebook publisher, the Fair extended its influence over both the way that tourists visited the grounds and ordered their memories of it. The author of the *Official Directory of the World Columbian Exposition* was the newspaperman Moses P. Handy, who served as chief of the Fair's Department of Publicity and Promotion.[48] W. B. Conkey and his Columbian Guide Co. won the concession to publish it by agreeing to a licensing fee of $100,000. The company also promised 10 percent of its gross sales as a return to the Fair. These sales amounted to about $232,000 worth

Agriculture Building, the White City. Published by official photographer C. D. Arnold, this view of the Agriculture Building shows amateur photographers at work shooting from one of the suggested perspectives of the Fairgrounds. (Library of Congress)

of catalogues published at $1 each, with condensed versions at fifty cents and ten cents. In effect then, there were well over 200,000 official guides of one sort or another sold.[49] Given the level of return and the hopes of the Fair administration, it is clear that this concession was expected to earn a considerable return. In turn, expectations for a lucrative market meant that Conkey's was by no means the only guide; indeed, scores of others were sold principally at railroad stations and hotels and booksellers or immediately outside the Fairgrounds.

The geography of the Fairgrounds was centered upon the White City whose unity of architecture and setting gave it a gravity and sense of purpose that was missing elsewhere. By limiting exhibition buildings to broad categories such as Transportation, Fish and Fisheries, Live Stock, Agriculture, Manufactures and Liberal Arts, and Mechanic Arts, commerce was divided into functional units. Here architecture was lavished upon commercial activities to disguise their very nature from the exterior perspective. This principle of architectural costume meant that the commercial purpose of the central core of buildings was not readily apparent. Indeed, many visitors mistook the purpose of the White City (as they were perhaps intended to) as a celebration of art and harmony when, in fact, the purpose of the exhibits was at least as much to display commercial products. If the White City exhibited a formal unity in its eclectic styles, it also had a less apparent intent: to provide the best possible setting for the wares of modern industrial civilization. This purpose was underscored by the central location of the huge Manufactures and Liberal Arts building. This centerpiece contained a remarkable juxtaposition of consumer items with displays of the liberal arts projects including education and prison reform.[50] By inference, product engineering was joined to human engineering.

William Dean Howells recounted a story told by Daniel Burnham that alluded to this unity of culture and commerce:

> At Chicago, Burnham, the Director of Works, at the Fair, who is of Swedenborgian training, told me that when he told his mother of the magnificent consensus of wills and aims in the capitalists and artists who created its beauty, she saw in it a vision of the New Jerusalem, and a direct leading of the Lord toward "the wonder that shall be," when all men work in harmony, and not in rivalry.[51]

What Mrs. Burnham sensed in this purported harmony was, in effect, a unity based upon proximities. Different orders of architectural exteriors and interiors effectively encased modern industrial and consumer products inside classical and historical motifs where their implications, their revolutionary qualities, seemed benign.

Even the physical experience of moving through an exhibit meant passing through allusions to cultures and styles linked together for the presentation of products. Once beyond the Corinthian exterior of the Manufactures and Liberal Arts Building, for example, a visitor came to a vast hall designed like a railroad shed,

Form, Function, and Fantasy. The interior of the Manufactures and Liberal Arts Building presented a cacophony of eclectic styles set against the visible beams and struts of the exhibition shed. (ICHI-02256, Chicago Historical Society)

consisting of gigantic, exposed iron and steel arches open wide to capture light. This purely functional interior merely enveloped a huge display field upon which were erected hundreds of exhibit pavilions. These kiosks were often designed as recognizable buildings or classical temples, or Gothic churches. Inside these, display cabinets were elaborately ornamented. And the products themselves— at last—were offered as items that could be purchased later. Often a display might be attended by a sales representative who would take orders for future purchases, although the exact item on display would not be for sale. Thus the visitor, moving from outside in, passed through several jarring turns of architectural styles, from white-painted neoclassical, to functionalist, to a jumble of eclectic kiosks, and, finally, to the product itself.[52]

One of the most interesting of these curiously framed interior displays was provided by the Western Electric Company of Chicago which erected a pavilion in the Electricity Building in the shape of an Egyptian temple. In it, Egyptian maidens were portrayed as telephone operators while "men of time" laid phone lines. These visual puns upon the timeless, extinct civilization of Egypt, used to display the liveliest of modern business and consumer products, made a conceit that was "very popular," as one guidebook noted.[53] It also demonstrated how eclecticism in the service of display could call attention to itself, to the very act of borrowing and unifying incongruities.

While something of this process was no doubt active in shaping the entire impression generated by the White City, it was not, perhaps, always successful as a strategy for the sale of goods. Indeed, several articles in the important advertising journal *Printer's Ink* suggest that attention to culture overwhelmed the regard for commerce. Editor John Romer minced no words in his negative appraisal: "As a universal exposition, the Chicago Fair is a huge, glittering success, but as an advertising and business venture, it is a magnificent failure."[54] What he intended was clear: orders for products were low, items were displayed badly, and information was lacking.

Writing from the Fair, the correspondant W. W. Brett was also scathing in his appraisal of the exhibits: "The awful, tiresome sameness of pillars, carved woodwork, and effects in white and gold, while pretty, become fearfully tiresome to the eyes. It is utterly bad advertising. The man who advertises soap would much better have spent his money in building a soap house."[55]

The implications of Brett's arguments hold true for the White City as a whole. While based upon commerce, selling, and advertising, this portion of the Exhibition with its ubiquitous statuary and classical giganticism, its planned walk and waterways, warred with the commercialism of its interiors. It was as if the planners of the Fair had chosen to work out from a treasured cultural core of the arts, through manufacturing, gradually, into cruder and cruder sorts of endeavors such as mining, agriculture, and fishing. Perhaps this strategy defined the shape of the city as Burnham and Olmsted intended it should become: the essential city was its culture, its art and architecture surrounded by rings of intensifying devotion to work, yet all cloaked in the same general architectural format.

This extravaganza in white-painted staff also defined a peculiar relationship between popular culture and enterprise. Despite the very obvious—glaringly obvious—control of design, and despite the formalism of the settings, the disposable White City was intended to impress an audience of millions of Americans with the possibility of completely redefining American urbanism. Whether or not it succeeded, it was intended to be accessible and to convey a simple message: it was possible through the exercise of control and taste to recreate the American city. The glistening, jarring artificiality of its architecture signified a kind of strength, for it emphasized the possibility of choice and unity in designing an urban backdrop. It was intended to be a lowest common denominator and accessible to all those who accepted its mission. The White City proposed itself as a kind of universal culture for all classes. It did not affirm what was but predicted what might be: it was a reproducible dream, a portable vision for urban America. In this heady moment, culture, it seemed, could be detached from its national and temporal meanings and placed at the service of dreamers of a universal, middle-class mass culture.

On this point some observers have suggested, and contemporary visitors often stressed, the religious quality of writing about the White City, portraying it as a celestial city or a "New Jerusalem." In its fashion it mixed culture, commerce, and evangelical expectations into one mission. Biblical vocabulary also illustrated that each step away from the central core of culture headed in a different direction, toward the infamous "Tower of Babel," a sobriquet often applied to the Midway. Before reaching this confusing place of foreign tongues and cultures, however, the visitor had several other important stops, again each with a carefully engineered purpose.

Adjacent to the White City and participating in its overall unity was the Woman's Building. Unlike the Philadelphia Centennial Exposition, the Chicago Fair granted women a separate building and a separate administration headed by Mrs. Bertha Honore Palmer. Although Susan B. Anthony had pressed the general administration for representatives on the Board of Managers of the World's Fair, the separate Board of Lady Managers was the most that could be achieved.[56]

Mrs. Palmer tried to make the best of this opening. A competition was set to select plans for the building, and Sophia Hayden won with her design. When completed, the building displayed a strategy that moved from demonstrating the contemporary accomplishments of women to the strong suggestion that, if given more opportunity, women could achieve much more. Mrs. Palmer tried to explain this: "[T]he Board has with ceaseless vigilance endeavored to secure for women the opportunity to show what they also could do, if given the opening." Quietly and carefully chiding men for prejudice, she continued, "In no other way might woman ever hope to receive the proper recompense for her services than by actual demonstration that in industry, the professions, the sciences and arts, discrimination upon the score of sex was solely the result of mutable conditions."[57]

The exhibit itself included examples of high art, such as murals by Mary Cassatt as well as handicraft works and examples of bookbinding. It sampled the accomplishments of women in science, in literature, and the other arts. Contrasted to the White City, however, the difference in displays was striking. While there were certain similarities in the arts and cultural objects, machinery, consumer items, and the products of industry dominated the interiors of the White City. The Woman's Building, on the other hand, emphasized the arts that extended from domesticity, including house furnishings and a variety of handmade objects. Its murals and paintings by Cassatt and Mrs. Mary Fairchild MacMonnies depicted leisure and cultural and moral virtues, often associated with women. This distinction between female and male displays was crucial, for the fruits of modern industry clearly came from male invention and ownership while female creativity appeared everywhere but where it counted most: in the factory.

Despite this large exhibit and the attached Children's Building, there was little shown on two of the largest social problems of the late nineteenth century: the exploitation of women and children laborers, many of whom worked in the factories responsible for the consumer revolution of the White City. In the building's meeting rooms there were frequent talks on philanthropy, literature, domestic science, and temperance. But this was clearly an exhibition of progress within a confined sphere and a carefully constructed middle-class argument for enlarging that sphere. If Chicago women demanded an equal place with men, that sense of equality itself was limited and tentative.[58]

Nonetheless, the exhibit was accounted a success by many commentators on the Fair. The Woman's Building became an important orienting place for female tourists. Furthermore, scattered throughout the Fairgrounds in other pavilions, there were important analogous displays of women's accomplishments in handicrafts, the arts, and sciences. Most state exhibits, for example, copied the general format of the Fair and set aside exhibit space for women. And one could also find similar sorts of displays in foreign exhibits.[59]

The ambiguous location of the Woman's Building—between the White City and the remainder of the Fairgrounds, between manufacturing and entertainment, between organized and disordered fantasy, between two forms of public space—heightened its importance as a transitional place. As the souvenir book writer William Cameron explained, "One issues from the refined atmosphere and artistic decoration of the Woman's Building, and in a moment is transported into the borders of *terra incognito* [the Midway]."[60] The Woman's Building could either be seen as a bridge between the ordered and the exotic, a checkpoint between the White City and the Midway, or in many cases it became a place to begin, to meet friends, to locate a comfortable and familiar position before journeying into the disorienting confusion and crowds.

Located to the north and surrounding the Gallery of Fine Arts, the state pavilions had several purposes. In part they existed as advertisements for the wares and products made within their borders. In some cases, they boasted of tourist spots. A further purpose was to provide a meeting place for state residents and delegations and a headquarters for the "state day" celebration accorded to most.

Both intentions were served by the instructions of Daniel Burnham to construct pavilions that quoted the history or characteristic architectural style of the state.[61] In consequence, California erected a building based upon the Old Mission Church at San Diego; Massachusetts used a design based upon the John Hancock

Arts and Sciences. The Arts Palace, later the Field Museum, and finally restored as the Museum of Science and Industry (see Chapter 7). (Library of Congress)

House that stood on Beacon Hill in Boston; Virginia contrived a pavilion to resemble George Washington's Mount Vernon. Inside, most states divided space into display areas with information about products produced, cities, universities and schools, and famous sons and daughters of the state. The other space was devoted to receiving rooms for guests.

The Pennsylvania catalog described what was a typical interior: "The design of the building was, and is, the mental and physical comfort of guests. It is fitted in a comfortable and home-like manner, carpeted throughout and bountifully supplied with cushioned chairs and lounges."[62] Facilities included a gentleman's parlor and smoking and toilet rooms, ladies' parlors and toilets, a grand reception room, a postoffice, and information and parcel rooms.

State residents frequently visited these facilities, and reports to legislatures afterward proudly boasted of the large number of residents who appeared. For example, Connecticut listed 26,000 citizens of the state who signed the registry book. It even calculated a statistical profile of the visitors, determining which areas sent the highest numbers. As expected, these came from Hartford which was "accounted for by the fact that per capita, it is Connecticut's richest town."[63]

New York's exhibit had a special mission in addition to the common functions of state exhibits. This was revealed by the summary report of *New York at the Fair* published in 1894. New York had competed against Chicago to host the Columbian celebration, and it never really gave up the claim that it should have been selected. Consequently, when Chauncey Depew spoke at the dedication of the pavilion, he noted, "New York stands to the American continent in much the same position as Florence to Europe in the fifteenth century."[64] The report proudly noted the contribution of New Yorkers to the Fair, with the work of Millet and Olmsted and several important New York architects.

Foreign exhibits, including the German, French, Japanese, and other displays were also grouped together between the White City and the Midway. Like the state exhibitions, they had multiple functions: to display their products, to provide a resting and greeting place for their own citizens, and to promote tourism. Like the state exhibits, they too, in their architectural designs, played upon the fantasies and expectations of the audience, so that each pavilion looked as if it were representative of the nation it symbolized. Perhaps most surprising—and interesting—was the Japanese pavilion which contained a huge variety of consumer products. The progress of that nation in such manufactures obviously contradicted racial stereotypes about Asians that were elsewhere emphasized in the anthropological exhibits.

Perhaps the most interesting building of the Fair was never constructed, although a concession was granted to build it. Planned for the east end of the Midway at the nearest entrance to the White City, this gigantic edifice would have, like the Eiffel Tower at the Paris Exposition, provided a monumental symbol for Chicago.

When first proposed in early 1891, the structure bore a remarkable likeness to the Eiffel Tower, only grander and taller. After several more versions of the tower—one rumored to be a project of Andrew Carnegie and the next a triplet of structures for bird's-eye photographers—the last project in the summer of 1892 was to be an amphitheater under a gigantic, bell-shaped steel structure. A guidebook to the Fair published in 1892 described its soaring dimensions:

> At the east end of the Plaisance will stand a tower 100 feet in diameter at the base and 400 feet high. An electric railway will follow a spiral course to the top of the tower, where an excellent birds-eye view of the Fair Grounds and surrounding country can be obtained, and where various scientific experiments in the meteorological line will be conducted. A full chime of bells, of beautiful tone, will be placed in the top of the tower.[65]

Some guidebooks, such as Rand McNally's *Handy Guide to Chicago and the World's Columbian Exposition*, published in early 1893 (while the tower was still under consideration), referred to it as the "Tower of Babel." Never constructed, the tower changed in concept from a copy of the Parisian monument to an outlandish design that readily invited biblical analogies.

This idea of a huge tower representing the accomplishments of civilization was not new in world's fairs in the nineteenth century. Nor were the associations of progress with the biblical tower of Babel.[66] Indeed, even after the Fair opened (without the tower), the idea of Babel was a particularly popular way to refer to the Midway, for here were ethnic and foreign displays of culture that emphasized oddity, exoticism, and difference as much as the White City celebrated the sameness and regularity of high culture.

The parable of Babel, employed as a metaphor to the Midway, is a fascinating application and deserves some attention. In *Genesis* in the Bible, Babel was a mythical place whose citizens, in their arrogance and overconfidence, built a tower to celebrate their accomplishments. Offended by this presumption, God strikes it down and confuses the tongues of the people. But what did the symbol mean when applied to the Midway? Was it the unity of all cultures— the secular part of the myth—or the divergence and confusion, or both that commentators intended?

This question is further complicated by the history of the Midway. As originally planned (when placed under the direction of the anthropologist F. W. Putnam), the Midway was to be a unitary exhibit of ethnic variation tied together by concepts of evolution and movement through stages of civilization. Yet, as the Midway evolved and changed, it became more chaotic and confused in purpose, with the initial order of exhibits disrupted, and the gradual triumph of commercial over pseudoscientific considerations.

The Babel referred to by guidebooks, visitors, and even Exhibition officials, was, in reality more like the second than the first part of the myth—a world of confused tongues and customs. Still, there remained an unstated coherence of sorts: the harmony imposed by commercialism and profit making. But to many observers, ethnic variety, not the commercialism of the Midway, made it appear a Babel. Indeed, the whole experience of visiting the Fair was sometime likened to a tour though that biblical land. As Ben C. Truman et al. wrote in their history of the World's Fair:

> There are Germans and Scandinavians, Frenchmen and Poles, Bohemians and Russians, Spaniards and Greeks, white men and negroes.
>
> Hundreds, did you say? Thousands. For they are pouring out in a very deluge, which will inundate the approaches to the grounds.[67]

Rapidly outgrowing the objectives of ethnology, the Midway developed into a vast amusement park that, nonetheless, retained certain elements of its original purpose. Professor Putnam originally hoped to demonstrate an evolutionary movement of cultures and civilizations toward the ideals of Western (and American) society. Ultimately, however, the Department of Ethnology was confined to much smaller quarters while the Midway expanded into a huge, money-making concession area.[68] And plans for a centralized Bazaar of All Nations to sell goods and souvenirs gave place to individual concessions representing various foreign nations and exhibitions.[69]

Putnam's ethnological exhibit and his classification system of cultures contained some of the best contemporary anthropology, which is, from today's perspective, racist and sexist. In his book,

Oriental and Occidental Northern and Southern Portrait Types of the Midway Plaisance, Putnam clearly revealed his biases, using language like "rude" to describe the instruments and tools of the Africans.[70] Perhaps the most remarkable and extreme example of this ethnocentrism was the display in the anthropology department of the naked figures of the perfect man and woman, based upon a composite of measurements of 25,000 American subjects. This Adam and Eve, unlike the denizens of Eden, were the end product of human history and evolution, not its innocent originators.[71]

Despite his loss of control over the Midway, Putnam tried to maintain his hold over the tourist's impression of it. In his souvenir book of the Midway, *Portrait Types,* he extolled the instruction a visitor would receive in the customs of other cultures in addition to the pleasures available at concessions. His words are worth quoting at length because so many of his interpretations are telling:

> We must not forget however that in the midst of peoples so new and strange to us there were others nearer akin. To many Americans "Old Vienna," the "German Village," and the "Irish Villages" gave information of the customs of their fathers; while our own crowning achievement, in mechanics, the great Ferris Wheel, arising in the midst of this magic gathering enabled us to view this mimic world as from another planet, and to look down upon an enchanted land filled with happy folk.[72]

In some respects, Putnam had only appropriated for his illustrated lesson from tradition, from an older popular painting and photo genre, the street crier or the portrait type. In the nineteenth century such works focused upon oddities of ethnicity or calling found in the city. In these photographs, pictured alone, against a white backdrop, curious figures wore costumes or carried symbolic objects, suggesting their trade or origin. Putnam used the same technique to present his anthropological "types."[73]

If Putnam intended to teach Americans about the superiority of their civilization and the cultural or racial inferiority of other nations it was probably not a lesson in which most Americans needed instruction. A popular newspaper printed at the Fair, called *World's Fair Puck,* exhibited such attitudes in much cruder and probably more familiar terms. Its cartoons and jokes were often anti-Semitic, anti-Irish and anti-German, anti-women, and anti-American farmer. To commemorate Colored People's Day at the Fair (the only concession of the Fair administration to African-Americans), it printed a racist cartoon entitled "Darkies at the Fair." And its very last issue featured a full-page cartoon of a huge Uncle Sam kicking up his heels in a row of diminutive dancers of other nations.[74]

Despite its origin as an ethnological exhibition, the Midway evolved rapidly until commercialism came to control and shape even its anthropological displays. There continued, of course, to be exhibits that appeared to have no other purpose than exoticism such as the Dahomey Village located toward the west end of the grounds. But even most of the cultural displays featured performances designed to make money more than instruct. Commercialism vied with science with the result that most concessionaires subordinated anthropology to entertainment.[75]

From a map's eye view, the Midway was a coherently designed city of pleasures, with a broad avenue and concessions along either side. On the east was the White City, and on the west Cottage Grove Avenue which itself contained many of the same sorts of amusements as the Midway (such as a smaller version of the Ferris Wheel) although on a more modest scale. Thus, on the east, the Midway merged into Burnham's planned culture; on the west, it blended into the commercial popular culture of Chicago.[76]

There were three distinct sections of the Midway. Closest to the White City was a large group of displays including the German and Irish villages, the Japanese Bazaar, the Libby Glass Works, the South Sea Islanders Village, and the Hagenbeck Animal Show. The Ferris Wheel dominated a large section of the Midway devoted to Middle Eastern exhibits: the Moorish Palace, the Street in Cairo, and the Algerian and Tunisian villages. This section also featured a one-fiftieth scale model of the Eiffel Tower, a nod to the 1889 Paris Exposition, and an invidious comment upon its diminutive significance when compared to the American-built Ferris Wheel. The farthest section of the Midway again featured a number of cafes, restaurants, and cultural exhibits. With its Chinese Village, American Indian Village, and Lapland and Dahomey villages, it might have appeared to represent Putnam's notion of a primitive to higher-order evolution. But this continuity was broken by other displays: the Aus-

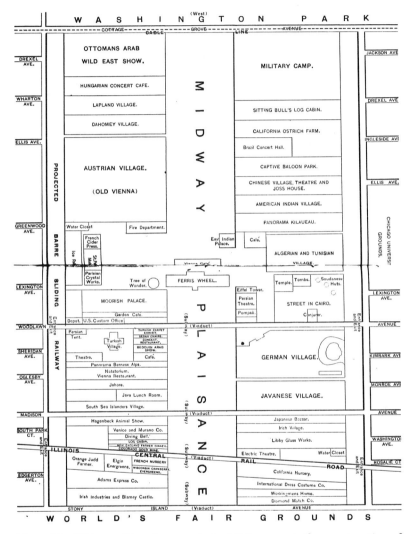

Map of the Midway. The placement of exhibits suggests the construction of this area around the central feature—the Ferris Wheel and the Middle Eastern pleasure palaces—showing the hand of Sol Bloom. (John Flinn, *Guide to the Midway*, Library of Congress)

The Algerian Theatre at the Center of the Midway. One reason why a great many photographs of the World's Fair are set from a distant perspective or picture empty scenes is illustrated here. Slow film meant that moving objects, like people, would be blurred. (Library of Congress)

trian Village, the Hungarian Concert Cafe, a military encampment, and the Ottoman's Arab Wild East Show.

If anything, the arrangement of the Midway reflected Sol Bloom's delight in "oriental" fantasies which he placed at the center of the Exhibition and his shrewd guess that this midpoint area would bring the highest returns to the Fair. His gamble paid off. The Algerian, Moorish, Turkish, and Egyptian exhibits, along with the Ferris Wheel at their center, brought very impressive profits.[77]

The coherence of the central point of the Midway based upon Middle Eastern fantasies lent the area a very special character. The harmony was borrowed in part from the 1889 Paris Exhibition where the French had designed a sort of midway made up of exhibits from French colonial possessions—many of them comprising Muslim cultures. This *Esplanade des Invalides et ses scandales* featured Javanese dancers and a Street of Cairo with belly dancers. While in Paris, Bloom had seen, admired, and even arranged to display one of these exhibits in America.[78]

Guidebooks and official commentary generally insisted that a visit to this Middle Eastern center represented, in fact, immersion in another culture. John Flinn's *Official Guide to Midway Plaisance*, for example, noted that visitors lost "all consciousness of being in that extremely modern city called Chicago" while strolling through the Street in Cairo. As the Rand McNally guide noted of the whole area, "[I]t is the purpose to introduce the typical people of Northern Africa, and showing them as they naturally are in their own country."[79] While the Cairo-Street did have reproductions of old buildings and curiosities from Egyptian museums, it also featured camel and donkey rides, long a staple of tourist life along the Nile.

In fact, however, these oriental exhibits combined tourist concessions and anthropology with more or less faithfulness to science. A quick trip through the Moorish Palace would certainly confirm this. After paying an entrance fee of twenty-five cents, the tourist could roam freely through the Palm Garden, Magic Maze, Spain's Alhambra, the Devil's Cave, and a Room of 1000 Reflections. In the Collection in Wax, the guest might see the "original guillotine" that executed Marie Antoinette as well as wax tableaux of Christ and the Samaritan Woman, Little Red Riding Hood, the Assassination of Lincoln, Luther in his Family, and a Moorish Execution.[80] If this was the least "authentic" of the cultural displays in the area, it nonetheless indicates how exotic culture became a pretext for an eclectic collection of money-making curiosities.

In some respects the centerpiece of the Midway, and even the Fair, was the Ferris Wheel. Not completed until well after the Exposition opened, it still earned a significant amount of money and was one of the most visited amusements. A bridge builder, George Ferris won the concession to build his gigantic steel construction. Certainly not the first such attraction, its scale and popularity were so overwhelming that it was thereafter known as a Ferris Wheel.[81] With its slow motion and large cars, the concession offered a safe and comfortable ride for the entire family.

As a symbol of the Fair, the Ferris Wheel must be given as important a rank as the White City. Just as Burnham's glimmering city provided a coherent vision of middle-class culture in which commercial culture was carefully measured, divided, and enclosed, the Ferris Wheel represented an undisguised display of technology in the service of enterprise. It was a structure in which form had no other purpose than the function of entertainment and profit. The great wheel was like an upended elevated railway, like a commuter line bent from carrying workers to jobs to carrying tourists toward an exhilarating sense of pleasure (the future Loop rendered vertical).

Together with its surrounding ensemble of oriental culture, the Ferris Wheel epitomized the triumph of popular culture freed from the moderating controls of classic architecture and censorship. The eclecticism, the rough juxtapositions of exhibits in the area, the merger of anthropology and "hoochy-kooch" dancing, the association of freedom, invention, immigrant exoticism, and ingenuity with commercialized culture was the opposite of the White City. But it was a good deal closer to the reality of the city of Chicago, with its incredible juxtapositions of cultures, than the uniform blanket of white staff that choked the exhibits around the Court of Honor. This association of enterprise and artistic license has probably always been a characteristic of fairs; in Chicago, however, it assumed equality with the White City that was so elaborately planned and promoted by the Fair administration.[82]

Besides this magnificent and profitable central area, there were other displays that attracted considerable attention on the Midway. Especially important were the Irish Village and Blarney Castle and the German Village. These two exhibits appealed to the two largest foreign-born Chicago populations, and there is no doubt that they were popular among local visitors.

Other cultural displays were also popular, especially the Javanese Village and the Dahomey Village. It is particularly the latter that offered a brief—perhaps obligatory—glimpse of "barbarism." The guidebooks and commentators that described it were quick to

Looking through the Ferris Wheel toward Chicago. This view of the wheel, like similar ones of the Eiffel Tower and the Brooklyn Bridge, is a good example of the power of function to determine form. Sometimes, from the top of the Ferris Wheel, the city appeared shrouded in smoke (see Chapter 7). (ICHI-17426, Chicago Historical Society)

lament the conditions of its inhabitants. Unlike the oriental pleasure palaces, these rudimentary exhibits had no entertainments associated with them. Anthropology was their sole purpose. As John Flinn noted in his guidebook of Dahomey: "Those who have visited the Javanese village will observe at once that there are very striking degrees of barbarism. The habits of these people are repulsive; they eat like animals and have all the characteristics of the very lowest order of the human family. Nearly all the women are battle-scarred; most of them are captives."[83] That these were distressing exhibits is confirmed by a sign reported at the entrance to Dahomey village requesting visitors not to ask the natives if they were cannibals.[84]

If this exhibit (and the reaction of visitors) was thoroughly consistent with the prevailing racial attitudes of the day and the notions of the Fair administration, it was also a sort of anomaly. Very few of the exhibits of the Midway were without a high content of entertainment, dancing, or salable items. Many had attached theaters and restaurants. Only a few were as dismal or as isolated as Dahomey. Proof of this intentional distancing came when all of the other nations and cultures of the Midway were invited to join a parade to celebrate Chicago Day—except Dahomey.[85]

Beyond the cultural and entertainment, restaurant, and amusement areas of the Midway, there were two interesting but jarring inclusions which appeared in the jumble of small exhibits at the beginning of the Midway: these were the model Workingman's Home and the New England house. As the report of New York State noted: "The "Home" is intended to demonstrate how good a living can be had for a family on an income of $500 a year. The house could be built and rented by a capitalist at a rate not exceeding $10 a month; or it could be built by a man himself in New York State outside of New York City, for $1000."[86]

The curiosity of this exhibit lies in its exile to the Midway, relegated to appear among the foreign cultures of the area. There was, indeed, no place for workers in the White City, no evidence of their presence. In the concentric circles of culture and industry that radiated out from the Court of Honor, there was little concern for the problem of housing in the modern urban area. Inclusion of the ideal worker's home as a curiosity among the menageries, anthropological exhibits, and amusement concessions represented a striking way to distance the visitor who was presumed to be middle class from the workers who built the Fair but did not visibly participate in it.

Another interesting act of distancing occurred in the Log Cabin and Restaurant, where Ye Old Tyme New England Dinners were served, as Moses Handy wrote, by "handsome young ladies from New England States in colonial dress."[87] This was one of the few American historical exhibits (another was Sitting Bull's Log Cabin), and it too, like most of the other exhibits, bore the marks of transla-

tion into popular culture. Thus even the past, like the anthropological exhibits, was transformed into a foreign land, yet made accessible because it offered itself for consumption by tourists.

The contrived exoticism and the improved alien environment of
the Midway depended upon a sleight-of-hand. The unfamiliar was
couched in familiar terms; what was foreign was made acceptable
and commonplace. The tourist was reassured that what he or she
viewed was authentic and, at the same time, fantasy. Only Dahomey broke this rule—isolated, miserable, and shocking to its viewers. Exoticism did not challenge the visitor by inverting expectations, but it did threaten, as it always had, to test limits or to justify
the presentation of scandalous exhibits. The Fair administration
recognized this danger and kept an anxious watch, especially over
the dancing in the Oriental center of the Midway. Nonetheless,
belly dancing and other forms of female undress were the rule in
these areas.

The display of nudity provides a fascinating contrast between
the way the Midway and the White City were perceived and how art
and culture functioned in each. In the statues and the paintings and
murals of the White City, there were considerable numbers of large-
scale human nudes. Although these figures were generally dis-
cretely half-covered, viewers were intentionally invited to comtem-
plate the undraped human figure. In the Midway, there were frequent hints of nudity in dances, although figures were usually carefully covered and shaded. But without the justification of art, in this
popular setting and veiled only by exoticism, the association of the
body in motion and sexuality became more explicit and controversial. Context and purpose, in effect, meant everything.

Contemporary observers were quick to note the contrast. One
of the most interesting theories about the acceptability of nudity in
the White City was offered by Julian Hawthorne in his *Humors of
the Fair*. Distance from the familiar, wrote the author, made nude
art acceptable. Thus, the generic male and female of Greek, Roman,
and Egyptian art was totally acceptable, and "[l]adies and gentlemen
from among our most prominent and cultured famlies go and con-
template them by the hour and never once blush or hold their hands
before their eyes." The case for contemporary art was much less

sure. Even further down the scale of respectability was the Midway's *danse du ventre*.[88]

If authenticity and distance transformed sexuality into art, they also provided a larger justification for much of the Fair itself. There were "original" objects—from the national medium of measurements of the ideal American man and woman to the considerable number of American historical artifacts such as George Washington's Diaries and the first electric chair used at Sing Sing Prison, to a scale model of St. Peter's at Rome, to the "hilted sword worn by Judge John Hathorne of Salem during all the trials of the 'witches,'" and, finally, to relics of Columbus. The combined weight of these collections lent credence to the solemnity and importance of a visit to the Fair.[89]

Perhaps this emphasis is what inspired a rampant cliché about the Midway: that it represented a Street of All Nations or a visit around the world. This ethnic/historical pageantry was thoroughly consistent with the nineteenth-century tradition of using diverse folk customs to enact its opposite in a ritual of common identity. Thus, diversity could be conceived as a preliminary for the unity of civilizations.[90]

Despite the amazing popularity of this area, some guidebooks to the Fair neglected to mention the Midway or only briefly described its features. Even those that did justified their attention in terms of the idea of a world trip. Thus, White and Ingelheart wrote that the Midway was "a place of good nature and gaiety, and, after returning from a day spent in investigations of its wonders, one feels indeed that he has returned from making a trip around the world."[91] This cosmopolitanism extended to the visitors themselves as observers noted that tourists were as varied as the exhibits themselves. In effect, the guarded cosmopolitanism of Chicago guidebooks reappeared in the cautious exoticism of the Midway.

So successful was this exhibit area that, in 1894, Anne Sergal published a popular guide to setting up miniature midways across the country. In describing how to construct a local midway, Sergal identified what she believed to be the essence of the Chicago exhibit. She stressed the idea of the street of all nations in her choice of crucial displays. These should include the Street in Cairo, the

A Parade on the Midway. This posed picture in front of Hagenbeck's Animal Show underscores the circus-like quality of the Midway. (Library of Congress)

Casino, the Congress of Beauty, a Candy Bazaar, Japanese Bazaar, an Art Gallery, Blarney Castle, and the New England Home. Like the Chicago exhibit, the local version would mix girlie shows, exotic displays, "art" (tastefully displayed), ethnic heritage shows, and snippets of American history. Where appropriate, she advised holding special ethnic days—for German, Irish, or other immigrants in the area. And to assure that it would all be taken in the right spirit, she encouraged noise: "[E]very one will recognize the show as a huge joke and the place will always possess a peculiar fascination just as it did on the original Midway."[92]

Was the Fair with its carefully divided cultures and special messages what visitors to Chicago actually experienced? To measure who came and what they saw is a particularly difficult problem because of a paucity of records. For example, the aggregate figure of 27 million paid admissions does not indicate how many visitors made multiple entries—and these were probably considerable. Furthermore, this tally does not include the large number of passes issued to special individuals or groups. The best conclusion is that if there were at least 27 million visits to the Fair there were considerably fewer than half as many different patrons.

Those who came, particularly for a lengthy stay (as most guidebooks advised), had to expend considerable amounts of money. Although the "sturdy young man" could sojourn "in a part of the city occupied chiefly by 'working people,'" it was more common to seek hotels either around the Fairgrounds or near the downtown area. For this purpose, hundreds of new structures were erected (making 750 available), supplemented by boardinghouses and rented rooms. In general, a hotel cost from $3 to $5 a day, sometimes including meals. A boardinghouse ranged from $7.50 to $15 per week.[93] This amount had to be added to train fares which could be considerable. So two weeks in Chicago might cost $55 plus train fare. For the worker who might live "comfortably" on $500 a year in the Midway's model house, a trip to the Fair from out of town would be unusual if not impossible. Inevitably, the clientele (as the Connecticut survey of visitors suggested) would consist of each state's wealthier citizens. Among workers, perhaps only Chicago's could afford to attend the exhibitions.

There were many opportunities for organized tours of the Fair. For example, a trip from Salem, Massachusetts, for ten days in late May and June offered travelers a packaged tour, including meals, train, and hotels, for $125. This did not, however, include admissions to the Midway. Entrepreneurs also offered membership in groups like the World's Fair Tourist Accommodation Society. For $5 this organization would book rooms and greet visitors at the train station. For international tourists there were organizations like the International Exposition Company offering much the same services.[94]

Although guidebooks and official publications tried to steer the visitor to the White City, this was clearly not always successful. This attempt to structure the experience continued the general strategy of guidebook descriptions of Chicago itself. But the more likely itinerary of the visitor began with a visit to an appropriate place of orientation: a state or national exhibit building, the woman's building, a relevant immigrant exhibit like the German Village. Furthermore, as the gross proceeds of various concessions indicate, the Midway was enormously popular. The German Village probably had close to 2 million guests; the Street in Cairo even more. George Ferris's wheel lifted at least 1,500,000 paying tourists high over the park skyline. The Moorish Palace, the Turkish Village, and the Algerian Village probably had close to 1 million visitors each. Hagenbeck's zoological displays drew at least 1 million while the French, German, and Viennese restaurants all did considerable business.[95] Given these substantial numbers, it is probable most visitors went to at least one of these major exhibitions.

Visits to exhibits in the White City are harder to measure since no figures were maintained. But since admission was free and because so many visitors purchased guidebooks that would lead them to the various buildings there, it is certain that this section too was well-visited. Moreover, a great deal of the commentary on the Fair, by distinguished visitors such as William Dean Howells, Theodore Dreiser, Henry Adams, and others stressed the importance of not just the displays in the White City but the impression made by the ensemble.

Yet, curiously, most of the photography of the Fairgrounds, including Arnold's official views as well as illustrations in guidebooks, revealed a contrast between the empty White City and the teeming Midway. For example, the *Chicago Tribune*'s "Glimpses of the World's Fair" typically showed the White City from an elevated camera angle with a few tourists in view strolling leisurely. On the other hand, the Midway was shot from a much closer angle and stressed the huge and unorganized crowds. This gave the impression, if nothing else, that the Midway was far more popular.[96] Per-

Breaking Home Ties by Thomas Hovenden. This genre painting in the exhibit of American paintings at the Palace of Fine Arts captured the attention of a great many visitors. One reason was its undisguised sentimentalization of the late nineteenth-century trip to the city—a representation of the flow of Americans into places like Chicago. (Philadelphia Museum of Art)

haps this was intended to indicate a class difference between the two areas. If so, it succeeded but at the price of making the White City appear empty.

Despite the directions and exhortations, if the World's Fair had a heart it was probably not the science celebrated by Henry Adams or the neoclassical architecture encouraged by Daniel Burnham— or, finally, even the Midway—but a simple portrait hanging in the Fine Arts collection. Among the largely academic paintings from Russia, Europe, and the Americas, one painting was repeatedly described by observers as the most popular and the most moving. This sentimental genre portrait by Thomas Hovenden (*Breaking Home Ties*) shows a young man standing in a New England kitchen preparing to leave home. As George Ade described the painting, the mother "is warning him of the dangers he will surely meet and beseeching him not to forget the mother and the father and the old home in the hour of temptation, that he may never bring disgrace and sorrow to those who have loved and sheltered him."[97]

Although not explicit, the boy's destination was undoubtedly the city, and the scene is reminiscent of the tale of the Prodigal Son. Why this sentimental portrait should be accounted the most popular of the exhibit surely relates to this message and to the story within the story it tells about the Fair itself. With the massive movement of Americans (and immigrants) into the city in the late nineteenth century, of sons and daughters into the vast and lonely—and tempting—grids of urban life, there was no doubt a strong sense of loss. The tale of the prodigal had become something of a cliché in the late Victorian esteem for motherhood and sentimentality.[98] That is the sentiment upon which Dwight Moody based so much of his preaching and why, perhaps, he constructed his ministry in the heart of the most changeable city in America. His most compelling sermon was that of the Prodigal Son. It appealed to his audiences and, as evidenced by Hovenden's popularity, to the larger audience at the Fair.

If a trip to the Fair was, as intended, a visit to the ideal city, then the discovery at its very core of a painting exploring the ambiguous emotions of that trip is both remarkable and appropriate. For even Columbus could be considered a prodigal son, and if his discoveries led ultimately to the great monuments to Western Civilization in the White City, then there still lay at the center the possibility of loss, a whimsical and nostalgic vision of the home in America that was being abandoned—Utopia notwithstanding. At the heart of every nineteenth-century American city lived the prodigal sons and daughters from America's heartland as well as millions of foreign immigrants.

If the Fair represented an idealized city with its appendages of popular culture, it also paid homage to problems of the real city that surrounded it. For one thing, the strong element of boosterism and competitiveness with New York was obvious and strong. Chicago had a reputation for vulgarity, crudeness, and commercialism that made something like the White City (in the very denial of these qualities) almost inevitable. In some sense, then, the White City compensated for a characterization that was perhaps justified but not welcome.

Just as the demands of self-promotion and the search by Chicago's elites for a respectable culture helped shape the White City, the Midway was also molded by the special problems of Chicago's urban environment: the cultural mixing of the city's vast immigrant populations. The Midway was a fantasied model of this element of the real city, and the association of exotic customs and pleasures with foreignness was certainly not accidental. Moreover, the Midway seeped out of the Fairgrounds onto nearby areas which had their own miniature concession stretches. Taken as a whole, the Fair itself was a meeting ground of two larger cultural ideals—one respectable and regulated and associated with elite control. The other was imbedded in a different form, based upon the marketplace with its open access to immigrant cultures and immigrant social mobility. These differences were symbolized by the Swedenborgian Daniel Burnham who focused his energy on the White City, and the Jewish entrepreneur Sol Bloom who helped organize and run the Midway. Between them stretched the competitive field upon which modern popular cultures contended.

Chicago itself in 1893 was as much on display as the Fair. This was visually inescapable. As visitors mounted the Ferris Wheel, seated in their plush swivel chairs, they were elevated above the two cities: "The horizon grew; the great blue lake, the White City in dazzling whiteness, moved into view, and then sank downward; the smoky city of Chicago rose, and fell into the shadows."[99] Whether by contrast or extension, such visual, physical links united the visit to the World's Fair with the city. If Chicago was the nation's emporium, so was the White City. If Chicago was the nation's most cosmopolitan city, then the Midway reflected this remarkable heterogeneity. No matter what the issue, there was an implicit comparison to be made between Chicago and its idealized essence, its metaphor in Jackson Park. Visitors moved through the city as they did through the Fair itself, between public monuments, breathtaking views of skyscrapers, into theaters, burlesque houses, the stockyards, even the notorious Levee district. As much as the Fair, Chicago was a sprawling carnival of cultures.[100]

Both the city and the Fair could be described in the same terms. Thus the poet James Wright Dickinson wrote in commemoration:

> O mighty City! Earth's historic page
> Knows naught like thee. Alone, unrivaled, thou
> Hast sprung to life, like fabric of a dream;
> Like tale of magic from Arabian mind!
> E'en Desolation gives to thee new strength,
> And, from thy flames, like to the fabled bird,
> Has thou arisen, thus renewing youth
> E'en from thy ashes.[101]

Or as a Wisconsin visitor wrote of her trip: "I hardly know what to say of the city. It was worse than the confusion of tongues at the Tower of Babel. Humdrum noises and confusion existed all day and all night long."[102] The vocabulary to describe city and Fair was interchangeable: Atlantis, Babel, Phoenix, Utopia, or Hell. They were all versions of the same city.

In an off-site satellite of the Fair in downtown Chicago in what would shortly become the Art Institute building, there were important international professional meetings called "parliaments." With an estimated 200,000 attendees and over 1,200 sessions, these meetings were intended to spread the idea of ecumenical culture, to prove the coherence of worldwide thinking on a wide variety of subjects from religion, engineering, science and philosophy, music and literature, temperance, and moral and social reform. Not surprisingly, the largest of the conventions was devoted to religion. Speakers representing Protestants, Catholics, Jews, Muslims, Hindus, and Buddhists were represented. There were also evangelicals (although Moody declined to participate) and even Inquiry Rooms where different religions could explain themselves.[103] Lucinda H. Stone spoke of this union in her remarks on the "Higher Lessons of the World's Fair" before the Congress of Women:

> In the olden times men could have seen in the face of every
> stranger whom we welcome to our Midway Plaisance, an

enemy to be met with an armed defense against himself, his customs, his thought, and above all against his religion. Now, thanks to the new spirit of our times, we may see in him a human brotherhood from whom . . . we may yet agree in broad human sympathies, and who, has the same claim to the Fatherhood of God as we have.[104]

Nonetheless, as at the Fair itself, there was an attempt to construct out of this heterogeneity not a compromise or a parliament but rather a consensus—something akin to the white veneer of the Court of Honor. This agreement on a fraternal kinship between religions was intended to validate an American, Protestant, Christian view of mankind. In his closing address to the last session, the Reverend George Danna Boardman made this agenda explicit by claiming that Christ was the only true unifier of mankind.[105]

But here, as at the Fair, the outcome in the balance among differences remained in question. Indeed, at the Fair, two events occurred which signaled a movement away from the predominance of White City ideals and cultural control. The first involved a dispute over Sunday closing of the Fair. Written into the enabling legislation for the Exposition, Sunday closing pleased many ministers and several Chicago newspapers like the *Record*. But labor unions like the Knights of Labor urged opening the Fair on Sunday "for the education of the masses." So, too, did several Chicago newspapers, concession holders, and administrators who feared lost profits and attendance.[106] Although the Fair was opened on Sundays after a series of lawsuits, attendance never did match other days, and the *World's Fair Puck* noted on July 24 that, "had you taken a microscope to aid you last Sunday, you would hardly have found a trace of the Workingman, whom Sunday-opening was expected to benefit."[107] Perhaps exaggerating, the paper accurately noted that the Fair was an expensive venture for a working family.

Whatever the results of this endeavor to attract working families to the Fair, the symbolic message was clear: the commercial considerations of the Fair proved more powerful than the effort to impress conservative religious customs onto Chicago's amusements. This reflected a similar and similarly unsuccessful ongoing struggle to close Chicago's theaters and other places of commercial leisure on Sunday.

A more telling shift in the focus of the Fair was the failure of the Theodore Thomas classical concerts. Highly touted and supported by Chicago's elite, Thomas promoted serious music, most of it modern and much of it Germanic. Concerts at the Fair only attracted scanty audiences. As the *Chicago Herald* reported on July 5, the fireworks display at the Midway outdrew Theodore Thomas: "The crowd was too busy seeking choice spots from which to view the fire works that began to paint the sky at 9 o'clock to pay more than passing attention to the music."

If this sort of thing was an ominous sign of failure, Thomas did not finally recognize it until very late. In August, he decided that expenses should be reduced and music considered "solely as an amusement." In early October he resigned. As the Chicago *Inter Ocean* gleefully noted: "At last there is to be some popular music at the Fair and plenty of it."[108]

Of course, both of these events are only small signals, but they nonetheless suggest the direction of events and the growing importance of a different version of popular culture than that most prized by Burnham and the Fair administration. It underscored the growing importance of the Midway as a center of the Fair and the increasing acceptability and necessity of commercial considerations in the presentation of culture.

That, finally, is the outcome of the shifting balance achieved at the World's Fair. Initially there was an attempt to create a universal culture, a unified merger of disparate elements, a cosmopolitanism based upon the predominance of the White City, with popular culture from the rest of Chicago admitted as a "concession." The two grand parades that opened and closed the Fair signaled this commitment. The dedicatory parade of October 20, 1892, featured a huge confabulation of trades, bands, ethnic groups, occupations, and organizations. As one reporter noted:

> In the great process . . . were Teutons and Slavs and Frenchmen, and their hearts and feet beat time to the same music—that of "The Star Spangled Banner." Orangemen walked in that procession and for the first time in the history of 300 years,

the Irish Celts walked with them in common cause. Hereditary foes were brothers, and for once the descendants of warring European clans marched under the same flag.[109]

The Chicago Day parade, which virtually ended the Fair on October 9, repeated this design, with another grand parade of Chicago citizens joined by marchers from the Midway. Nothing could have better matched the purposeful eclecticism of the whole endeavor. Organized, passing in review before dignitaries, and deliberate, this organized heterogeneity embodied a vision of cosmopolitanism thoroughly consistent with cultural designs of the White City. It carefully included marchers representing Chicago immigrant groups plus floats celebrating the history of the city. Float number two was particularly interesting, with its theme, "Chicago, I Will." As the official souvenir book exclaimed: "Guided by Love and Liberty and surrounded by all the States of the Union welcoming all peoples of the globe: at the four corners, Music, Sculpture, Science, Literature" (but no commerce).[110]

This omission of commerce, undoubtedly purposeful, is enormously revealing of the intentions and purposes of this display of high culture and political power. It replicated the abstractness of the White City itself and its relegation of commerce from the central role to a subordinate purpose. And yet in a curious way, this slight revealed a fundamental truth about the relationship between types of cultural displays at the Fair. While it might have been freely offered, the grandiose architecture, paints, sculptures, and classical music depended not only upon the commerce it embellished but also upon the profits derived from popular culture on the Midway. This relationship reproduced the larger reality of the commerical aspects of Chicago culture itself. While the institutions of high culture strove to disguise their dependence upon commerce and presented themselves as public institutions open freely to all, popular culture was unabashed in its search for profits.

In contrast to the opening and closing spectacles, on the Midway there was a different sort of parade appearing daily—a disorganized mass of individuals moving in contrary directions but held together, nonetheless, by their participation in the commerical culture of the concessions. If Burnham and the organizers of the Fair did not see this analog, it nonetheless defined something very different that was occurring in Chicago.

At the Fair, in Chicago, and at the very center of American culture, a different measure of cultural order existed beyond the organized parades through the White City. It competed with the ideals of the White City. That was the standard of the commercial market which held sway on the Midway and which created a different sort of unity and familiarity. Just as powerful in its ability to transform and shape culture, this commercial marketplace created a different sort of pastiche, a collage of cultures, customs, and ideas that eventually predominated and absorbed the disparities of American life into what became modern mass culture. The Midway that could be recreated anywhere—and even the disposable White City—were part of the same essential attribute of modern mass culture: it could be reproduced anywhere for anyone.[111] What better place to exhibit these characteristics of modern mass culture than the Phoenix city of Chicago, which itself had risen up once on a lonely plain and then emerged again after the terrible fire of 1871. Burnham's great debate at the Fair posed a question which perhaps even he did not fully anticipate. Which would predominate in American life: commercial culture, or a culture defined by history, custom, and morality? The impossibility of any easy answer has meant that this question would be asked again and again throughout the twentieth century.

Five

SECOND CITY

Our Town

O N THE WINTRY EVENING OF January 9, 1883, a special train of six new Pullman Palace cars crept slowly out of the Illinois Central depot in Chicago. It stopped, as the elaborately printed invitations announced, first at the Van Buren Street Station, then near the Pullman residence on Prairie Avenue, then at Twenty-second Street, and finally halted at the little brick terminal in the village of Pullman. Despite the snow and blowing wind outside, the cars were cheerful and warm, and the almost 300 guests of the Pullmans chatted with animation amidst the luxurious appointments of the coaches. Dressed in evening clothes, Chicago's social world was augmented by friends from New York City and the guest of honor, the Civil War cavalry hero General P. H. Sheridan.

In the obscurity of the night, only shadowy outlines of the little company town were visible, like a darkened stage: the clock tower and works on the left; then across the small park the grand Hotel Florence (named after Pullman's favorite daughter); then to the right the destination of the party, the Arcade with its shops, library, and theater. Protected from the weather by a canopy strung out over a carpet leading all the way from the station to the Arcade entrance, the invited guests made their way to the theater. Once inside, they settled into special boxes or in the orchestra surrounded by the opulent, Moorish decor. Most of the Pullman family seated themselves

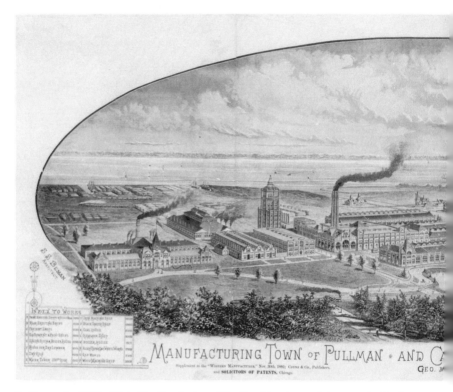

MANUFACTURING TOWN OF PULLMAN · AND C

Pullman in 1881. This idealized view, like the Currier and Ives portrait of Chicago (see page 47), rendered this most industrial of settings as a pastoral Utopia. (ICHI-01918, Chicago Historical Society)

in an elaborate, fantastically designed box on the right-hand side of the proscenium. The general's party was on the left. As the gas lights dimmed, the intricately designed curtain, given by Marshall Field, rose to reveal George Pullman in the center of a line of Chicago dignitaries and prominent businessmen. As the *Chicago Inter Ocean* reporter noted, "As the audience saw this strong company of actors in everyday life, there was loud applause." The performance had begun.[1]

Lieutenant Governor Stewart L. Woodford of New York stood to give his opening celebration of George Pullman and his new company town. To an audience enthusiastic to the edge of applause, he

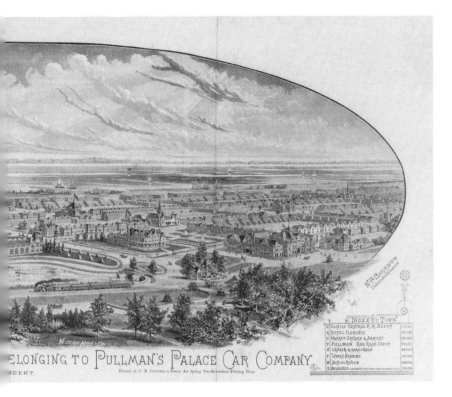

described the virtues of the housing arrangements, the workplace, the cleanliness and facilities of the city, and finally and more particularly its culture. Pullman's town would, he promised, produce a new sort of manhood, impossible to conceive of emerging from the obscure and dismal slums that the party train had raced through on its way to this new Utopia. Then the group on the stage filed out to their seats, and at nine o'clock the performance of *Esmeralda* began. Like the new house it inaugurated, the play reflected the enthusiasm for theater of George Pullman and his wife Harriet. Pullman would never allow a "questionable performance, and no company of secondary merit [would] be allowed on stage."[2] As in every venture undertaken by these elegant, wealthy, and powerful Chicagoans, there was an assumed continuity between morality, good taste, and profitable enterprise.

The Pullman Clock Tower. This building, through its height and symbolic importance, dominated the town. (Library of Congress)

The elite audience that traveled out to the suburb of Pullman that blustery night saw not just a performance at a new Chicago theater. They also participated in the opening of a new environment, a stage upon which George Pullman played out his ideas about the relationship between culture and work, between the engineered surroundings of his model town and the behavior he hoped it would solicit from his workers. Everything about the village was designed to create the impression of a special new urban culture. As Richard Ely wrote for *Harper's* two years later, it was "very gratifying" to pass quickly through the new town and observe the material comforts of its residents. "What is seen in a walk or a drive through the streets," he continued, "is so pleasing to the eye that a woman's first exclamation is certain to be, 'Perfectly lovely!'"[3]

This striking visual quality of the town, based upon its carefully staged elements, is exactly the impression that Pullman tried to create for the thousands of visitors who made it an important Chicago tourist stop and for the workers who lived within its confines. What the visitor or new arrival saw from the Illinois Central train station was a proscenium with the extraordinary works, clock tower, and engine building (holding the great Corliss Engine purchased from the Philadelphia Exposition of 1876) fronted by a small lake. At the center, across the park, was the Hotel Florence with its wide veranda, impressive restaurant (with black waiters reminiscent of the porters and servers on Pullman cars), and sumptuous saloon. On the right was the multipurpose Arcade, containing the town postoffice, the Pullman Loan and Savings Bank, and covered shops on the first floor. Up one flight was the library, the Arcade Theater, and offices. On the third floor was a lodge room for town meetings and societies. Between the hotel and the Arcade sat the lovely Greenstone Community Church. Employees of the company maintained the parks and streets of the town. In the wings, behind and stretching beyond these public buildings, were the workers' houses, arranged in neat rows and designed and appointed in quality according to their distance from the central area. Looking from a passing train or standing at the station, a visitor could observe workers passing across the central area to and from work or home to lunch at noon. Wives and children filled the park and the shopping area.[4]

This was the scene that thousands of World's Fair visitors beheld during the summer of 1893. One of the three or four great tourist attractions of Chicago during the Exposition year, the town attracted more than its share of curious travelers (10,000 foreign visitors alone). Indeed, this summer saw more visitors than ever before or after, for Pullman's reputation and fortune were at their height. Frequent trains and trolleys connected the Fairgrounds with the town, and on several occasions Pullman himself conducted guided tours of the area. Pullman was also a leading investor in the Fair and one of its early promoters. Like the Glessners and other Prairie Avenue neighbors, he and his wife Hattie used the Fairgrounds as a social rendezvous, a festive part of their extended social season in the city.

Pullman's interest in expositions was a longstanding one. A central feature of his company town featured one of the major exhibits taken from the 1876 Centennial Exhibit, the Corliss Engine that he and Hattie had viewed in a visit to Philadelphia. His purchase of the engine, installed in an elaborate ceremony in 1881, with Florence Pullman starting the works, meant more than delivering power to the town. It represented an engineering triumph; but even more important it was a display of power, polished and surrounded by walkways for viewers and, in part, visible through glass to the outside. It was a symbol of Pullman's interest in technology and a token of his power to command this monumental engineering triumph for his personal use.[5]

For visitors to the Transportation Building in the White City at the Chicago Fair, Pullman offered two displays linking his Utopian town and its car works. The first was a scale model of the town; the second was an exhibit of several newly designed palace cars. The chief of the exhibit, Fritsch, sent Pullman a daily report on his activities and a record of visitors. His work was divided between entertaining the merely curious and soliciting business from railway men interested in franchising Pullman cars. A select few expressed the desire to purchase palace cars for their private use. For many visitors, there was the brochure, written by Duane Doty, a publicist for the company, extolling the virtues of the planned community, entitled *The Story of Pullman*.[6] As the Chicago novelist Ernest Poole remarked later, Pullman used his town during the summer to entertain special guests to the Fair. Dressed in his Prince Albert coat, he escorted visitors through the exhibit or took them out to see the town and the works.[7] Some friends and acquaintances might stay in Pullman cars or at the Hotel Florence or in specially constructed (in a Venetian motif) flats around the Pullman marketplace.

Despite competition from the Wagner Palace Car Company (both Pullman and Wagner built and named cars in honor of Isabella and Ferdinand of Spain), Pullman dominated the industry; his dining and sleeping cars were packed bringing visitors to and from Chicago. The fortunes of Pullman remained high during 1893 despite the terrible downturn in the economy in the United States. The throngs who took the trip out to the suburban works had no sense of the impending disaster that was to doom the town during the Pullman strike of 1894. Instead, the visible future they encountered was a carefully engineered vision, a prophecy in brick of the coming relationship between work, leisure, and culture.

On the surface, it seemed that Pullman had resolved the two greatest problems striking every major metropolitan area in America: the formation of permanent social classes and the terrible confusion of manners, taste, amusement, and public behavior that resulted from sharing city space. The Pullman solution, like the World's Fair that it in some respects resembled, offered a controlled environment. His cultural strategy, however, was different, with a harsher, more extreme separation of the White City and Midway polarities. While Pullman used the Fair to advertise his community, his own ideal city actually represented a distinct alternative to the balance between diverse cultures sustained at the Exposition. The great railroad car builder simply banned what he did not like and promoted his own tastes. His complete ownership and control of the community gave him vast power which he did not fail to exercise. The result was a very different urban vision than that promoted by the Fair at Jackson Park. Still, to the parade of visitors who viewed the town in 1893, it must have appeared to be a comfortable and familiar prospect in which middle-class values and American traditions existed; it bore little evidence of any impact from the huge immigrant city around it. Only its population—upon close inspection—was foreign.[8]

The origin of this remarkable dream were the fertile imaginations of George Pullman and his wife Hattie Sanger Pullman. Like so many successful men of his acquaintance, George Mortimer Pullman was born in upstate New York, in Brocton, (Chautauqua County), in 1831, the third of ten children. His father was a farmer and carpenter. The family, like many others in this religiously agitated part of New York, was Universalist. The children were raised strictly, and two sons became Universalist ministers.

George grew up in this same family mold but devoted himself to secular pursuits. He left school at fourteen to take a job at a general store in Westfield, New York. From about eighteen to twenty-one, he was a carpenter's apprentice in his brother's cabinetworks in Albion, New York. After a brief period working on raising and removing buildings and houses along the Erie Canal in preparation for widening the waterway, he set out for Chicago in 1859. By chance that city was also struggling to raise itself (literally) out of the mud and swamp of hasty, early constructions. Pullman used the skills he had learned to raise buildings for placement on new, higher foundations. With a flair for publicity, he successfully lifted a number of buildings, including the famous Tremont Hotel, without disturbing its guests, who watched in awe as hundreds of men, on command, slowly turned screws that inched the building out of the ground.[9] There was something apocryphal in this raising of the hotel, something symbolic about hoisting the city above its crude beginnings, in raising luxury and wealth out of the unseemly muck from which it had emerged. This was a task that Pullman returned to time and again.

George Pullman did not invent the railroad sleeping car, but he revolutionized the quality of its interior, taking the crude idea of a traveling dormitory and transforming special cars into a more luxurious, middle-class environment. He believed that by developing a more sumptuous interior, he could persuade increased numbers of middle-class voyagers, especially women, to take extended train trips. And he successfully argued that this class of patrons would willingly pay extra for a conveyance that carried with it all of the comforts of a middle-class home.[10]

Although Pullman had this remarkable vision for transforming rail travel, he lacked capital. Like many other young men, he struck out for the West, spending almost three years in Colorado. As he wrote enthusiastically to his mother on July 2, 1860, from Denver: "If the gold mines yield anything like the supply that is now confidently expected this is destined to be a large city, and a splendid opportunity is presented to enterprising men with a fair amount of capital to realize a fortune in a few years and at the same time enjoy all the comforts of a pleasant home."[11]

Pullman Car. This car was lent by the fledgling company to the federal government for the cortege of Abraham Lincoln in 1865. (Library of Congress)

Although very young at the time, Pullman's habit of mind is rather clearly revealed by this eager letter. He believed in the power and prospects of the venture capitalist, convinced of the limitless opportunities for men with ideas and means. But at the same time, he was solicitous of his own comfort. Home (and family) meant a great deal to him. And in merging these two notions, he held the kernel of an idea that transformed middle-class rail travel.

When he returned to Chicago in 1863, he began work on his first, wholly new sleeping car, the "Pioneer." Dubbed "Pullman's Folly" by some unbelievers, the car became the subject of national attention when Pullman lent it to the federal government to bear Abraham Lincoln's body to Illinois in the funeral cortege of 1865. After persuading several railroad companies to eliminate obstacles along the right-of-way to passage of his slightly wider coaches, he incorporated the Pullman Palace Car Company in 1867 and expanded production. By the time of the Great Fire in 1871, he had become a leading Chicago businessman and served energetically on relief and reconstruction in the amazing frenzy of building that

The Pullman Residence at 1729 Prairie Avenue. This fashionable street housed many of Chicago's great entrepreneurs in the 1880s and 1890s. Today, only a block of this district remains amidst a wasteland of warehouses and broad through streets. (Chicago Historical Society)

erected a new city out of ashes.[12] As a trustee of the Relief and Aid Society, he helped oversee the distribution of charity in the city after the fire. Furthermore, like others of his class and background, he worked energetically for Chicago's new institutions of moral order and mutual benefit: the YMCA, the Citizen's Law and Order League (1877), the Mutual Benefit Association (1873), as well as civic clubs such as the Calumet, Commercial, and Union clubs.[13]

In 1869, Pullman bought land in the Lake Calumet area, south of Chicago, for the expansion of his works. In 1875, he was building not just sleeping cars but also parlor cars; indeed, the Pullman idea embraced a comprehensive world of homelike appointments that middle-class travelers would never have to leave. A train might have dining cars, sleeping coaches, a barber shop, parlor cars, and so on, all linked together by the vestibule—a flexible link between coaches so that passengers would never have to risk exposure to accidents or the elements in moving about the train.

At the same time, Pullman had begun to create, with his wife, the elaborate and complex and intertwined social and business worlds through which the family rushed during the next decades. All during this time, Pullman kept building new environments for himself, his family, and his workers, almost all of them constructed by the architect Solon Spencer Beman whom he brought to Chicago in 1879. These major undertakings included the Pullman Building for the company's administrative headquarters in Chicago and the town of Pullman around the works. (Both were completed at about the same time.) The Pullman Building at the corner of Michigan and Adams in downtown Chicago was one of the last elevator constructions in the city, that is, it had a masonry construction but a height that required elevators. The first two floors were devoted to Pullman headquarters; the other stories were made over into other offices and a few flats, apparently, as the *Chicago Tribune* reported, designed to house his "employees, seventy in number."[14] These "superior" apartments were for families and bachelors. On the ninth floor a restaurant was planned with a summer promenade and private dining rooms, a parlor, and a reading room.[15]

The second construction was the town of Pullman south of the city, next to Lake Calumet, and adjacent to Roseland and the town of Hyde Park. Here, Beman greatly expanded the idea of associating living arrangements with business activity and work. In this case, because it was designed for working-class laborers and a class of foremen and engineers, it was built on a much larger scale, a whole town instead of, simply, a building.[16]

Beman's other enterprise was to transform the Pullman castle— no other word could describe it—on Prairie Avenue into an even larger environment for lavish receptions and dinners and cultural entertainments. Here, when the family was in town, there were dinner and card parties, receiving days, plays and musicals, lectures, French classes, dancing classes, and receptions for visiting dignitaries, musicians, and actors.[17]

The Pullman family's home life was not confined to Chicago. It extended on rail corridors along which the family traveled in its luxurious private car to New York's Thousand Island district, where Pullman purchased an island and had constructed a huge summer house, designed by Beman, and named Castle Rest. Closer to New

York City, at Elberon, New Jersey, the family built another vacation spot they frequently visited for the summer. Even the Pullman crypt at Graceland Cemetery was designed by Beman. Carrying the accoutrements of home, which meant a train car of children, servants, clothing, and sundries, Mrs. Pullman also made a yearly circuit of extended trips to West Virginia, Florida, New Orleans, and California, during which, occasionally, George joined her. In each of these places she was able to recreate the social life of Chicago with its round of parties, dinners, and card parties, and calling upon important business and social leaders.

Harriet Sanger, who became Mrs. Pullman in 1867, came from a background somewhat similar to that of her husband. Her father, Lorenzo P. Sanger, moved from New Hampshire in the early part of the nineteenth century to upstate New York, around the area of the Erie Canal. From there he went to Pennsylvania and finally to Illinois. As a young woman, Hattie was much admired: a somewhat stout, clear-skinned, dark-haired, energetic beauty. A newspaper described her in the mid-1880s: "Mrs. Pullman is a plump little woman of about forty, with beautiful blue eyes, black hair, teeth of cocoanut whiteness and dear little hands and feet that were only made to wear jewels and walk on roses."[18] Her granddaughter related that during the Civil War she rode by horseback to distribute "delicacies" to wounded soldiers in Union hospitals, an early indication of her abiding interest in horses.[19]

With the immense wealth and prestige of her husband's business, Mrs. Pullman carefully constructed an elaborate social life of almost restless intensity and amiability. An acknowledged leader of Chicago society, she spent much time away, in health spas or escaping the heat or frigid weather of the city. Her letters to her husband are filled with health complaints: headaches, fevers, grippe, and, again, headaches. There are also laments about loneliness, being away from her husband or confined to bed or bored by the company of fellow sufferers. Yet she found ample time to ride, read, play cards, dine, and call, even in her most indisposed times. She admitted as much in a letter to George written during her stay at Jackson Sanatorium in Dansville, New York. She quoted, without comment, their son Sanger: "He says 'Mama was very gay and danced about every dance' pretty well for an invalid."[20]

Harriet Sanger Pullman. (Library of Congress)

If there was, perhaps, a note of anxiety in the relationship caused by frequent absences during the stressful year of 1894, there were also, on George's part, at least, forthright indications that Hattie's health problems had long been a major obstacle. As he wrote in February 1894 to her in Danville: "[A]m awfully lonesome and I do sincerely hope that you will soon recover permanent health so that we may have a few years of happy home life that will make us forget the sorrows of the past."[21]

This problem was not confined to the last years of Pullman's life nor inspired by the dismal business conditions of early 1894; indeed, Pullman had complained before. So despite the frenzy of letters, telegrams, and protestations of loneliness and love, both partners managed to spend a great deal of time apart. For several years Hattie passed a large part of the winter season in New York City. And even when both were at home, George frequently went to late-night card parties at Marshall Field's home or, occasionally, spent the night at Pullman.[22]

If the relationship was sometimes distant (both physically and emotionally), the Pullmans had much in common. They both shared a belief that they had been called upon to launch and then steer a new cultural life for Chicago. George Pullman became a master builder of environments for middle-class travel and the workers in his plants; working in tandem with Harriet, he sought to construct a social world designed to rein in the crude, maverick, entrepreneurial elite of Chicago. If the Chicago elite was coarse, deficient in manners, grace, the skills of dancing, speaking French, appreciating music or Shakespeare, Hattie Pullman arranged instruction for herself and her friends. Like other prominent Chicago families, she enthusiastically supported the new symphony orchestra of Theodore Thomas. But she also extended her cultural enterprise to the citizens of Pullman. There she founded and encouraged a version of the elite institutions found in her own social world of Prairie Avenue. Together she and her husband fashioned a partnership to instruct several levels of the cultural life of Chicago.

George Pullman had a contradictory personality. Always controversial, either because of his engineering innovations in the railroad industry or because of his activities in Pullman, he was both reviled and admired by commentators who visited the company town. A man of extraordinary ideas and energy, he was nonetheless almost totally lacking in introspection and self-examination. Toward the end of his life—a white-bearded, ruddy looking man, with prominent cheekbones and wearing pince-nez glasses—at the christening of his grandson George Mortimer Pullman Lowden, in August 1897, he espoused this opposing philosophy: "The principle of my life has been that all wealth beyond one's own need is held in trust for the benefit of all. No one has a right to so expend money that it will not legitimately and naturally benefit others as well as himself, even though such money is used primarily for one's own ends." He concluded this short talk by claiming he happily shouldered a "sacred trust to equalize the differences which fortune brings to different ones."[23]

Seen through the events of Pullman's life of peripatetic luxury and his tragic stubbornness during the 1894 strike, this statement seems almost self-consciously ironic, even cynical. The distance between Pullman and his workers was in every respect immense. Looked at objectively, there is no way to justify the incredible extravagance of the Pullman household. But that, of course, is not the point. His lack of introspection blinded him to see beyond the self-created scenery of his life. Having been born into a culture that sanctified the transformation of each individual, Pullman could not perceive, as perhaps other observers could, that his actions had outstripped his understanding. He mistook the veneer of culture for a solid reconstruction of consciousness. What he created at Pullman, what he and other Chicago entrepreneurs established with their grandiose schemes and investments, provoked a huge range of social and economic problems and opportunities. But these could scarcely be understood in terms of an ideology of self-reliance. What might have worked for young George Pullman had become largely irrelevant for his employees. The Pullmans had helped create a world in which it was increasingly difficult for others to emulate their success and mobility.

Yet it was Pullman's genius to understand, if only instinctively, the importance of transforming the culture of modern urban life in ways that would change the behavior of the new groups that were

George Pullman. This highly stylized portrait was a common way to picture the faces of famous people even in the late nineteenth century. (Library of Congress)

flooding the city. For him there never was any distinction between culture and business; indeed, his business was founded upon the manufacture of a new life-style of travel. In realizing this idea, he followed two fundamental strategies.

The first developed around the franchise. No matter what environment he created, George Pullman demanded continuing and absolute control. The Pullman company only sold cars, on exception, to very wealthy or important political men. Every other Pullman car was built to be leased to railroad companies, which attached them to trains. Pullman furnished all the services: conductors, porters, cooks, waiters, plus linens and other provisions. In this way the management of the company could supervise the quality of the services provided.[24] This successful system was carried in its entirety into planning for the workers' community.

Pullman's meticulous attention to monopolizing the means of supervision also had another purpose. He wished to change the behavior of his customers and his workers through manipulation of the cultural environment—to transform them into better customers and workers. This notion was the principal explanation for the Pullman car: by providing luxurious surroundings, Pullman elicited better behavior and, hence, the patronage of growing numbers of middle- and upper-class travelers. By 1893, the recounting of this stratagem had become something of a business legend. Duane Doty of the company wrote in the booklet distributed at the World's Fair,

> We know now that men will not climb in between the sheets of a Pullman sleeping-car bed with their boots on, and that they will not regard sleeping-car carpets and upholstery in the light of convenient cuspidors. We know that the same instinct which makes people conform in their habits to elegant surroundings in homes, will make them proportionately conform to them in public vehicles.[25]

Confronting the reality of rail travel in the second half of the nineteenth century, Pullman persuaded increasing numbers of customers that it could be comfortable and refined, perhaps even more than home. To create this illusion, the train of Pullman coaches reproduced the separated spaces of the middle-class home with its separate dining, sleeping, and living quarters. Comfort was maintained by porters whose obvious role was to act as surrogate domestic servants. For an aspiring and increasingly mobile middle class this was a remarkable solution to the inconvenience of travel and also a reminder of their elevated station. As Pullman saw it, there was ample reason to apply the same principles of engineered environments to the company town he constructed around his new works near Lake Calumet.

Pullman's most important venture was the company town south of Chicago. Into this enterprise, the entrepreneur poured his hopes and aspirations for a reformed society. Here he fully articulated his faith that culture and enterprise could mutually reinforce each other for personal and social profit. As in designing his sleeping cars, his purpose was to change the behavior of those involved in his enterprise. While certainly not the middle-class patrons who slept in his coaches, the workers of Pullman were nonetheless immersed in a total environment that made them actors under the businessman's direction. Furthermore, from the very beginning, the town of Pullman had a theatrical bearing clearly intended for an audience of visitors: for those who might glimpse its tidy proportions from the Illinois Central Railway as the passed by; for tourists to Chicago who wished to witness Pullman's experiment in social planning; for customers who, in being reassured about the happiness and contentment of the workers, could be certain that operating Pullman coaches would guarantee steady and reliable service.

There were also other objectives. Duane Doty predicted in 1887 that Pullman would someday become a city of 100,000, a "model city not only of the western hemisphere, but of the world."[26] So stated, the goals of this elaborate undertaking included nothing less than resolving the severe urban problems that Pullman perceived in Chicago and which were doubly demanding in the railroad industry. Persuaded of this purpose, the Massachusetts Bureau of Statistics of Labor reported after an inspection tour through the town in 1884: "Let the model factory and the industrial community of Pullman City . . . be held up to the manufacturers and employers of men throughout the country as worthy of their emulation."[27]

In response to the larger problem of cultural diversity and confusion, the town also represented a controversial solution. The difficulty of creating urban space to be shared by widely different people and social classes suggested the importance of defining the meeting ground of cultures. A commonly shared culture that did not expose or threaten the established world of Chicago might also allow social and class differences to continue and even flourish. The purpose of Pullman's town was, therefore, not to create a democratic society but rather a uniform culture as a model for Chicago itself. That culture, which the elite treasured, the working classes would also be persuaded to revere. Expounding on this thesis, Pullman told the visiting French observer, Paul de Rousiers:

I have no wish to mix all my workmen in a vast community, but only to prove to them that decency, propriety and good manners are not unattainable luxuries for them; that it is not necessary to be loosely or carelessly dressed in order to do good work, to save money, and to raise themselves in the social scale.[28]

There were also returns of a more practical nature that the town promised. By providing a clean, moral environment, guided by accepted manners and the behind-the-scenes manipulations of the company, workers would remain loyal to the company and resist labor unions. Built after the terrible railroad strikes of the late 1870s, the company town was clearly designed to produce a more docile labor force by manipulating the environment in which workers lived. Furthermore, as Pullman repeatedly declared, the town was meant to be a money-making enterprise, and he insisted that every dollar spent should return a 6 percent dividend.[29]

The Pullman idea germinated in the soil of these objectives, but it was also nourished by the entrepreneur's reading of the British reform novel by Charles Reade, *Put Yourself in His Place.* Quite possibly, while visiting England in 1873, he took a trip to Saltaire, an experimental industrial community in York. Furthermore, in his fascination with town planning, Pullman shared a belief, widespread in the late nineteenth century among builders and home designers, that architecture could affect behavior. Solon Beman was also a fellow proponent of this notion, although he carried it out on a much grander scale than most architects of his era.[30]

Together with Pullman and landscape architect Nathan Barrett, Beman laid out the model town. After three years of construction, it stood completed in 1884. For many of those who saw it, it was a marvel of order and neatness, in stark contrast to the smokey and rancid slums that surrounded the factories and meat packinghouses of Chicago. To the labor statisticians, such as Carroll Wright, who visited in 1884, it revealed the "Christian inspiration of Pullman." This phrase referred not just to a view of workers as the object of stewardship, benevolence, and paternalism. The visitors rightly detected traces of a secularized evangelical view of human character that Pullman had imbibed as a child. The malleability of human nature and culture were, for him, assumptions that nourished his hopes for Pullman and a regenerated Chicago.[31]

As Beman and Pullman planned it, the town followed a grid pattern imposed upon a central focal point: the factory and town square. All of the buildings, except the Greenstone Church, were constructed primarily of brick. Dominating the vast works was the clock tower with a huge water tower and, close to the Illinois Central tracks, and in full view of the passing travelers, was the glass-plated observatory building housing the Corliss Engine.[32] The large gates to the factory had substantial open spaces for billboards to announce company social and cultural activities.

The Florence Hotel, with its wide veranda and impressive structure, dominated the central part of the town, as if to underscore the importance of visitations by guests and, frequently, by George Pullman who always kept a room reserved for himself.

To the south rose the Arcade building in which the social and mercantile facilities of the town were grouped together. By placing all of the dry goods shops together in a covered space, Pullman preserved a kind of market motif that nonetheless revealed a strong kinship to the department stores then flourishing in Chicago. This working-class version of the elegant downtown establishments looked backward to the idea of a market or high street and also forward to the modern notion of the shopping mall. Like the World's Fair exhibits erected shortly afterward in 1893, the exterior of the building was elegant and impressive, while the interior remained visibly functional with space divided into display sections. Pullman intended to provide every necessary service for the community so that residents would not have to, nor feel inclined to, go elsewhere in the city.

As Henry Koopman, longtime resident of Pullman, wrote in his photo essay of the town, [even] "[t]he different seasons of the year have been specially selected to impress the observer more fully with the beauty and originality of its architecture and general landscape effect."[33] Koopman's reaction to landscape (as if to say that every season of the year unfolded new delights) was certainly an intended visual effect of the community. Pullman left nothing to chance. Thirty thousand trees and shrubs were planted along the streets and in parks and were fully maintained by the company.

The Arcade Interior at Pullman. A working-class market, shopping center, and department store, the Arcade resembled some of Europe's covered markets and anticipated more modern shopping centers. The Arcade Building with its multiple uses combined commerce and culture in one place. (ICHI-01889, Chicago Historical Society)

Housing for workers consisted of brick row houses of differing quality and size. Those closest to the center, reserved for engineers and foremen, were the largest and most elaborate; those beyond the town center were less so. Stressing the importance of preventing diseases like cholera, Pullman constructed a model water and sewer system, whose compost was added to the profitable vegetable farm at the outskirts of the town. Besides numbered streets (extending the pattern of Chicago), there were north-south avenues: Pullman and Florence boulevards, and then, appropriately, avenues named after inventors: Morse, Watt, Whitney, Bessemer, Stevenson, and Fulton. This pantheon of mechanical wizards with whom Pullman associated himself and his family paid no reference to the employees of the works. Street names like landscaping created a "scientifically and artistically built" environment that was both visually apparent and emphasized in the promotional documents of the community.[34]

In the carefully selected and maintained scenery of the town, there was a noteworthy absence of certain sorts of familiar institutions: saloons, gambling or prostitution houses, police stations or courts, orphanages, or governmental institutions (aside from a post-office). This "negative adornment," as Joseph Kirkland called it in his 1892 history of Chicago, was one of the attractive features of the town and that most remarked upon by visitors (who were often guided to this conclusion by the literature of the company).[35] Within the confines of the community there were none of the "vicious amusements" against which contemporary reformers crusaded.[36]

Vicious amusements and their synonym, "baneful influences" (used by Pullman), were strong words of disapproval employed by middle-class reformers to distinguish between amusements such as saloons, cheap theaters, and dance halls favored by working-class and immigrant Chicagoans and approved culture. To any observant city dweller of the late nineteenth century, however, these dubious institutions were thriving—despite the censure—and frequented not just by working-class men and women but also in some instances by members of the new middle class. How to divert this patronage to a higher form of culture remained one of the objects of Pullman's Utopia. This effort, however, was not solely directed at workers who might aspire to the privileges of middle-class culture, but extended also to a whole city ostensibly in need of the cultural leadership which George and Hattie Pullman enthusiastically supplied. In this effort they were guided by the assumption that higher culture was a privilege cherished by everyone.[37]

Pullman's strategy for governing the diverse immigrant cultures (he carefully kept a record of the ethnic composition of the town), for suppressing the temptations of emerging urban leisure and the baneful influences of alcohol depended upon banishing them from his community. He offered only healthy institutions in exchange. As many observers have noted, this was an attempt to mold docile and cooperative workers, to prevent strikes and labor organization. But it also had its roots in the evangelical culture from which Pullman had emerged, which matched the watchful energy of the reformer to the ambitions of the successful entrepreneur.

Like the brick clock tower that dominated the town, Pullman maintained a regulatory eye over the activities of his workers. A ban on the sale of alcohol (except in the swank and expensive Florence Hotel available to visitors) headed the list of prohibitions. It was hoped that banishing such influences from the immediate environment would promote good manners and self-improvement.[38] Workers would remain sober and isolated from the influence of union organizers who frequented saloons. Nonetheless, workers could, and did, cross the boundaries of the town into Roseland, a neighboring village that housed the saloons and brothels unavailable in Pullman.

Pullman's competing culture centered around self-improvement. The major centers were the library and the Arcade theater. Both were closely scrutinized by the company. The appointments of the library were lavish, if not intimidating, with a $3 a-year membership fee, and the librarian, Frederick A. Bisbee, seemed happiest when he could report a decline in fiction reading. Reflecting the accepted wisdom of contemporary custodians of learning, Bisbee in 1895 lauded a large increase in reference reading and history and a slight decline for fiction.[39] Plays at the Arcade Theater were approved by Pullman or his representatives so that no cheap or degrading performances would take place. Admissions were also set substantially below Chicago prices to encourage patronage. The weekly *Pullman Journal* noted the meetings of its clubs and cultural institutions and recorded the steps taken by the enterprise toward social progress.

Another proud institution of the town was the Pullman Band that played concerts in the central park of the village during the summer and which in 1893 performed frequently at the World's Fair. The town also sponsored bicycle races and other athletic events. In the meeting rooms of the Arcade, self-improvement clubs could gather and, in the later construction, Market Hall, there was a room used frequently by Dwight Moody and Ira Sankey for their revivals.[40]

In her 1893 pamphlet on Pullman, Mrs. Doty drew upon this idyllic culture to sketch a scene of the town that resembled nothing so much as the popular dioramas used widely at the Fair and other popular nineteenth-century exhibits: "Evenings the arcade present an animated scene, hundreds of people visiting it and engaging in social chat, discussing in an animated way the political situation, the labor question, the prospects of a visitation by cholera, and other topics of current interest, reading in the library-rooms or trading in the elegant stores."[41] This and almost every favorable visitor's account always returned to the same point: the town was self-sufficient. It contained all the institutions, a theater, library, stores, meeting places, athletics, savings bank, band, and religious and self-help organizations required for an ideal urban life. Although reminiscent of the ideal small town, Pullman also had the feel of an urban environment. It had, indeed, "solved" the problem of balancing the new city cultures by selecting some and banishing others entirely.

Slightly apart and back from the secular institutions that commanded center stage at Pullman stood the architectural anomaly of the town, the Greenstone Church. This handsome but expensive building was designed by Pullman and Beman to be the ecumenical center of the town's religious services. Extending the notion of franchise even to religion, Pullman intended that various church groups would rent the building for services; it was not offered for sale to any group. Unfortunately, no sect was able to pay to hold regular services in the church, and, in a sense, religion like alcohol had to establish itself outside of the town.

No doubt Pullman meant to encourage religious worship, but it was not the centerpiece of the town, nor would he sacrifice his financial principles for the sake of faith. Quite possibly, Pullman also hoped to avoid reproducing the broad, competitive sectarianism of Chicago, with its immigrant churches and competing Protestant and Catholic groups. The idea of the ecumenical Protestant community church was as appealing to Pullman as it was to some of the Protestant participants in the World's Fair Parliament of Religions.

They and Pullman tendered their own beliefs as the basis for a universal religion.

The construction of Pullman culture also represented an extension of the family's larger endeavor to fabricate a culture for Chicago's elite groups. In this effort, and in the founding of institutions at Pullman, Hattie as well as George Pullman became a leading figure. The notion that informed their efforts was aptly summarized by George: "I have always held that people are greatly influenced by their physical surroundings. Take the roughest man . . . and bring him into a room elegantly carpeted and furnished and the effect upon his bearing is immediate."[42] What was true of society could also true of the working class. As Dr. De Wolf, commissioner of health of Chicago, noted in 1883 (speaking of the town of Pullman): "Men who are accustomed to lounge on their front stoops, smoking pipes and in dirty shirt-sleeves, soon dress and act more in accordance with the requirements of society."[43]

If environmentalism was the general theory, how was it practiced in the competitive social world of Chicago's upper classes? The Pullman's social life in Chicago was far more than the typical elite rounds of calling, visiting, and dining, although these were major activities. In fact, much of what Mrs. Pullman planned had two purposes at least. She fully intended to establish herself as the doyen of Chicago society, the arbitrator of taste and fashion in cultural matters. In a humorous, very long piece in the *Chicago News Setter* in 1886, the paper reported a serious split of high society into two warring camps led by Mrs. Pullman and Mrs. Marshall Field. At issue, the paper reported, was control of the opera season which the Pullmans had, apparently, seized. This ploy had divided the South Side into two enemy armies as implacable as "Rome and Carthage." The paper continued:

> One faction is presided over by Mrs. Marshall Field, the other is led by Mrs. George M. Pullman. Each of the ladies aspires to the position of *grande dame*, for which each is eminently fitted. Mrs. Field is an accomplished woman, speaking several languages fluently and being *au fait* in all the arts and graces of the cultured woman in modern society. Mrs. Pullman is quite the equal of her rival in graces and talent. Both have unlimited

wealth, and each has a very long clientele of admirers and followers. The origin of the feud is lost in obscurity, but it exists and flourishes.[44]

Although there is a good deal of evidence that Messrs. Field and Pullman remained close friends throughout the period (there are a number of diary entries that record late-night card games at the Field home), it is quite possible that the rivalry for leadership did take this form. Perhaps one reason has to do with the other purpose of Mrs. Pullman's social activities: the establishment of an accepted culture. To achieve this goal, Hattie did much more than hold soirees and parties. During the brief seasons she spent in Chicago, she organized instructional classes in French and dancing which both she and George attended. An early diary entry records another self-help activity: "January 28, 1878: George returned this morn from New York. We took a (5th) painting lesson this morning."[45]

Theater was also especially important to the family, and George and Hattie went frequently to plays in Chicago and, later, to their theater in Pullman. After the construction of a small theater at their residence at Prairie Avenue, there was ample room for amateur theatricals. Hattie even carried this practice to Castle Rest on the Thousand Islands. As she noted in 1871, "We arranged a beautiful little stage on the back end of the Platform today and this evening had some pretty charades acted with . . . speeches and song, afterwards."[46]

The Prairie Avenue mansion, when completed in 1876, was furnished with a library, music room with pipe organ, and a theater, and, after Solon Beman's later additions, a large conservatory (the "Palm House"). In these huge spaces, Mrs. Pullman held dinner parties and musical performances (parlor concerts). Besides organizing these activities, Hattie began a Shakespeare appreciation group. The *St. Louis Post Dispatch* reported in early 1885 that the Pullmans held Shakespearean readings at their residential theater and, for a month, sponsored classes for ninety-five ladies in the poetry and plays of the bard. At her famous lunches, there was quite often an amusing guest: a singer, an actor, a clairvoyant, a fortune-teller.[47] In the autodidactic elite culture of Chicago, these activities made a wide mark.

Much of what Hattie did for herself and her friends to develop a new Chicago culture she also encouraged at Pullman. As the *Chicago Inter Ocean* noted in January 1889: "Mrs. Pullman gives much time and thought in inventing means for amusement and profit for those working people." Evidence appeared everywhere on the cultural calendar of the company town. There were French and German classes, a Shakespeare class, instruction in painting, an amateur dramatic society, a ladies' charitable union, dancing classes and a whist club (a game to which Mrs. Pullman was partial).[48] As the Massachusetts Bureau of Labor Statistics reported, "Pullman has really wrought a greater change for the women than for any other class of its dwellers." By this the bureau inspectors meant that the tasks of motherhood—child rearing, keeping house, and encouraging cultural development— were far easier in Pullman than in other Chicago working-class districts.[49]

This interchangeability of culture between Prairie Avenue and Pullman raises a fascinating question. Did the Pullmans believe in an integral middle-class culture for all Chicagoans with no distinctions of class or station? The answer is both "yes" and "no." Cultural institutions at Prairie Avenue and Pullman were closely related, often replicated. They did seem to follow a single cultural standard made available for everyone to admire even if they could rarely afford to attend. Yet, within this universalized democracy of their extended tastes, they demanded first place—a box, as it were, at the democratic opera. Furthermore, the Pullmans did not acknowledge the validity of culture beyond their own tastes which they hoped to impress upon Chicago society and the Pullman working class; hence, their aspiration to instruct the tastes of society as well as the workers and their families. Moreover, the Pullman family treated the town as a stage upon which to perform or call for performances from the residents. This practice of using Pullman as a setting for entertainments was established early, at the gala opening of the Arcade Theater, and maintained throughout the heyday of the town, culminating in the frequent display of the town during the World's Fair summer.

The Pullman's social calendar records the frequent uses of the town. George Pullman stayed occasionally at the Florence Hotel in the special suite reserved for him overlooking the car works. He may

Hotel Florence. One of many of George Pullman's residences, the hotel served tourists and potential customers and family, not the residents of the town. (Library of Congress)

have done this to escape the flurry of activities (or loneliness) at Prairie Avenue. Often Pullman took a party of potential customers to the town, to the hotel, to see the works or attend some cultural event. The family also often attended theatricals at the Arcade, sitting in their glorious box above the stage. As Hattie wrote in June 1883, "George and I gave a party of 20 guests at Pullman to see Regatta this afternoon, dined in private-car, went to theatre after, and got home at 11:30."[50]

Something of a high point was reached at the 1890 Arcade Theater Benefit for the Pullman Library. The performance that night included the Pullman Military Band and an orchestra of Chicago society children playing kazoos, including Pullman's children (George and Sanger and Hattie), with his elder daughter Florence directing.[51] In this celebration, the Pullman family treated the town as an extension of their own social world. But its residents remained either the objects of an experiment or the witnesses to a miracle: the cultural transformation of working families into middle-class citizens. That they had little choice in the matter was not relevant in matters undertaken for their own benefit.

While the Pullmans created a cultural environment in the town that reflected their own preoccupations and tastes, it was decidedly directed and manipulated.[52] It was both democratic, in the sense of reflecting what Hattie and George believed was best for themselves, and elitist in denying to the residents their own tastes and initiatives. Like every other endeavor of Pullman's life, this reflected the entrepreneur's belief in the transforming qualities of middle-class culture. Anything else was to be repressed. George and Hattie Pullman lived life grandly; they surrounded themselves with the most powerful men and women of Chicago and the United States. Under the circumstances, it would be unrealistic to challenge their tastes.

Beyond his business friends and associates whose mansions adorned Prairie Avenue and the North Side, George Pullman maintained an active civic life, belonging to Chicago's most important civic clubs such as the Athenaeum, the Citizens' League, and the Commercial Club. More prestigious even were his highly visible and active acquaintanceships with Ulysses S. Grant and the Republican presidents who followed him. Abraham Lincoln's son, Robert Todd Lincoln, became a business associate and director of the company; eventually he assumed the presidency of Pullman. Despite their often separate lives, split apart by George's inevitable business trips and Hattie's extended vacations and cures, the Pullmans both participated actively in the creation of Chicago's nineteenth-century social world—as pupils and instructors.

Maintaining control of this far-flung enterprise plus directing his business was, for George Pullman, an overwhelming task and perhaps, predictably, a source of his eventual failure. While he believed in the power of culture to sway men's souls, he added a stern measure of direct control to assure the triumph of his ideals, especially in the company town. The town agent, approved by Pullman, effectively ran the village through commissions that he appointed. Only the school board had elective posts. Pullman's refusal to sell any housing gave him social rights that flowed from property owner-ship. Restrictions on behavior in the rental units was excessive and minute, suggesting that "tenants should always enter or leave the building quietly" down to prescriptions about how to split wood, when to play musical instruments, and where to smoke.[53]

In justification, Pullman declared:

> If any lots had been sold in Pullman it would have permit-ted the introduction of the baneful elements which it was the chief purpose to exclude from the immediate neighborhood of the shops, and from the homes to be erected about them. The plan was to provide homes in the first place for all people who should desire to work in the shops, at reasonable rentals.[54]

Pullman also attempted to guide the voting habits of Pullman residents in national elections and urged them consistently to vote Republican. This pressure, plus the absence of any local politics, effectively disenfranchised workers. Together with the reported use of company "spotters," hired to prevent any complaints from being made public, independent political expression was an unwelcome intrusion and evidence that Pullman lacked trust in his own princi-ples. But too much—the health of his whole company—was at stake, and the power to intervene was a fatal temptation.[55] Having created a Utopia, so deeply personal, Pullman surrendered to the lure of power that was inherent in his concept of work, culture, and class.[56]

In the summer of 1893, the Pullman's celebrated their own and Chicago's accomplishments. For many years, George had used the company town as a combined business and pleasure resort. As his granddaughter noted, "Mr. Pullman took many distinguished per-sons to the Hotel Florence to dine, going to and fro in a private car."[57] When the Fair opened in 1893, its grounds became part of the Pullman social itinerary that included Prairie Avenue, Jackson Park, and the company town and its works.

During the Fair, the Pullmans spent considerable time in Chi-cago. Mrs. Pullman broke her habit of almost continual travel for an extended early summer stay, and George remained in town for a good part of the season. Like much of Chicago society, the Pullmans frequently visited the Fair. Together with parties of ladies and gentlemen, the Pullmans visited the attractions of the White City and the Midway and dined in its restaurants. They participated in wining and dining visiting European royalty and important politicians and businessmen from the East.

Although George and Hattie frequently attended the great middle-class popular culture display on the lakefront, they did so from a position of conspicuous privilege. While they watched performances on the Midway and explored the cultural curiosities of its sanitized ethnicity along with hundreds of thousands of other Chicagoans, they remained separate and demanded special treatment. Just as at Pullman, the especially constructed cultures of the Fairgrounds became something of a vast theater, a demonstration of the ingenuity and accomplishment of the master builders of Chicago like Pullman himself. As a large investor in the Fair corporation, George Pullman could be justly proud of the achievements of the exhibition. In the same measure, he was handsomely rewarded by the rail travel generated for his palace and sleeping cars by visitors pouring into Chicago.

When Hattie Pullman took guests to the Fairgrounds, she often did so armed with special permission to take her carriage inside. For example, on October 24, 1893, she carried a special note from Fair President Higinbotham: "The Guards and gatekeepers at Jackson Park will admit Mrs. George M. Pullman and friends, with carriage, at her pleasure." When George accompanied a party of gentlemen, he often explored the Midway. An itinerary, with expenses, records that Pullman with four guests spent the huge sum of $52 in a visit that included the South Sea Islands Theatre, Street in Cairo and *dance du ventre*, Ferris Wheel, Museum of the German Village, dinner, the Wild Beast Show, Bedouin Camp, Eiffel Tower, French Ballet, and chairs to transport the party around.[58]

Entries in Hattie Pullman's diary give an incomplete but revealing picture of the number of times the family went to the Fair. There are mentions of at least twenty-three separate trips, but undoubtedly more went unrecorded. In addition, the family often conveyed guests from Pullman to the Fair. For example on May 30, Hattie recorded the following: "George, self, and all visitors and I went to Pullman to see Bicycle Race. Came back to the Fair at noon, and reached home about six o'clock."[59] In their rounds of visitations, the Pullmans made no distinctions between the cultures exhibited at the Fair; they were equally comfortable in the Midway and among the consumer and scientific and artistic exhibits of Daniel Burnham's lagoons and pillared city. But, just as at Pullman, they expected and received privileges. Culture might remain open and accessible to all, but the Pullmans reserved their special place in the audience.

If 1893 was the very height of Pullman's influence, prestige, and, perhaps, happiness, what followed shortly thereafter began a reversal of extraordinary proportions. During the summer of 1893, the Pullmans participated in the great Chicago festival as its leading citizens. Thousands poured into the company town to admire its prosperity and engineered culture. Pullman's two daughters, Florence and Harriet, came out in their spectacular official debut before Chicago society. The Pullman company continued to work while the rest of the nation shut down in a gloomy depression. Yet in a few months, all this crashed down with an amazing finality.

Pullman's construction of special cultural environments for travelers, workers, and the Chicago social world was amazingly successful, but it was based upon self-delusion. Banning working-class culture from Pullman did not eliminate it, it only displaced it outside the town. Outlawing unions did not eliminate or even temper the resentments of workers. Franchising the lives of Pullman families in rented houses and planned cultural events did not, and could not, transform them into a middle class. Building environments on Prairie Avenue, Castle Rest, Elberon, and the Monitor did not define a successful family life. A frenetic social life of parties, calling and visits, musical soirees, and Shakespeare classes did not guarantee the unity and coherence of Chicago's elite. Each of these aspirations faltered in 1894 when the strike at the company town dragged down the curtain on Pullman's carefully constructed worlds.

Despite appearances, Pullman had never achieved the labor peace at the works that he desired. When business slumped badly toward the end of 1893, Pullman began to cut the wages of his factory workers although he did not reduce rents or town utility rates or administrative salaries, and the operating company for Pullman cars continued to show a profit. When a walkout, aided by Eugene V. Debs and the American Railway Union occurred in May 1894, grievances were compounded by the very factors that Pullman had counted on to prevent such a happening. Wages, working conditions, and, particularly, the functioning of the company town infuriated workers and intensified their resentment.[60] The United States Strike Commission, appointed in 1894 to investigate the strike, determined that rents at Pullman, where workers had to live, were 20–25 percent higher than comparable accommodations elsewhere in Chicago. The commission report concluded: "The aesthetic features are admired by visitors but have little money value to employees, especially when they lack bread."[61]

Perhaps as disheartening for Pullman as the collapse of his dream was the bitterness that his actions caused in Chicago society. Mrs. Potter Palmer wrote to the reformer Ralph Easley of the Chicago Civic Federation in August of 1894 that people in the East did not understand the strike: "The general impression is that it was a fight for higher wages and that Mr. Pullman performed a public service by putting down the strike; that he has saved the country, as it were, from anarchy and future aggressions from labor organizations." Mrs. Palmer urged Easley to correct this misapprehension and reveal how unfairly Pullman had treated his workers.[62]

An even sharper critique came from newspapermen. George C. Sikes of the *Chicago Record* wrote to Madeleine Wallace in July that there were rampant rumors that Pullman had fired men for voting Democratic in the 1892 national election. Pullman did have his rights, Sikes said, "But society does not want a man to insist on his rights arbitrarily simply because they are his rights when great suffering is caused thereby." He concluded by saying: "Pullman is cursed on every hand. Even the *Tribune* and *Record*, that refer to Debs as an anarchist and the A.R.U. [American Railway Union] as an outlaw organization curse Pullman for his pigheadedness."[63] There were even rumors that Pullman explained the depression as a reprisal visited upon his workers for voting Democratic in the 1892 election: they could now "take the consequences."[64]

During the strike, the issues were not confined to wages and high rents but went to the very core of the Pullman experiment, the town itself and its management. Although Pullman ultimately won the strike by persuading the federal government to crush the boycott of trains that pulled Pullman cars, this was a hollow victory indeed.[65]

Pullman Headquarters in Chicago. This massive structure is pictured here in another typical sort of urban photograph: the single, massive building standing alone. (Compare this perspective on the city to pages 31 and 70.) (ICHI-19460, Chicago Historical Society)

Nor was George Pullman's personal life restored to order. During the period immediately before the strike, while Hattie was away from Chicago during one of her frequent cures, George wrote to her: "I find myself wishing that I might get you every morning to act as a tonic in helping me through the labors and worries of the day." At the end of August 1894, after the strike had collapsed, Hattie, who was in France, in a letter to George alluded to the fact that he had to flee Chicago in fear for his life.[66] Being apart and under the severe strain of the turmoil at Pullman also caused George a severe "nervous depression" both during and after the strike.[67]

A pall of despair spread. On the evening of July 5, at the height of the strike, a huge fire at the deserted Fairgrounds consumed much of the White City. Frances Glessner (wife of an important International Harvester official and Prairie Avenue neighbor) recorded in her journal three days later: "I am anxious about the news of the riot and strike at Chicago where the rioters have burned all of the buildings around the Court of Honor at the Exposition."[68] Although there was no evidence to link the strike and the fire, the symbolism was clear enough for Chicago: two of its greatest cultural environments had been destroyed—the fate of the Fair and Pullman's experiment were overcome by neglect and exploitation.

Despite a return to work at the end of the summer and the quelling of union agitation, Pullman's troubles continued after 1894. Perhaps his severest disappointment came from his twin sons. Sharing her husband's melancholy, Hattie, writing from St. Augustine, said, "I am just heart-broken at what [daughter] Harriett wrote about Georgie!" She continued that she longed for a place, like one she had heard described in France—a reform school for "gentlemen's sons who cannot be controlled at home."[69]

Burdened with hard work, his anxiety, compounded by continuing separation from Hattie (she noted, coolly, that at their wedding anniversary that summer she had given him a silver toilet set—"but had nothing from him"), George Pullman died on October 16, 1897. Commemorated in newspapers throughout the United States, even his final rest was uneasy. Despite the statuesque, solitary column erected by Beman at Graceland to mark his grave, the family took the precaution of encasing the body in concrete and steel to prevent desecration. Even more remarkable was his will in which he left a significant endowment for a Manual Training School at Pullman, a fortune to his wife and daughters, and a trivial bequest to his sons, citing his deep disappointment in them.[70] After a period of mourning, Hattie resumed her life of travel and social events, remaining, until the end of her life, a force in Chicago society. Yet her commitment to the city became more tenuous. By the end of the 1890s she had constructed a large mansion in Washington, D.C., where she and widowed neighbors Mrs. Marshall Field and Mrs. Norman Williams helped preside over the capital city society.[71]

In a hyperbolic but accurate depiction of Pullman's lifelong motivations, Dr. N. D. Hillis proclaimed in his eulogy for the dead entrepreneur: "What ideals he cherished for this city, of whose people and achievements he was so proud! What plans he had for its libraries, its galleries, its houses, its people." What London was to Milton and Florence to Dante, so was "this much loved city by the inner sea" to Pullman.[72] Pullman had tried, throughout his life, to translate the ideals of a secular evangelism into a culture for the cities he helped to construct. Believing in the malleability of human character and the importance of environment, he made culture instrumental, a force for persuasion of customers, workers, and friends. Hostile to the "baneful" influences of the immigrant world that he helped to attract to Chicago with employment in his works, he tried to banish their cultures, offering, instead, an approved cultural ideal derived from his own tastes.

Yet, like so many men of his generation in Chicago, he lacked the poet's sense of introspection, of self-understanding. When he advised frugality and hard work for others, even to explain his own success he did not recognize that these virtues had long since ceased to be the secret. A meticulous, even fastidious man, he did not acknowledge the immense distance between Prairie Avenue and Pullman, nor recognize the isolating privileges exacted for himself and his family. High in his opulent box at the Arcade Theater, he did not appreciate that the pageant playing before him did not represent the reality over which he actually ruled. Pullman had created a kind of mass culture for the working classes, an ersatz and eclectic spectacle modeled faintly upon the life to which he and his family aspired. But Pullman residents were players, not, ultimately, consumers of this culture; they were part of the decor. The town appeared dramatically more successful to the tourists who saw it. In some respects, they were the most important audience for this cultural experiment.

Pullman did not recognize that components of culture could not be banished nor people isolated from their heritage or from the culture that surrounded them in the larger environment of Chicago. In engaging the diversity of cultures in Chicago, in his strategies for constructing an urban vision, Pullman took an extreme position. He did not trust the marketplace nor its decisive role in shaping what was becoming modern mass culture. He excluded its mechanisms of competition from his company as well as from his town; he insisted on maintaining jurisdiction over culture. There is a deep irony in this because Pullman, along with other Chicago entrepreneurs, did much to create the modern capitalist market economy. Yet he opposed its extension to cultural matters.

Pullman's attempt to regulate the cultural marketplace and suppress the emergence of mass culture was significant. But as his (and his family's) various trips to the Midway in 1893 reveal, he could enjoy at least one important version of modern mass culture in the negotiated and balanced confines of the World's Fair. He had not entered the competitive market of popular culture as, we shall see, Dwight Moody had. Indeed, he represented an extreme alternative to the evangelical's plunge into the center of urban culture. Perhaps he saw a kinship between the controlled environments of the town of Pullman and Jackson Park. But even in this comparison, Pullman was unique—and extreme.

After George Pullman's death, the town survived only a short time as a company entity. The Supreme Court of Illinois ordered the company to sell the town property in 1898, and the experiment quickly ended. The Arcade Theater closed in 1902. Middle-class employees at the factories soon moved out of town. Eventually, the Hotel Florence became a flophouse, and, during the 1920s, the town boasted several speakeasies.[73] The very success and coherence of the town now accelerated its downfall. The workers, who played their parts successfully in the middle-class cultural world constructed for them, perhaps because of this, nourished a deeper resentment against the roles they had to play during that one, great, last summer spectacle of 1893 when they were scrutinized by so many visitors. No doubt the universal middle-class culture that the

The Corliss Engine. This massive engine purchased by Pullman from the 1876 Philadelphia Exposition was a proud and very visible celebration of the entrepreneur's interest in science and invention. It was one of the most important sights in any tour of the town. (ICHI-01913, Chicago Historical Society)

Pullmans tried to impose in their model city heightened class consciousness rather than suppressed it. Nearby cultural resorts appeared more inviting and natural than the cultural delicacies served up from the cultural kitchens of Prairie Avenue. The strike and depression stripped off the veneer to expose class antagonisms and community solidarity. The "baneful" culture once dammed up in Roseland had provided a refuge from the strictures, making life in Pullman tolerable. Eventually, as the compromised experiment at Pullman ended, the culture of Roseland washed back over Utopia.

Six

THIRD CITY
The Evangelical Metropolis

THE ECHO OF IRA SANKEY'S strong, unadorned song died slowly in the lavish Haymarket Theatre auditorium as Dwight Moody strode toward the podium on center stage. A small, burly, patriarchal-looking man with a broad forehead, broad cheeks, and a thick, flourishing beard, he took his place confidently. Behind him rose the large choir, and to the side stood Sankey. Looking out over the people packed into the theater rows, Moody appraised his audience. They were enthusiastic but not stirring; some still clutched their green admission tickets. Moody shifted his substantial weight and looked down at his notes. The writing was oversized, round, and hurried, and almost illegible to anyone else, scrawled on six small, folded quarto sheets. He knew for sure, as he confided to friends, that with the end of the Fair approaching, and crowds increasing daily, the "hottest" of the battle was before him. His sermon, preached several times that summer of 1893, remained one of his favorites: "The Prodigal Son."

Beginning slowly, he talked deliberately, as if his speech might break into a stammer. The "text" for the evening was the story of a young man who had come to the city setting out to make his fortune, without God. The ancient tale mixed imperceptively (even confusingly) with its modern version. The young man of the parable left home in Judea to go down to Egypt. There, in the city, he "used to go to the opera four nights in the week, and the other three nights he spent at the theater and billiard rooms." Quickly exhausting his money and

169

his parcel of his father's fortune, he became the lowest of the low: a swineherd. Losing everything but his father's love, he finally returned home, to be greeted with love and great rejoicing.

Searching their faces, Moody projected his words out over the audience: "Wanderer, arise and go to thy father, who loves thee; to thy mother, who weeps over thee." And then he softened his words, bringing the audience forward to catch his personally grieved message. After his own father died, his older brother Isaiah ran away to make his solitary fortune in the city. "For years and years we heard nothing of him. Sometimes it seemed as if my mother's heart would break," he confessed.[1]

Then, when his mother's hair was tainted with gray, a dark-looking, sun-stained stranger approached the house. He was even unknown to the old mother, until she invited him in. Stooped by shame, he looked silently at her until the tears erupted from his eyes. The son had come back, penitent, full of apologies and explanations. But his mother "made him come right in," forgiving him everything. "And that is just the way God forgives all the prodigal souls who come back to him," Moody ejaculated. "O wanderer, come home! come home!"[2]

To Dwight Moody, the great urban preacher, shepherd of the souls of Chicago, the World's Columbian Exposition was a great challenge and opportunity. In many respects, his lifetime of preaching and organized revivals were channeled into a great six-month's contest for an audience of millions who had come to the Fair and to marvel at the ideal city on the shore of Lake Michigan. For a man of many distant crusades, his flock was finally coming to him. "I have been swinging around the world for twenty-five years," he reflected, "and now the world is swinging around me."[3]

If anything revealed the qualities of his life's effort to preach salvation in the city, to redefine urban life, this moment did. Moody, gathering a crowd of fellow ministers and helpers and singers, promised nothing less than the blueprint for a celestial city to the newcomers to Chicago. For those who wished to remain, there was also the actual, redeemed town of Harvey, Illinois, skirting the edges of the South Side. This real estate venture, launched by Turlington Harvey, Moody's longtime benefactor, and an evangelical enterprise in which Moody, Sankey, Moody's brother-in-law,

Dwight Moody. Before a sermon. (Moody Bible Institute)

and leading Chicago philanthropists had purchased shares, promised new settlers a prosperous new town free from the shame of alcohol and scandal.

Seizing the occasion of national attention, Moody mounted one of his greatest and most comprehensive evangelical campaigns in the summer of 1893. In direct competition with the Fair and its banal Parliament of Religions, he offered his morally arduous vision of a sanctified city. Instead of the carefully negotiated and controlled dualistic culture of the Fair, he contrived a different solution to the problems of urban cultural diversity. Rather than reject or distance himself from the popular culture materializing around him as Pullman did, he sought to master it with his religious message. The problems of diversity and heterogeneity that excited the worries of the Fair planners worried him, too. The troubled, seductive environment of the city that distressed Pullman also distressed him. Like the social elite that constructed the White City, he worried about the impact of technology, enterprise, and social and cultural diversity. He, too, hoped to divert modern consumer culture. His solution, however, required nothing less than fusing secular popular culture to evangelism. He aspired to integrate the new world confined to the Midway (or banished to Roseland) into an unabridged, modern, Christian society.

The World's Fair evangelization campaign conducted by Moody in 1893 displayed his uncanny talent for adapting popular culture to this task of Christian social engineering. Moody refused to abandon popular institutions, however much he might disapprove of them. Nor did he, like the designers of the Fair, maintain two visions of culture (the White City and the Midway) bound together in tension and competition. Instead, he attempted to exploit the secular popular culture institutions he discovered around him. He sought to graft middle-class business ethics and evangelical revivalism onto some of the newest instruments of mass culture and communication that he discovered in the modern city. The result was perhaps more complicated than he imagined—an influence that flowed in two directions. True, he tried to open popular institutions to contemporary evangelical ideas. At the same time, he altered the nature of evangelical Protestantism, making it more accommodating to modern popular culture. If this did not exactly amount to the

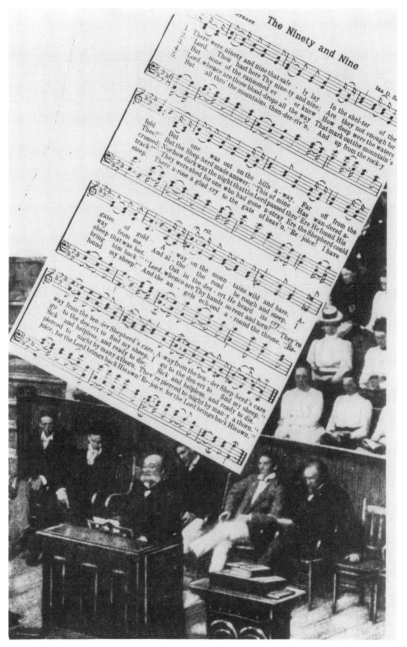

Ira Sankey and the "Ninety and Nine." This publicity photograph shows Sankey at the organ, presumably playing one of his and Moody's favorite hymns. (Moody Bible Institute)

secularization of evangelical religion, neither did it result (as he intended) in the purification of secular institutions. Indeed, a new
word is required to capture the syncretism Moody and his assistant,
the singer Ira Sankey, established—some term to define the recipro-
cal, transforming process that occurred as they renewed and revived
the fusion of religion and popular culture. Moody was not the first
or last Protestant revivalist to perform this act of refreshing evangelical culture. Indeed, there is a long history of interaction between
religion and popular secular institutions. Nonetheless, Moody's
achievement of a new form of religious counterculture was dramatic.[4]

One reason for this success can be laid to Moody's instinctive
evocation of nostalgia for the rural life then being abandoned as
young men and women wandered into the city. Mixing the biblical
parable with current events, Moody repeatedly preached the emotional story of the Prodigal Son who succumbs to the temptations of
the city but eventually returns to "the homestead" to seek forgive-
ness of his parents. Countless times, the evangelist also called upon
Ira Sankey to sing their favorite hymn, the "Old Ninety and Nine,"
a musical version of the same notion. The verses, portraying the
Good Shepherd, intone God's concern for the single lost sheep:

> There were ninety and nine that safely lay
>   In the shelter of the fold,
> But one was out on the hills away
>   Far-off from the gates of gold—
> Away on the mountains wild and bare,
>   Away from the tender Shepherd's care.

An observer at one of Moody and Sankey's early revivals wrote:

> When you hear the "Ninety and Nine" sung, you know that
> down in this corner, up in that gallery, behind that pillar which
> hides the singer's face from the listener, the hand of Jesus has
> been finding this and that and yonder lost one, to place them
> in his fold.[5]

The theme of hymn and parable is lost and found, straying from
home and community, and rescue through God's determined desire
to gather in His lost flock; in other words, the story of emigration to

the city. Its perspective mixes Bible parable, nostalgia for the past and rural life, based upon the values of an older generation and its conflict with new and bewildering experiences of the city. Reverend H. B. Hartzler, an assistant during the 1893 campaign, in his extensive account of the summer's events explored this problem in reporting on Moody's culminating Chicago Fire Anniversary Sermon October 9, 1893. Hartzler took the occasion to describe this pervasive estrangement from the modern city:

> With this closing appeal the speaker turns to God with a fervent prayer of thanksgiving, consecration, supplication, and tearful intercession for the city and for the multitudes coming up to the Fair. Then once more the people unite in singing, and are dismissed with the benediction to meet again no more until all the earth shall stand before the judgement-seat of God.[6]

In this description, anguish and sadness well up as a powerful sensation after the brief feelings of community. Yet Hartzler intended the sketch to be a positive evaluation of Moody's mission in the modern city. Moody knew, instinctively perhaps, because he saw the city this way himself, that feelings of nostalgia for a rural past affected immigrants to the vast new metropolises like Chicago—as a last resort of memory and the imagination.

Moody's autobiography itself offers a story of frequent attempts to recreate that fellowship in the urban churches of Chicago, the crusades he preached throughout the country, and the communities he helped establish. His own life story furnished a rich source for sermons on the subjects of alienation and restoration and the disruptions of moving to the city. Born in Northfield, Massachusetts, he grew up fatherless, although he imbibed typical Protestant virtues of his day. As he often tearfully reminded audiences, his own family had been wrenched by the story of the Prodigal Son. As a young man, Moody set out for Boston in 1854 to became a shoe salesman (perhaps even feeling that in leaving he resembled his prodigal brother). Moving shortly afterward to Chicago, he plied the same trade with considerable skill and success. Joining other young Easterners like Marshall Field, Moody became a traveler. This was obviously a seminal experience, and he never forgot the competitiveness

The Moody Homestead. Northfield, Massachusetts. (Moody Bible Institute)

of the trade: "I can make money quicker than anyone except Marshall Field," he once remarked.[7]

But the lure of evangelism proved too strong. From the beginning Moody plunged into church affairs in Chicago. Neither a trained minister nor theologian, he joined lay institutions such as the YMCA and eventually organized Sunday Schools, prayer groups, schools, then a church, and finally a major evangelical institute. If not completely rootless (he often returned home to Northfield where he established a summer religious camp and missionary school), he led a peripatetic life similar to others who searched for a new profession at the turbulent end of the century.[8]

Moody's special calling, as he described it, was to evangelize his chosen venue, the industrial city. Yet abandoning commerce was not easy: as he reported, the greatest emotional struggle he ever endured "was when I gave up business."[9] In effect, he never did abandon secular enterprise; he merely transferred his account to religious ventures. Like many contemporary reformers he discovered that his experience in the competitive world offered lessons and cautionary tales to shape a response to the new urban America. In moving from small town to city, he recognized a common experience he shared with fellow migrants to the heartland of industrial society. He responded to many of the problems of this transition that beset other observers and social reformers. He worried about a church grown "cold and formal" and a modern urban society filled with strangers and alien, threatening cultures. In the city, this cultural modernism expressed itself most dangerously in the profligate growth of theaters, Sunday newspapers, drinking, lust, worldly amusements, and threatening scientific ideas like Darwinism. Through this changing world, Moody made his progress. He was a man who in his own itinerant search for career confronted the most extreme changes of the era, sharing with many Americans their confrontation with the modern city and its daunting new mass culture, industrialism, and consumerism.[10]

In many respects, Moody also resembled his great predecessor Charles Finney. Beginning his great preaching in the 1820s after a profound conversion, Finney searched the Burned-Over District for souls to convert. A handsome, imposing young man, he had studied law. As an itinerant minister, he brought business acumen to his work, and his organizational skills helped to solidify the awakening that swept upstate New York. Preaching free will, conversion, and Sabbatarianism, Finney eventually moved his crusades into the cities where he found substantial support from wealthy merchants such as Arthur Tappan and David Dodge. In his approaches to the laity, he developed a far more theatrical mode than the prevailing style of preaching. His protracted meetings, inquiry rooms, and plain, direct, and illustrative speech, moved religion from the isolated pulpit to center stage.[11]

Yet Finney came from a culture that also flowered into moral perfectionism and social reform. The evangelist took up causes like the Graham vegetarian diet, abolitionism, and education—always, it should be added, with the expectations of millennialism. Although Moody grew up in the heat of these evangelistic disturbances and adopted many of Finney's practices, there were distinct differences. Moody made a different mark upon urban evangelism. For example, he had a far more distinct urban orientation than Finney. He preached at an even farther edge away from established churches. He developed new preaching practices which other evangelicals then adopted. And, theologically, he tended toward premillennialism (emphasizing preparation for Christ's judgment) rather than Finney's perfectionism. Nonetheless, the similarities and continuities which linked both men established a tradition that worked to fuse popular culture and revival Protestantism.[12]

Marshaling his forces against a church grown cold, the proliferation of institutions strayed beyond the hegemony of traditional Protestantism, and a population wandering away from home and mission, Moody took his evangelical message directly to the contaminated and questionable institutions and populations of the city. He insisted upon challenging them on their own grounds. Very early on, this strategy caught the attention of a Catholic satirist who expressed outrage at Moody's first great American crusade in 1876 in Philadelphia. In a thinly disguised parody of Moody, the satirist mocked "Reverend Eliphalet Notext," who was neither theologian nor minister but a modern businessman who "had been originally the business manager of a circus." This vulgar and blasphemous performer, he continued, perverted religion into a sideshow. "When he was at a loss for words to continue one of his disjointed discourses, he took refuge in music and hymns."[13]

The critic was right—at least from his traditional perspective. But he failed to appreciate that Moody's offensive use of popular culture was, in fact, one explanation for the great evangelical's success. By directly engaging modern popular culture, about which he certainly had grave reservations, by exploiting its forms for his own purposes, Moody touched his audiences and mapped a clear pathway for future revivals to follow. By pouring old wine into new vessels, Moody could, as Reverend Hartzler expressed it, empty "Sunday theatres and other places of sinful amusements by filling churches, halls, theatres, and tents, and displacing the Godless Sunday performances with Christian song services and Gospel preaching."[14]

Although Moody's goals were traditional, his strategy, as he developed it, centered around institutions that existed in the empty space between philanthropy and the established Protestant churches. This became apparent immediately. After quitting business, he became a librarian at the Chicago YMCA in 1861. He worked diligently with Civil War organizations like the U.S. Sanitary Commission and the Chicago Y's "First Presbyterian" regiment. Turning then to mission work, Moody, after the Civil War, organized the "Yokefellows," a group dedicated to searching saloons and bars for converts. Eventually, he established the Chicago Bible Work and the Chicago Evangelization Society which, after his death, was renamed the Moody Bible Institute.[15] With this institution, he helped to train the young men and women who would spread out from this center to evangelize the city and the nation.

Besides the temptations of secular popular culture, Chicago was particularly threatened after the 1870s by outbreaks of class warfare. Along with his wealthy patrons like the Cyrus McCormicks, Moody worried that newcomers to the city and the heterodox beliefs and populations that they encountered there would adulterate religious faith and incite disorder.[16] To the evangelist, religion and order occupied the same tray of the social balance. He also understood the appeal of drawing such a picture when he solicited funds from wealthy benefactors. As he wrote a Chicago businessman in 1889, "[T]here can be no better investment for the capitalists of Chicago than to put the saving salt of the gospel into those dark homes and desperate centers from which come the criminals."[17]

According to Turlington Harvey, lumber magnate and financial backer of Moody for many years, Moody's decision to expand his urban ministry in Chicago derived partly from the turmoil around the Haymarket riot in 1886. As he wrote in a letter explaining the history of the Chicago Bible Institute, Harvey said:

> The tragedy of the Haymarket had brought to the knowledge of our citizens the depressing consciousness of the extent and danger of the communistic element in our midst, and many earnest Christian people were feeling pressure of the conviction, that the only way to convert this dangerous element

Turlington Harvey. Moody benefactor, lumber magnate, and founder of Harvey, Illinois. (Moody Bible Institute)

into peaceful, helpful citizens was through the transforming power of Christ, so that when Mr. Moody made his appeal [for funds], it was very cordially received and liberally responded to.[18]

Yet, as is always the case with Moody, it would be a mistake to interpret his appeal too literally. Just as popular culture and the World's Fair presented both threats and opportunities to his ministry, so did the labor violence of the late nineteenth century both menace the social order and enhance the attraction of his evangelical enterprise for businessmen searching for charities in which to invest.[19]

Reverend Hartzler, in his chronicle of 1893, offered a perceptive account of the dual attraction and repulsion of the city and the World's Fair that summed up Moody's vision of the modern world:

But the aggregation of individuals in the cities creates perils on the one hand and offers opportunities on the other, which call for evangelistic effort on a larger scale, of a more comprehensive character not alone for the salvation of the individual sinner and the edification of the individual believer, but also for the salvation of society itself.[20]

To Moody the World's Fair especially exemplified, in its promiscuous mixing of uprooted populations and competing religions and cultures, all the dangers of the urban environment. The ambiguity of the city and its institutions were reproduced and magnified in the Fair. As Hartzler noted, Chicago in 1893 filled up with diverse sorts of groups, Americans and foreigners, and especially "vicious" people. As one Methodist publication commented, the 1893 campaign aimed to "neutralize to the greatest extent, the bad influences which beset World's Fair visitors."[21]

This negative appraisal, however, disclosed only a portion of his assessment. When Moody answered a questionnaire on the effects of the Fair, he wrote that it enhanced the education of the common people and broadened their sympathies (presumably for the various ethnic groups displayed on the Midway). Furthermore, he noted, "I have been impressed with the fact that it is the Christian people of the land that take an interest in and patronize such expositions as the World's Fair."[22] While this may be only a commentary on the predominance of middle-class visitors to Chicago during the summer of 1893, it surely displays optimism about the possibilities of evangelization among World's Fair visitors.

In many of his views—with his ambiguity toward popular culture; his desire to create a stable, Protestant Chicago; his economic conservatism; and typified by his talents for organization and dreaming on a grand scale—Moody closely resembled the grandest Chicago businessmen who were his benefactors and friends. The devotion of this group of entrepreneurs to evangelical Christianity is noteworthy. From their mutual involvement in business affairs, their support of lay Protestant organizations like the YMCA, the Moody Bible Institute, their tenure on the boards of reform organizations, universities, and cultural institutions, and their support and work for the success of the World's Fair, this was a remarkable, stable and homogeneous group. Such men as wholesaler John V. Farwell, Cyrus H. McCormick, banker Lyman J. Gage, Marshall Field, George Pullman, hotelier Potter Palmer, Gustavus F. Swift, and Turlington Harvey constituted a group whose geographic and generational origins and economic successes bound them closely. Moody shared their background, their successes, and, to some degree, access to their social world.[23]

Although Moody made his headquarters in Chicago and expended his greatest efforts there, he always retained a strong link to Northfield, Massachusetts, where he established an important training school and summer programs. In the process, he helped to refurbish the town of his youth, thereby participating in the contemporary rejuvenation and restoration of New England towns. If this helped to recreate a nostalgic past for the sons and daughters of the region who had long moved away, it also provided a second center for Moody's life, set in an idealized and revived "homestead."[24]

What the *Springfield Daily Union* called "a Modern Eden," in Northfield consisted of several new buildings constructed because of the activity of Moody's Mount Harmon School for Boys and the Northfield Seminary for Girls, and Moody's countless summer

Sunday School Class in 1876. This early class was led by Moody and his supporter, J. V. Farwell. The names of the boys are remarkably Dickensian: Red Eye, Darby the Gobbler, Smikes, Butcher Kilroy, Billy Bucktooth, Green Horn, Madden the Butcher, Indian, Jacky Candles, Black Stove Pipe, Sniderick, Old Man, Billy Blucannon, Rag Breeches Cadet. The original caption of the phtograph reads: "Go out into the highways and hedges and compell [*sic*] them to come in." (Library of Congress)

conferences. The town was graced by a modern hotel, library, and Congregational church. These new structures were designed in contemporary styles of the Italian Renaissance and not New England revival designs. Yet the whole effort was, as the *Union* exclaimed, to create "a spot whereon the eye of God dwells lovingly!"[25] Moody

Moody Church. This building was later renamed the Moody Bible Institute. (Moody Bible Institute)

even constructed a large, new homestead for his family at North-field, remodeling, as it were, the environment of his youth.

Because many of Moody's friends and allies were deeply involved in financing and planning the World's Fair, he could not attack it openly without offending them. But he did object to the secularism of the Exposition. Whatever his motivation for undertaking the campaign that summer, whether it was genuine opposition to the celebration or opportunism, he disguised his decision in the form of an anecdote that claimed God's miraculous intervention. In London in 1891, the revivalist visited a medical specialist who confirmed an earlier diagnosis of serious heart disease. The ship returning home was struck by a dangerous storm, and in a prayer Moody promised that, if he survived, he would "come back to Chicago and at the World's Fair preach the gospel with all the power He would give me."[26] Whether it was God's bargain fulfilled or, as Moody explained elsewhere, the "opportunity of the century" to convert a wicked city, does not much matter. In 1892 planning was well under way, and by May 1893 Moody and his specially gathered staff of ministers and gospel students prepared to meet the challenge.[27] The urban evangelist was ready to offer a major counterattraction to the secular Utopia that promised to attract millions of travelers to Chicago.

When it came to providing an alternative spiritual "city" to the secular Columbian Fair, Moody's organization enjoyed the advantage of long experience. Although the relationship between the Fair and Moody's campaign was mostly a cordial one, two issues threatened to split the celestial city from the White City. The first involved Sunday closing of the Fairgrounds. The original stipulation by the U.S. Congress in providing funds for the Exposition mandated Sunday closings. This condition had support from many, although not all, Chicago Protestant organizations. Moody, for one, was ambiguous. Although he opposed the Sunday opening, he also refused to be drawn into the dispute, saying, "Let every man decide for himself. You can't force people to observe the Sabbath. It would prove a boomerang."[28] Perhaps stimulating his ambivalence was a vote by the Fair Council of Administration on June 1, 1893, inviting him to preach on the Fairgrounds the next Sunday.[29]

A more antagonistic note was struck in arguments over the World's Fair Parliament of Religions. Philosopher Paul Carus summarized its possibilities when he said that the Parliament would remind "us anew that the narrow Christianity will disappear, for its errors have become palpable."[30] Many in Chicago's Protestant community would have agreed with Carus's intimation that the unfortunate purpose of the Parliament was nothing less than to spread secularism. As the leader of Chicago revivalism, Moody was alternately urged to join or denounce the proceedings. But his aloof strategy proved to be more effective. As one of his lieutenants caustically wrote:

> When the ecclesiastical menagerie gathered from all quarters of the globe made its appearance, Mr. Moody was asked again and again to take part, he only replied that he had his hands full of work and declined to go. When it seemed to some of us that our Lord was belittled and disgraced by the motley crew who disported themselves upon the platform day by day in the wonderful "Parliament" we suggested that we should attack them all along the line. Mr. Moody was very emphatic in his instructions. "Preach Christ," said he, "hold up Christ, let the Parliament of Religions alone, preach Christ." And he was right.[31]

Despite the heavy emphasis upon revivalism and converting World's Fair visitors, Moody in fact offered two substantially different forms of urban evangelism in 1893. The first stressed individual conversion and salvation and offered a temporary Christian community for the tourist during his stay in Chicago. The second promised a more lasting chance to invest in a permanent residence in the evangelical city of Harvey, Illinois, on the outskirts of Chicago in which the immediate Moody entourage had a significant investment of money and prestige.

Moody's primary efforts transformed Chicago into a vast camp meeting. For the casual visitor and the summer tourist at the Fair, the revivalist planned a crusade that encompassed the geography of the whole city. He decentralized his ministry, carrying the campaign to a variety of churches, and then into those places of the city—the pleasure resorts—where visitors might wander seeking amusement. He divided Chicago into districts and designated a church headquarters in each. He further segmented his "congregation" by holding special services for selected populations: young men, young people, children, foreign visitors (sometimes in their native languages), and even survivors of the Civil War. By the end of the campaign in October, his organization was sponsoring as many as 125 services and meetings on a single Sunday.[32]

Many of the principal services occurred in churches, but Moody himself appeared to prefer the more confrontational environment of theaters and public halls such as Tattersalls where Buffalo Bill performed and where political conventions took place. In fact, his favorite spot, where he frequently began his Sunday itinerary, was the infamous Haymarket Theatre in downtown Chicago, located, as Reverend Hartzler described it, "in the midst of a very hell of saloons and vile resorts of all kinds."[33] This represents a fascinating choice, since the Haymarket recalls the notorious riot only a few years before—an event that had encouraged Moody and his supporters to establish a continuous Chicago ministry. Whether this allusion was recognized, the choice signified a challenge to the theaters of Chicago and their normal fare of risqué entertainments. The campaign spent $2,125 in rentals of the Haymarket, second only to payments to the more neutral Central Music Hall.[34]

Because Moody spent considerable time preaching in secular amusement centers, he concluded that he must advertise his meetings in the Announcements section of Chicago newspapers. There, amidst notices for performances at the Trocadero (which he also rented upon occasion), Buffalo Bill's Wild West Show, cycloramas, theaters, and World's Fair events, Moody listed his evangelical meetings. For example, the notice for his "Chicago Day" rally in October appeared between advertisements for the local race track and Stoddard's educational lectures. As he told a *Chicago Tribune* interviewer, he had "taken a new departure by advertising his meetings in the amusement columns of the newspapers, and found that it paid. It brought in the crowds." The result convinced him of the virtue "in advertising, even in the service of the Lord."[35]

While most other Protestant ministers of the city clung to traditional patterns of church worship, Moody moved religion out of the church building to find audiences wherever they might be found. This strategy demanded the erection of mobile circus-like tents around the city for Sunday services. Pitched in neighborhoods away from the downtown area, they brought evangelical preaching to Chicago's hotel and residential districts.[36] Other facilities guaranteed, for those who desired it, a visit in Christian company to the city. Moody's organization passed out handbills for the Hotel

Moody Preaching. This publicity drawing captures the aura of theater and rapt audiences for which the great evangelical was known. The thoroughly secular environment, emphasized by the prominent American flags and the stereotyped perspective from the elegant box seats, was transformed by Moody's words into a sacred environment. (Moody Bible Institute)

Endeavor, "For All Christian People," located in a "prohibition area" of the city at Seventy-fifth Street and Bond Avenue near the Fairgrounds. The hotel boasted a chapel and a dining hall and charged the moderate rate of $2–$3 per room.

To promote tent meetings and other religious services, the organization often distributed free tickets. Designed primarily to encourage audiences to remember the dates and addresses of meetings, they, like many of Moody's adaptations of popular culture, also served a larger purpose. Contrived to resemble theater tickets or World's Fair entry passes, the tickets were part of a strategy to claim popular culture for evangelical Christianity, to create an evangelical counterculture in which the participant could share in what looked like popular culture but which had a religious content.[37]

Perhaps the most celebrated of his descents into the resorts of popular culture was Moody's meeting before an audience of 15,000 at Forepaugh's Circus which he hired for the purpose. Speaking to jaded circus workers "used only to rough words and oaths and condemned to a life of hurry and bustle," Moody inspired listeners to allow their "thoughts to wander away to the old home"—or so the *Chicago Tribune* imagined it. "The trapeze wires were pulled up to the top of the amphitheater," wrote the reporter, " . . . where the performing lions do their turn, was the pulput from which the great preacher was to tell his story." Attempting to cash in on this success, Forepaugh asked Moody to lend an evangelist to travel with the circus and preach on Sundays.[38] Although the evangelist refused the offer, the Forepaugh management clearly saw an advantage in the kinship between their performances and Moody's. Indeed, it acknowledged this in an advertisement printed in the form of a poem:

> Ha! Ha! Ha!
> Three Big Shows!
> Moody in the Morning!
> Forepaugh in the Afternoon and Evening![39]

In tendering this proposal, Forepaugh insinuated that both revivalism and popular performances shared the same perspectives and audiences. Moody's borrowing of certain elements of popular culture made his preaching seem comfortable and appropriate to

Admit Two to the Haymarket Theatre. Tickets like these were issued during the great evangelical campaign of 1893. (Moody Bible Institute)

audiences that attended circuses. So it was on that special circus Sunday. Sentimental and simple in his message, he again preached the parable of the Prodigal Son. Other elements of the typical evangelical production were also familiar. Moody understood the emotional power of music and used it extensively. The harmonium, massed choirs, congregation hymn singing, and Ira Sankey's melodies and words particularly appealed to popular audiences. In part, this is true because they shared a common kinship with the sentimental ballads such as those written by Paul Dresser, composer of "On the Banks of the Wabash," and brother of Theodore Dreiser.

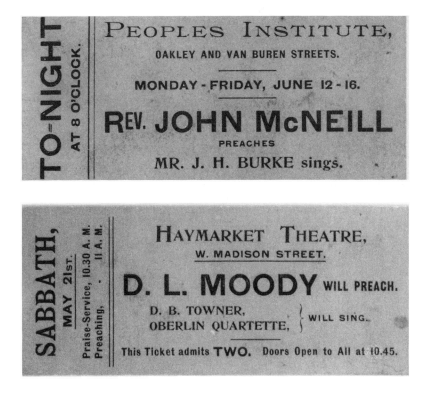

Moody's use of music during revivals had long since become a trademark of his appeal. And observers had quickly recognized the affinity of Sankey's hymnody with popular culture. In 1876 the *Nation* remarked: "Determine the pleasure you get from a circus quickstep, a negro-minstrel sentimental ballad, a college chorus, and a hymn all in one, and you have some gauge of the variety and contrast that may be perceived in one of these songs." Later historians have also commented on Sankey's technique, finding it scarcely distinguishable "from the ordinary secular songs of the day"—that is, similar to music hall and vaudeville styles.[40]

Inevitably, this practice also provoked contemporary criticism. As an accusing letter to Moody in 1893 admonished, "You are not a

Christian. You are serving the money god. You are preaching to please the people. You are no Christian." That Moody made this letter public testifies to his confidence that every observer would recognize the charge to be patently false; he only intended to Christianize secular institutions and culture. But the writer was perceptive to imply that influence could flow in the opposite direction too.[41]

One last strategy rounded out Moody's ingenious campaign. Equipping wagons with lanterns, a small organ, and two horses to draw them, he assigned young students to advertise his services in tough sections of the city, such as "Little Hell." These "Gospel Wagons," the "flying artillery of the evangelical forces," as Moody dubbed them, later became the basis for his Colportage Society, which also sent out wagons equipped with evangelists and a supply of religious tracts to peddle throughout the countryside.

A perusal of the expense ledgers of the crusade reveals how extensive and costly the campaign was, totaling $60,000 in extraordinary outlays. These included rental of theaters, advertising in newspapers for Sunday events, transportation and hotel fees, supper for gospel wagon men, and printing of tickets and announcements. Obviously, the campaign required an extensive administrative and financial commitment beyond Moody's normal summertime activities.[42]

This movable evangelical crusade in no way exhausted the efforts of Moody's organization to evangelize the city during the opportune year of 1893. On the outskirts of Chicago, in the small, new industrial town of Harvey, Illinois, existed the religious, counterculture city made real, waiting for real investors and permanent residents. The World's Fair campaign publicized this special endeavor. At many of his meetings, Moody exhibited a map picturing Harvey as "an earthly paradise which had never been defiled by painted windows and the music of gurgling bottles."[43] Before and during the World's Fair summer of 1893, advertisements for Harvey filled the evangelical press, to appeal to prospective visitors to the Fair who might be thinking of a permanent move to Chicago.

The story of this other city erected shortly before the World's Fair, at the confluence of the Grand Trunk and Illinois Central railroads at about 155th Street South, belongs to two chronicles: the history of planned communities and real estate ventures in Chicago such as Riverside, Oak Park, and Pullman; and the efforts of Moody and his friend and patron, Turlington Harvey, to create an environment that would advance the principles of a Christian culture. To some extent, it is also illuminated by the distant light of the Utopian experiments of the 1830s and 1840s.

Like most of Moody's Chicago business friends, Harvey was born in upstate New York in the 1830s. Growing up near Oneida, he initially learned the trade of sash and door making. Moving to Chicago at the age of nineteen, carrying a box of tools and a single lucky penny (which his grandson testifies he never spent and had set inside a watch fob surrounded by opals), he labored for three years in a carpentry shop. Gradually, he worked his way up in the lumber business until he had organized a huge and thriving enterprise, embracing vast tracts of forest in Wisconsin, and lumber yards and mills throughout Chicago.

Like others of his social and business group, he carefully surveyed and supported several emerging lay Protestant institutions in Chicago. After the Great Fire of 1871, he purchased cheap lumber and rebuilt tenement houses for homeless workers. He became president of the Chicago Bible Society, vice-president of the Chicago Evangelistic Committee, and president of the YMCA for six terms. In this position, he helped Moody finance the YMCA and, later, helped raise money for Moody's Bible Institute. After the Fair ended, he served as chairman of the committee that helped organize Chicago's Civic Federation.[44] In the words of an early historian of the city, Harvey achieved the "high rewards that are attainable in fortune, character and influence through a life of industry and probity, guided and regulated by a sense of Christian obligation."[45]

Following the example of the planned workers' community at Pullman (although not so rigorously managed), Harvey, Illinois, had at least two purposes. Turlington Harvey fervently believed in the principles of sobriety and community morality, and he wrote restrictive covenants into every contract forbidding "any bone-boiling establishment or factory, or saloon of any kind, or for any other dangerous, vexatious or offensive purpose or establishment what-

ARRANGEMENTS ARE BEING MADE WHEREBY

✳·HARVEY!·✳

Will be enabled to accommodate

Thousands of World's Fair Visitors

The HARVEY LAND ASSOCIATION

Who founded and platted the whole town, are now selling lots at original prices, and at figures that will be advanced very materially March 1st.

THE HARVEY LAND ASSOCIATION

HAVE CHOICE PROPERTY

Near the Factories
Near the Schools and Churches.
Near the Hotels and in the Business District.
Nine Factories .in Operation, others will soon be running.

Seventy Passenger Trains Daily.
Twenty-five Minutes Ride to the World's Fair Site.
Forty-five Minutes to Union Depot.

Better Chance for Investment than any Suburban town in the vicinity of Chicago

In addition to our three large hotels, one new hotel, "The Transit House," is just completed on 148th street near Marshfie. avenue. Plans for another large hotel on the main boulevard near the Illinois Central depot are reported by a strong compan. **Build your own Cottage:** You can either rent it or sell it at a handsome profit. Send to us for plans. Sent free.

NOW IS THE TIME TO INVEST.

·Send at once for our new pamphlet that will tell you what you want to know about the most successful temperance man facturing town in the world.

THE HARVEY LAND ASSOCIATION

extend a cordial invitation to the readers of the INSTITUTE TIE to visit Harvey any afternoon at 1:55 p.m., returning arriving Chicago at 5 p. m. Transportation will be furnished including a ride through Harvey on the new electric railway. Call at t. city office, 819 The Rookery for tickets.

HARVEY LAND ASSOCIATION,

819 to 825 ROOKERY BUILDING.   **CHICAGO, ILL**

Advertisement for Harvey, Illinois. There were two typical ads for Harvey in 1893, one stressing the investment possibilities of the new town, the other its prohibition regulations and Christian environment. (Moody Bible Institute)

soever . . . nor any gambling to be carried on thereon, nor any house or other place of lewd and immoral practie hereupon."[46] Like his restrictive neighbor to the North, Harvey sought an idealized urban environment.

But Harvey also hoped to capitalize on the building and industrial boom then at its height in Chicago. From this perspective, the evangelical tone of the town can be explained as its strongest selling point. It offered rural or small-town Americans a safe urban haven and manufacturers a sober and orderly working force.[47] Noting the number of businesses enticed from other small towns, advertisements for Harvey proudly referred to the relationship between opportunities for industrial jobs and the temperance ambience. To increase the sway of religion, the land association built the Methodist Episcopal Church and donated the basement space to the town for meetings.

A subtle part of Harvey's appeal, to both future residents and employers, was aimed at American-born men and women, more likely to be attracted by a prohibition town and presumably less unruly than the foreign-born who filled Pullman. Yet Harvey only contained some aspects of the rigorous social planning of Pullman's ideal town and purposely avoided monopoly control over the lives of its inhabitants.

After purchasing 700 acres and surveying the area, Harvey incorporated the village in May 1891. Originally, he had fancied the name Turlington, but he was persuaded that Harvey was a more appropriate name. He then erected his American Fire-Proof Steel Car Company on a choice property in the industrial section of the town. To entice other industries into the city, he offered free plots of land, cash premiums, and the lure of sober and industrious workers.[48] As an 1892 promotional history of the town noted, "Its founders believe that the highest good for both the employer and employé requires the absolute prohibition of the saloon. This will keep some people out of the town, but it will be a strong inducement for others to become residents."[49]

Harvey clearly believed in temperance as an effective inducement for manufacturers to relocate in his new town. He aggressively courted industries in Chicago and in small cities to move their businesses. For example, he wrote to J. P. Adams, a small manufacturer in Sandwich, Illinois:

> We propose to make the town as free from saloons and the bad element as possible, and some gentlemen from Iowa—Messrs. Crane, Steele, and Austin, propose to come there and manufacture headers and spring wagons and also propose to live there. I have no doubt that we shall make the place an attractive one for residences.[50]

In a little less than two years, the city had sprung up from nothing to a total population of 5,000 with roads, churches, newspapers, civic organizations, and ten manufacturing plants. Dubbed "The Magic City" in advertising brochures and favorable newspaper stories, the new town compressed the miraculous history of Chicago itself into its brief moment. But there was a significant difference. Harvey was a temperance town, while Chicago was an aimlessly expanding cosmopolitan giant.

The Harvey Land Association set up offices in the Rookery Building in Chicago near Rand McNally Publishers and the Chicago World's Fair headquarters. The association's officers included Harvey as president, publisher Fleming H. Revell as vice-president (Moody's brother-in-law), and some of the most important bankers, businessmen, and lawyers of Chicago and regular contributors to Moody's campaigns as directors. Principal investors were Ira Sankey, Moody's own Northfield Massachusetts Institute, his brother Will who "owned one of the best lots in town" and leading businessmen and churchmen.[51]

Like other land companies, the Harvey Land Association widely advertised its properties. Interested clients could schedule a guided tour of the town by company agents who took groups out on Saturday rail excursions from the Rookery. But unlike other contemporary real estate developments, Harvey emphasized its religious character. The evident fruit of these intentions, local branches of the GAR, Young People's Society of Christian Endeavor, Knights and Ladies of Honor, Equal Suffrage Association, the Prohibition Club, the Women's Christian Temperance Union, and the Royal Templars of Temperance had all been founded within the first few years. As one of the earliest residents recalled, "Mr. Harvey believed in mixing religion with business and on occasions brought to town such people as R. A. Torrey, a nationally renowned evangelist [and Superintendent of the Moody Institute]; Ira B. Sankey, an equally famous gospel singer; and Susan B. Anthony of woman's suffrage fame." The association representatives in Harvey also tried to close places of "public resort" on Sundays and even made half-hearted attempts to prevent Sunday newspapers from being delivered.[52]

Publicity about the new town made its way quickly to other parts of the country and received very favorable comment in local papers. This was partly due to generous tours provided to visiting editors by the Harvey Land Association. After one such trip, the editor of the *Kansas City Progress* wrote:

> Nowhere is there nobler impulses manifested, or grander accomplishments for the elevation of Humanity.
> It has been left, though, to the genius, philanthropy, and Christian courage of T. W. Harvey, the noted lumberman, and other prominent businessmen of Chicago, to build a manufacturing city, which shall be free from the curse of the saloon, and its manufactured products, known in commerce, politics, and law, as hoodlums, paupers and criminals.[53]

To reach the proper purchasers, the Harvey Land Association mounted an extensive advertising campaign in national journals and newspapers. Most of these had a dependable middle class, farming, and Protestant readership. Periodicals included the *Ladies Home Journal, Banner of Gold, Farmers' Advocate, Christian Herald, Rams's Horn, Chicago Inter Ocean, Farmer's Voice, News Record,* and *Free Methodist.* In addition, Harvey sent traveling salesmen across parts of the country, particularly to neighboring farm states and upstate New York and England, seeking recruits for his evangelical Utopia. The response aroused from these efforts was large, closely following the routes of salesmen and the subscription lists of journals. Not unexpectedly, the greatest returns came from areas like Michigan, Illinois, Minnesota, Pennsylvania, and New York.[54] Typical of inquiries was a letter from Freeman Manter of Kennebec County, Maine: "I have seen notices in newspapers of your famous town of Harvey. I would like to know more of its wonderful prosperity. I go for both temperance and prohibition. I believe any town

would be greatly blessed to do like Harvey, *go for prohibition*—
Please mail me if convenient a few circulars, Harvey papers, anything."[55]

The height of Harvey's advertising efforts came during the
World's Fair summer of 1893, and, in fact, it is reasonable to assume
that the ideal town was planned, in part, to appeal to some of the
thousands of tourists who planned to visit Chicago with the thought
of staying. Notices in national newspapers and magazines proposed
a side trip to Harvey as part of a World's Fair visit. Moody publicized
the town during his meetings. Pamphlets distributed by the Harvey
Land Association and by national temperance organizations showed
the location of the World's Fair and the best routes to reach Harvey.
Famous visitors were invited to the town during the Fair. Harvey
itself planned to accommodate its share of visitors. Groundbreaking
for two large hotels occurred in 1892.

Writing from one of these, the Harvey World's Fair Temperance Headquarters, General Agent Walter Mills promised Turlington Harvey that the hotel would be ready for dedication on April 25,
1893. Although some of the planned accommodations in the town
burned (one hotel was destroyed and never finished and Mills's enterprise was only partly rebuilt), as many as 2,000–3,000 visitors,
staying in the general area, used the Harvey train station daily to
reach the Fair. The Harvey Land Association even organized a kin-
dergarten for children whose parents intended to visit the Fair.[56]

Although the town attracted many visitors and certainly gained
new population from among World's Fair tourists, it shared in the
general economic misfortune that struck the nation in 1893 and
intensified over the winter of 1894 in the Chicago area. Land speculation around Chicago ceased, and land values plummeted. Investment in World's Fair hotels proved to be ill-advised, and Chicago's economic boomlet crumpled as it joined the rest of the nation
in depression. For Turlington Harvey there were personal misfortunes: his eldest son proved to be an alcoholic and the correspondent in a scandalous divorce, and his economic empire crashed at
the end of 1893. Shortly after the town of Harvey achieved stable
self-government, its citizens voted to allow the sale of liquor.[57]

Turlington Harvey's precipitous decline in 1894 and Moody's
death only five years later signaled the passing of an older generation

of leaders in Chicago's business and evangelical communities. Nonetheless, the mark they made was significant and lasting, discovering ways to link developing notions of Fundamentalism to the instruments of popular culture. Moody and Harvey helped conceive a religious counterculture to compete, on its own terms, with the secular and cosmopolitan world of Chicago in the late nineteenth century. Like the builders of the World's Fair, they regarded the emerging American city, represented by Chicago, as a dangerous but exhilarating place. Unlike the directors of the Fair, however, their Utopia promoted the priorities of a modern evangelism, not taste and culture.

In some respects Moody was a paradox. Despite his remarkable experiments in modern communication and advertising, his social views were only ordinary, even conservative. Sometimes, as in his support of the Harvey experiment, he revealed a very ambiguous attitude to the city. Unlike many of his reform-minded Social Gospel brethren, his answer to unemployment, immigrant adjustment to urban life, and the venality of modern culture lay in individual conversion. Still democratic and catholic in wishing to unite all demoninations and classes, he wrote, "[T]he churches can be crowded full and the masses reached if we go about it in the Spirit of the Master."[58] Yet the impulse he followed, both theologically and sociologically, clung to one side of the great developing schism in Protestantism between Fundamentalism and modernism.

Moody firmly believed in the work ethic, temperance, Sabbatarianism, and individual—not social—regeneration. He feared the growth of urban Catholicism and secularization. While he located the Bible at the very center of his teachings, it was an American Bible resonant with special meanings and analogies already established as familiar stories and parables in popular culture. It was certainly not the ambiguous text examined by contemporary biblical scholars or religious liberals. He did not countenance those who interpreted religion in the context of classical learning or philological science; he disparaged reform based in the emerging methods of social science.[59]

Ironically, Moody's attention to modern urban problems and his repeated attempts to evangelize the city may have exacerbated his pessimism and caused him to turn more and more away from the

Interior of Moody's Auditorium. (Moody Bible Institute)

corrupt, secular world at the end of his life. For all his efforts in 1893, the World's Fair campaign experiment probably signaled the decline of his ambition to mobilize the Christian city. The quickly corrupted Harvey experiment never occupied his full attention. Increasingly, he worried about the outcome of his crusade to evangelize the world. This pessimism placed him close (in disposition) to the camp of the premillennialists, whose ideas would emerge full-blown in the Fundamentalist movement of the early 1920s.[60] Even his apparent success at conversion was probably less abiding than he initially presumed. Great numbers of Protestants flocked to his campaigns. But many of those he touched only reconverted; certainly they could not be counted among the newly gathered. It is also unlikely he had much impact upon Chicago's huge foreign-born population. Yet thousands were undoubtedly affected by the experience in ways that Moody may not have anticipated. What they heard was a redefinition of religion that declared an affinity between evangelical ideas and popular culture.[61] Their religious experience, in Moody's hands, was molded into a thoroughly modern format.

What were the elements of this Christian popular culture? Despite his confident air, Moody held contradictory views about the direction of modern society that help explain the mixture of restraint and innovation in his thinking. One example was his attitude to technology. Moody seemed both engaged yet aloof from change. Certainly he appreciated the possibilities of adopting the tools created by modern communications technology. He directed that a telegraph machine be installed at his headquarters, and toward the end of his life had his voice recorded. Beyond tinkering with inventions, however, he adapted both the new communications media and selected practices from the emerging business culture to his evangelical operations. His urban crusades borrowed advanced forms of organization from corporate enterprise, and, in particular, he shared the modern penchant of business to identify its products and purposes with familiar and universal symbols of popular culture—a process that would practically define modern advertising. He even founded a short-lived, experimental journal, the *Christian Economist*, published as a trade journal for other preachers.

Yet as Martin Marty has aptly noted, Moody was "able to exploit modern technology [but] he was ambivalent about its ethos and content."[62] Moody happily appropriated what he required from modern technology, but he tended to ignore the implications of contemporary scientific theories, especially Darwinism. When Fundamentalism sprang up after Moody, it revived an older paradigm of science derived from nineteenth-century common sense philosophy. This philosophy assumed a continuity between the patterns of natural order and divine order revealed in the verses of Scripture; it dismissed contemporary scientific theories that implied a disjuncture between natural and divine law. Historians such as Marian Bell have concluded from this development that "Moody preferred to ignore evolution as a divisive force, and this refusal to deal with modern science alienated revivalism from contemporary intellectual currents of thought and ultimately estranged it from the mainstream of society." The first part of this evaluation seems quite correct; revivalism did swim against contemporary scientific intellectual currents. But it is wrong to conclude that modernism came to dominate the mainstream of American culture. Nor in 1893 was it predictable that modern evangelical movements would primarily acquire a lower-class and rural following. If anything, Moody's audience consisted of a mixture of middle-class urban Protestants and leaders of Chicago's elite. And even Moody's antimodernist science certainly does not exclude him from the mainstream of American culture. Moody's close relationship with the most important businessmen of Chicago belies this notion of isolation. So does the increasingly professional profile of membership in Protestant Chicago's lay organizations of which Moody was a leader at this time.[63] Characteristically, William R. Harper, president of the University of Chicago, explained to Moody in 1899, when inviting him to speak on campus, his centrality to the high purposes of the university:

> I can understand how it is not possible for you to have men like . . . myself speak at Northfield. We, fortunately, are in a different position, and the University is most anxious to have all sides represented. I do not understand, of course, that you, as a matter of fact, represent any other position than that which is actually maintained here at the University. The differences between us are merely differences of detail.[64]

Finally, "mainstream" American culture is more complex than it might first appear; in reality it has not one current but many that flow together. One of these—certainly obvious in Moody's attitudes—separated science and technology. Nothing could be more central to popular thinking in the twentieth century than accepting the fruits of technology without hesitation while remaining skeptical, hostile, or just unaware of the implications of scientific theory.

Even Moody's cautious adoption of the practice and technology of modern communications and his use of business methods had its critics among other evangelical Christians. Some contemporaries scored the evangelist for relying on "un-Christian," modern techniques. But in doing so they ignored the impact of Moody upon popular culture. By turning these tools to evangelical purposes, Moody simultaneously linked revivalism and popular Christianity with vital new forces in mass culture in a marriage whose offspring led the evangelical awakenings of the 1920s and the 1970s.[65]

As to the question of regulating cultural enterprises, the evangelist also picked his way through a serious contemporary debate. He remained an enthusiastic friend of American entrepreneurs, in part because of his experience as one of them as a successful salesman, and in part because they backed his efforts. It is therefore fully comprehensible—and in character—that Moody inaugurated his first great American revival in 1876 in a temporary tabernacle built on a portion of land in Philadelphia where his friend John Wanamaker planned to locate his famous department store.[66] Sharing this terrain symbolized the sympathy of both men for the competitive enterprise system, the consumer culture it portended, and their continuing commitment to evangelical Protestantism.

Still, Moody was nothing if not equivocal here too. While he celebrated business ethics and methods in his own organization, he never approved of unregulated cultural enterprise—a freedom that has come to define modern society and its commercial culture. Far more harshly than the planners of the White City, he protested developments in popular culture—the other culture that they had offhandedly relegated to the Midway. Moody viewed this part of the modern urban world more soberly than Pullman, although he sought neither to ignore it or to confine it. Moody chose to meet and overcome this culture on its own terms. He planned to transform the leisure resorts of American urban life and turn baneful influences to his own purposes. When he denounced saloons and theaters, this did not deter him from preaching inside them if that is where his audience abided—or to dramatize his point. This inspired rivalry made Moody's World's Fair Campaign into the remarkable event that it became.

On questions of social order, Moody stood shoulder to shoulder with his peers in the business community. He preached individualism and conservatism, displaying little interest in the budding social Christianity of urban reformers and social gospelers. Even though he reached out to convert immigrant groups streaming into the city in the 1890s, as his 1893 campaign demonstrated, his success was mostly among Protestants and among those who shared American roots.

By the time Moody's five months' campaign ended in October, his organization had expended a huge effort. It employed a roving staff of 220 men and women. By the organization's own estimate, it reached close to 2 million people or about 7½ percent of the estimated 27 million who attended the Fair.* Beginning in late May, the crusade began to keep attendance records for various meetings. Obviously crude estimates, the figures did not include smaller crowds at gospel wagons, Sunday schools, or mid-week meetings. Understandably, Moody was encouraged to believe that he had converted thousands of new people. To maximize this possibility, the organization issued tickets to meetings in hopes that the same audience would be discouraged from following him around the city. To confirm his success, Moody began asking crowds if there were Fair visitors. He was satisfied by a show of hands that most were. By his estimate, he had preached to the nations of the entire world through their representatives visiting the Fair. He also claimed practical results such as a decline in whiskey consumption; he took credit for preventing larger crowds from attending the Fair on Sundays. He had, finally, he noted, helped to educate "the common people."[67]

Taken by another measure, such as a comparison with World's Fair admissions and Midway concession receipts, Moody held his own against the competition. Only top attractions such as the Ferris Wheel, Cairo Street, the German Village, and the Hagenbeck Menagerie outdrew Moody's various events outside the Fairgrounds.[68]

Yet there is scant evidence that Moody accomplished any of his immediate goals. The records of the campaign, for example, reveal that most of the preaching was done in English or, occasionally, German. Few, if any, of the foreign ministers represented the other ethnic groups that lived in Chicago, although there were occasional local meetings held for immigrant groups. In the main, Moody's success lay with preaching to the city's—and the nation's—Protestants.[69]

---

* I have not corrected either of these figures for repeaters. Undoubtedly, many people went to the Fair twice just as thousands attended more than one Moody sermon.

By any gauge, Chicago remained a wicked city despite his efforts. In some respects, the World's Fair campaign and the abbreviated experiment at Harvey represented a high point of optimism from which the evangelist retreated after 1893. Although the town of Harvey represented a bridge between homestead and urban world and the possibility of combining the sanctified and the industrial, the experiment quickly aborted. Certainly not always so engaged, focused, or topical as during this year, Moody apparently became more and more pessimistic. He spoke of a world "getting darker and darker" and grown "worse and worse." At his funeral in 1899, John Wanamaker, in a eulogy for his close friend, paraphrased a recent conversation with Moody. The great preacher had wished with some sense of discouragement and finality, "If I could only hold one great city in the East before I die, I think it might help other cities to do the same."[70]

Nonetheless, evaluations based on numbers, conversions, and attendance reveal little. Could anyone expect a revival to eliminate moral corruption? Moody is important for other reasons. Throughout his career and summed up in this extraordinary crusade was a special approach to problems of modern industrial and urban society—a bold use of culture to overcome disunities, to affect behavior, and to apply technology and enterprise in the service of evangelical Protestantism. His was no mere accommodation of traditional America to the modern world. He discovered how traditional ideas might be heated with evangelical emotions and poured into the mold of a developing new popular culture in order to reshape them for contemporary relevance. He was (wrote a supporter) "a great advertiser. He is one of the children of light, who have learned from the children of this world. The newspapers, streetcars, billposters, and ticket distributors are all brought into requisition."[71]

If Moody requisitioned the inventions of the "children of this world," then they, in turn, borrowed some of his light. The tone of some of Moody's attitudes to popular culture, like those of many middle-class traditionalists, often seems censorious. But that does not summarize the effect of his—or their—efforts. Their efforts to restrict and change popular culture had more than negative results. If anything, such exertions ultimately broadened the appeal of popular culture to middle-class audiences and the interchangeability between diverse American subcultures by establishing parallels and shared formats.

One instance of this can be seen in a literary venture of Moody's brother-in-law Fleming Revell who, by the 1890s, was one of Chicago's largest publishers and a leading printer of religious works. Revell published many of the books and pamphlets intended for the new Colportage Society that Moody set up in 1894. In 1899, Revell embarked on a new enterprise: evangelical dime novels. Publishing at least ten works by Ralph Connor (Charles William Gordon), Revell established a genre in which a minister or religiously inspired person goes to the frontier, challenges the raucous popular culture, and converts the men to Christianity through his courage and good sense. The message was Moody's, but the form was the popular and often disreputable dime novel.[72]

Moody happily exploited the technology of emerging mass culture industries to communicate his religious ideas. It would be incorrect to say that he alone discovered the pathway between mass culture and evangelical ideas. The history of this connection is far more complex and his role less pioneering. Yet the great evangelist was a noteworthy player in the great cultural drama that has kept, and still keeps, religious ideas and emotions on the center stage of American popular culture.

Like his friends who helped design the Chicago World's Fair, he participated in the monumental enterprise of creating modern commercial culture. Attempting to contrive Utopias out of the most American and changeable of urban environments, Moody, Pullman, and the Fair builders created a plausible fiction about the possibilities of the new metropolitan world. They did so at a moment when fiction writing and reading had exploded with the spread of cheap books and magazines throughout the nation. The World's Fairgrounds and Pullman and Harvey, Illinois, despite their fleeting, hopeful moments of existence, articulated dreams of an idealized city life being explored in contemporary popular fiction.

Although many middle-class Americans had been used to obtaining their information from the dense and elaborate prose of the late nineteenth century (a fussiness that matched, in some respects, the ornate and busy facades of the White City at the World's Fair), there was also an increasing tendency to rely upon photographs which could now be more cheaply reproduced or in the journalistic style of the new urban observers and critics. In the face of the increasing cultural diversity apparent in American society, this format of simplified ideas and images and commercially mass-produced culture offered opportunities to those who wished to spread their messages to a larger segmented group.

Moody's place in this transformation is, again, central. Seeking to appeal to urban dwellers, he used the new means of communications being developed around him. He pared down and simplified his message to appeal across social and cultural divisions; his stories were as simple as journalism, his parables as vivid as photographs. It should come as no surprise, then, that Moody is one of the precursors of Fundamentalism, which itself offered a solid, concrete, and very direct message easily compatible with the demands of modern mass communications. Fundamentalism relied upon a unitary, nostalgic founding myth and a single magical historical text upon which all could presumably agree.[73]

In a certain sense, this argument is circular. Modern media developed partly to respond to the remarkable diversity and confusion of the city and its subcultures. It united disparate populations with accessible images and messages that denied the importance and relevance of distinctions. Moody's almost instinctive understanding of this process places him among the important inventors of this new American culture.[74]

Just as certainly, the new constructions of reality in the aesthetic Utopia of the Fair and the celestial counter-culture of the Chicago campaign were devised to offer an alternative Chicago to the one peopled by the new immigrants to the city with their dissonant cultures. A festival to urban possibilities, the celebrations of Chicago during the summer of 1893 offered the group to which Moody belonged an opportunity to expose their ideas and beliefs to the entire nation. With these revelations, they hoped to inspire its future.

Seven

EXIT

The Gray City

T HE OTHER CHICAGO—the black city of smoke, grime, poverty, hard work, and unfulfilled dreams—had always been present, even if a tourist might choose to ignore it. But departing the city, slowly gathering speed in reverse, this darkened perspective from the blurred, dirty train window became almost inevitable. The British author H. G. Wells, who was greatly distressed by Chicago, described it with revulsion:

> Chicago burns bituminous coal, it has a reek that outdoes London, and right and left of the line rise vast chimneys, huge blackened grain-elevators, flamed crowned furnaces and gauntly ugly and filthy factory buildings, monstrous mounds of refuse, desolate, empty lots littered with rusty cans, old iron, and indescribable rubbish. . . . And then suddenly Chicago is a dark smear under the sky and we are in the large emptiness of America.[1]

Through this somber cloud, the remarkable skyline of Chicago faded, barely visible as a looming, dark blur.

Having been reborn in fire, the grand construction of Utopian Chicago in 1893 was, in its way, also consumed by conflagration. After the Midway was pulled down in late 1893, once the great Fair closed, two devastating fires ravaged most of the White City. Writing in her journal on November 4, 1893, Frances Glessner had a kind of premonition of the coming destruction: "Wednesday we went to the Exposition. It was exceedingly interesting to see the wonderful change that had come over everything. It looked as though death had struck it."[2]

Another portent should have been the weather. Like the fire year of 1871, 1894 was exceedingly dry. The first fire at Jackson Park struck early on January 8 and consumed several buildings. Then, on July 5, most of the rest burned. As Hubert Bancroft wrote in his comprehensive *Book of the Fair* in 1895: "The burning of the Manufactures building was a sight that will never be forgotten by those who witnessed this tragic climax in the destruction of the White City"[3] The fire even inspired a poem on the "Vanishing Fair." H. H. Van Meter wrote:

> It has mounted, mourned forever
> On the fiery wings of flame—
> But its beauties fade—no never!
> From the fairest page of fame.[4]

Novelist Robert Herrick was not very optimistic about Chicago's transmutation into yet another Phoenix. In his novel, *The Web of Life*, he wrote in 1900, "The poor had come lean and hungry out of the terrible winter that followed the World's Fair. In that beautiful enterprise the prodigal city had put forth her utmost strength and, having shown the world the supreme flower of her energy, had collapsed."[5] His choice of the biblical metaphor, prodigal, to represent the exhausted city resounds with irony: it recalls Moody's reiteration of the parable; and it underscores the transitoriness, the instability of the city's foundations for the future.

Other specters peopled the nightmare that followed hard upon the World's Fair. Chicago's mayor, Carter Harrison, was assassinated on October 9, following Chicago Day. The terrible depression gathering outside Chicago swept over the city from the rest of the nation as if in retribution for the gaiety of the Fair. Novelist Ernest Poole later wrote, "Chicago plunged back into chaos and grime in the Black Winter of '94": again the somber metaphor![6] But what distressed Chicago most was undoubtedly the savage split of the city into two warring camps and classes around the prolonged strike at Pullman.

The cause of the strike at the works lay clearly with the Pullman company. Deep-seated hostility against the company and rigid regu-

Pullman. The Illinois National Guard in front of the Arcade Building during the bitter strike of 1894. (ICHI-21195, Chicago Historical Society)

lations of the town produced a well of animosity, but the immediate cause was undoubtedly the declining employment at the works during the winter of 1894. After Pullman refused to lower rents for the unemployed or underemployed, anger quickly turned into action. Ray Stannard Baker, writing of Chicago that year, evoked the sadness of this depression and strike: "What a human downfall after the magnificence and prodigality [again!] of the World's Fair which had so recently closed its doors! Heights of splendor, pride, exaltation in one month; depths of wretchedness, suffering, hunger, cold in the next."[7]

Despite Pullman's best efforts to control his workers, there had been previous labor strife at the works. But the worst came when, in

Pullman. A Pullman scene during the strike of 1894 taken by reformer Ray Stannard Baker. (Library of Congress)

late 1893, Pullman cut wages by about a third. Employees fell behind in paying rents and water bills. Crossing over into Roseland and Kensington to the bars and saloons they habitually frequented, workers met, debated, and then decided to strike on May 12, 1894. They received substantial support from Eugene Debs's American Railway Union which refused to service trains that carried Pullman cars. By this means, the local strike expanded over the entire franchise network owned by Pullman.[8]

Pullman won the strike and workers returned to their jobs, but he did so at enormous cost to himself. The Chicago press, whatever its ultimate defense of Pullman's property rights, displayed serious and probably long-held misgivings about the entire experiment. Worse was a split among businessmen, some of whom blamed the manufacturer's stubbornness and refusal to deal with the unions. By encouraging the federal government to step in with troops to break the strike, Pullman played the card he had always held but never intended to surrender: his friendship with the most powerful men in Washington.[9] When the United States Strike Commission, set up by the federal government to report on the events of 1894, drew its conclusions a year later, it published devastating testimony about conditions in the town. It lamented the hardening of organizational divisions between capital and labor but nonetheless urged the recognition of unions. It did not attempt to rescue Pullman's compromised reputation.[10]

In late 1894, George Pullman tried to put the pieces of his Utopia back together. But they were too fragile and brittle edged, and, besides, he had lost much of his drive and energy. After 1894, he and Hattie spent winters in Washington, D.C., giving lavish parties and lobbying for favors for the company. In effect, his ties with Chicago, which had betrayed his expectations, diminished.[11] After his death, with a hurried finality, the town of Pullman declined from Utopia to dystopia.

The story of Dwight Moody also had a quick although different culmination. Despite hints of discouragement with his endeavors, Moody plunged into a new publishing enterprise, the Colportage Society. These small, convenient publications, written in popular style, were something like a tract-of-the-month club, and designed to be sold throughout the United States. There were no more great campaigns. In only a few short years, Moody too was dead. He died in Northfield, Massachusetts—as if Chicago which had demanded so much from his life now had to relinquish his estate.

Other evangelists such as Billy Sunday stepped forward. Through the years the Moody Bible Institute continued its innovations in mass media, developing radio programs in the early 1920s and even visiting World's Fairs throughout the twentieth century. But the very special dynamism of Moody vanished. Evangelicalism, to which he had contributed so much, pressed quickly down the road of schism away from established Protestant sects. The town of

Gospel Wagons. Moody and his followers used these movable churches to bring an evangelical message to areas of the city without strong Protestant churches or where the population might be indifferent or even hostile. (Moody Bible Institute)

Harvey, Illinois, quickly evolved to an undistinguished industrial suburb of Chicago, with little of its evangelical pallor remaining. By 1897, the town had gone wet, abruptly ending the temperance experiment. And in 1909, Harvey himself had died. Indeed, with his death a whole generation had for the most part disappeared from Chicago.

Other signs of the transition were two curious sorts of guidebooks to Chicago published in 1894 that subverted the distanced and bedazzled prose prospective of the guidebook literature. The first was English publisher William Stead's shocking book *If Christ Came to Chicago.* This book gained instant notoriety for its unblemished realism about the city. Stead named names, described scandal and immorality, and placed blame where he thought it was deserved. He even included a map indicating gambling and sporting houses in the city: marks in red for brothels, black for saloons, and gray for pawn-brokers.

It was not that Chicagoans had denied the existence of prostitution, poverty, drunkenness, political corruption, and other sins of urban life, or that Stead was the first to describe them. These flaws mattered little to boosters and city builders in an era of expansion. But appearing in 1894, at the height of the depression, Stead's descriptions were sobering, terrible, and apt. Stead even turned upon the shaken heroes of Chicago business: Marshall Field, Pullman, Philip Armour, and others for their failure to offer leadership to the desperate community that they had, in effect, created.

Ironically, Stead reiterated the need for a great White City, but he went beyond the formal architectural structures that had celebrated high culture and muted consumerism at Jackson Park. Inspired by this architectural vision, Stead wanted Chicago to create a new, single culture of reform, a civic federation, an "ideal collective Humanitarian Episcopate on democratic lines."[12] The newly awakened Chicago would experience a dramatic, reformed political and economic life. It might find inspiration in the ideals of the White City: parks, art, a unity of religions, music, reformed theaters, no saloons, a decline of vice. But these conditions should be extended and deepened. So Stead supported the White City definition of culture. But he also encouraged something else, proposing cooperative housing, the eight-hour day, city-owned department stores, free medical service, and Pullman cars donated for tuberculosis patients.[13] This attention to the working-class world was probably shocking and unexpected to Chicago's elite. But then few of the builders of the White City sympathized with the Victorian socialism that he proposed.[14]

The other map of Chicago published in 1895 revealed an even less familiar city. This was outlined in Jane Addams and Florence Kelley's *Hull-House Maps and Papers*, which included a color-coded map and report prepared by Hull-House researchers of one Chicago neighborhood showing the income level, the nationality, and the residences of slum dwellers.[15] This remarkable document was like a vivid painting of exploitation brushed upon Chicago's monotonous grid system.

Jane Addams's Chicago represented, in some respects, a new characterization of the city. Erasing the distance between her settlement house residence and the immigrant districts by moving to Hull-House, Addams also strove to diminish the distance between elite culture and the best of immigrant culture, gleaned from the teeming Babel around her. She had not relinquished middle-class tastes in literature and the arts; in fact, she wanted to communicate these to the men and women who came to the settlement house. She also deeply disliked the culture of the city streets—the commercial culture that was increasingly popular with young immigrant men and women.[16] So the dream of a White City was not really gone from the Hull-House endeavor. The settlement house stood across the same median place as the Women's Building at the Fair, as a connection and a boundary between two cultures. From this vantage point, there was still a large part of Chicago popular culture excluded even from Jane Addams's sympathetic vision.

As if reaffirming the suggestion of the bazaar of all nations at the Fair, Addams and her coworkers founded the Arts and Crafts Society at Hull-House in 1897 and then the Labor Museum in 1900. Both of these institutions had the purpose of displaying the material culture of older generations of immigrants and reviving the value of labor from a nonindustrial setting.[17] This valorizing of handmade objects and cultural remembrance was certainly not revolutionary or even original. But it represented an effort to enter the world of the Chicago immigrants and an attempt to elevate their cultures to a kind of parity with elite culture. As a metaphor for those values compromised by modern industrial and consumer society, however, it was not entirely apt. And while sympathetic to some aspects of immigrant life, this strategy still deprecated the commercial culture in which many immigrants participated enthusiastically and through which some discovered a convenient new avenue of social mobility into the popular arts and media industries.

Despite the fires, not all was lost after the disappearance of the White City and the Midway. One monument remained, the Field Museum of Natural History, created out of the Fine Arts Palace building, and sustained by a $1 million gift from the department store entrepreneur. His friends Pullman and Leiter gave $100,000 each and Higinbotham $50,000.[18] In 1921, a new museum opened, designed initially by Burnham's firm to house the natural history exhibits. Originally, Burnham had planned four great statues to embellish the building: Columbus, Washington, Lincoln, and Marshall Field. When built, the museum did have four statues—dedicated to Natural Science, Dissemination of Knowledge, Research, and Record. This noteworthy shift into abstractions signaled a descent from the heroic era of Chicago's boomtime arrogance and self-congratulation. In 1930, gifts from another merchandising millionaire, Julius Rosenwald of Sears, Roebuck, made it possible to transform the now abandoned Arts Palace into a new museum of Science and Industry, opened in 1933 to greet visitors to Chicago's Century of Progress celebration and exposition.[19]

There was also one powerful attempt to revive Chicago's reputation as an inspirational white city. For a number of years after the World's Fair, Chicago's business and civic leaders and organizations such as the Commercial Club and the Merchants Club pushed for a comprehensive Chicago plan to incorporate some of the ideas of the White City. When proposed in 1909, the new Plan of Chicago, drawn up largely by Daniel Burnham, appealed to a number of long-standing traditions: late nineteenth-century European schemes to redesign cities; Burnham's own experience in formulating plans for Washington, D.C., and other American cities; and, of course, the experience of the World's Fair.[20]

The 1909 plan for Chicago proposed a park system, a rejuvenation of the entire lakefront, a system of radiating and encircling highways, and, perhaps most important, a civic center around which would be grouped government and cultural institutions, hotels, parks, and railway terminals. Burnham had long believed that centralization and aesthetic grandeur in architecture would keep wealthy Chicagoans at home, in the city, by creating a place that could compete with the tourist spots of Europe. To achieve this, it was important to construct new buildings displaying historical gravity in their architectural embellishments.

In the Chicago plan, Burnham also gave considerable attention to making public spaces available to nonelite members of Chicago's society. He believed the life of the wage earner would be greatly enhanced by the widespread park system and by cultural institutions accessible to all.[21] In many respects, these purposes were the same as those of the World's Columbian Exhibition; now Burnham suggested imposing the White City on all of Chicago.

Over the years that followed, some of the elements of the plan were put into effect. Several parks were built and the lakeshore was greatly improved. But the city center was never constructed, and the "ensemble" which would have given the plan its weight was never completed. Little attention was given to enhancing life in the slums. There were many reasons why Chicago accepted only part of this design, not the least being the archaic vision of Burnham. But a stronger explanation derived from a misunderstanding of the Fair itself. Although Burnham had done much to facilitate the success of the Midway, with its cacophony of cultures, he simply ignored this aspect of city culture in his later plans. The blanket of high culture he intended to cover the metropolis fit uncomfortably over the robust commercial demands of Chicago's many civilizations. Quite simply, the White City was not what everyone wanted.[22]

At almost the same time, Chicago's railroad entrepreneurs, in particular, proposed to create a different "plan" for the city based upon the success of the Midway. In 1905, at least four new amusement parks, located around and at the edges of the city, attracted considerable attention. The most important of these, the "White City Amusement Park," opened in May of that year. Owned by Edward C. Boyce, vice-president of Dreamland in Coney Island, New York, this was the largest of a chain of White City parks erected at New Haven, Cleveland, Portland, Louisville, and Worcester, Massachusetts. Aimed at the "working man with a large and clamorous family" who could only afford cheap amusements, the park was situated just south of the original White City and Midway, at Jackson Park and Sixty-third Street.[23]

Exhibits at this amusement park (like its name) conflated the two elements of the original Fair and dissolved visions of elite culture into popular amusement. Its central feature was a 300-foot electric tower, recalling the White City illuminations. It also featured the Canals of Venice and a picturesque gondola ride by the Doge's palace. There was a scenic railroad, a coal mine (later to become

White City Amusement Park, Chicago, 1905. This view bears a striking and intentional resemblance to the 1893 White City. (Library of Congress)

one of the most popular features of the Museum of Science and Industry). Other exhibits included a Midget City, Custer's Last Stand, a Chinese theater, and "a Midway" with various rides such as "the Chutes" and restaurants.

That the idea for all these exhibits came from Coney Island, Atlantic City, P. T. Barnum's American Museum, and other amusement parks is apparent. But there was also a visible texture woven out of the remnants of the 1893 Columbian Exposition onto the loom of commercial culture. The ease of this task of turning the White City into a symbol of commercial amusement reveals the inherent nature of the original grand design itself and its understated dependence upon "commercial."

In another respect, however, the alternative White City amusement park discloses how little had really been learned about the success of the World's Fair. Different planners for the city continued to scheme in their separate spheres. Burnham and his associates dreamed of a Chicago with little more than a nod to popular culture, while local entrepreneurs hoped to position several miniature midways throughout the city, generally at the ends of railway lines. Neither effort was entirely successful. Even amusement parks could become too much of a good thing. As *Midway Magazine* reported in 1906, "Chicago has many proposed parks. They are cropping up on all sides of that Windy City, but many of them seem to be full of wind."[24]

Chicago also experienced a metamorphosis in perceptions and expectations. The name of the city itself and the impressions it evoked shifted perceptively in this era. This subtle reorientation occurred gradually, but it was a change that would forever make the recent past of clamorous self-advertisement seem oddly quaint, even obsolete—as passé as the ornate elegance of Prairie Avenue mansions.

This transformation involved nothing less than a reinvention of the theatrics of cultural presentation. Such were the terms Louis Sullivan used to describe the overwhelming reality of the city:

> It may have been your habit of mind to consider drama as occasional; episodic; an artful presentation merely, as set forth on a stage within an isolated house called a theatre. . . . That is but a little truth. The broader, unescapable truth is that you are ever in the midst of a drama; a drama in the open. You are both spectator and actor therein.[25]

Sullivan was right. The city was a kind of on-going pageant. But gradually the scale and understanding of this drama shifted. A complex transfiguration began to eclipse the earlier sweeping vision of the city, to lesson the possibilities of command and the expectations of an orderly, unified culture. Thinking about the urban world and its peoples through abstractions like betterment, improvement, of imagining a visionary, universal uplifting culture declined with the disappearance of a generation of master builders and evangelical entrepreneurs. The creators of the perfect cities of 1893 had imagined a pageant of marching citizens, like the World's Fair opening-day parade, exhibiting order in diversity, purpose in change, and a public culture applauded by thousands of individuals in unison. They had imagined the city in such terms of command and spectacle. Over time, this vision ceded to a much more confusing picture of Chicago, one that was more intimate, diverse, and private spirited.

Renderings of urban reality as well as the imagination both expressed this reversal of aesthetic possibilities. This occurred most obviously in photography and literature. In March 1893, during the Fair, reformer Jacob Riis arrived in Chicago. Jane Addams arranged walking tours for him through Chicago slums, and he used his camera to record the horrible poverty he encountered. Like his previous work, these photos were stylized—one could hardly avoid that given the technology of the age. But Riis's contrivances, his cropping and framing, had the purpose of erasing distance between the viewer and the viewed. Breaking down this emotional gap, diminishing the safe formality, the quaint and picturesque style of much contemporary photography, Riis supplied the burgeoning settlement house movement with visual evidence of the reality its members confronted daily. Published by the reform press, such photography was a powerful instrument to awaken the conscience of the Progressive movement. Even more to the point, this style of photography altered the way even the press pictured the city. It pressed images of the "black city" onto the everyday consciousness of Chicago's residents and visitors.[26] There could hardly be a greater difference between this and the controlled perspectives of the official photographs of the White City sold at the World's Fair.

The literary texture of Chicago also obtained a rough, more realistic surface. This new style never completely triumphed, but a new generation of writers made the disfigured reality of the city the subject of their novels. Robert Herrick's *Web of Life*, published in 1900, was typical of the new sobriety in presenting Chicago's cityscape. Describing the South Side, he wrote:

> On the southern horizon a sooty cloud hovered above the mills of South Chicago. But, except for the monster chimney, the country ahead of the two was bare, vacant, deserted. This avenue traversed empty lots, mere squares of sand and marsh, cut up in regular patches for future house-builders. Here and there an advertising landowner had cemented a few rods of walk and planted a few trees to trap the possible purchaser into thinking the place "improved."[27]

This realism spawned the remarkable novels of Theodore Dreiser and the poetry of Carl Sandburg, and created a new stereotype of Chicago, as powerful an image even as the swelling skyline had been for a previous generation.

Although Dreiser lived only briefly in Chicago, it was an experience he revisited throughout his novel-writing career. Moving to the city in 1887, he worked at collecting money for a real estate firm and then as a feature writer for the Chicago *Globe*. He wrote later in his autobiography, "Chicago was like a great orchestra in a tumult of noble harmonies. I was like a guest at a feast, eating and drinking in a delirium of ecstasy."[28] But, not all was bliss, for what Dreiser also remembered from his travels throughout the city was immigrant life, slums, and social disorder.

Leaving Chicago before the beginning of the Fair for newspaper work in St. Louis, he shortly went on to Pittsburgh and then, finally, to New York where he stayed. During this period, he worked for several journals including Joseph Pulitzer's *World* and Orsden Swett Marsden's *Success*, where he did sketches of prominent businessmen. In 1899 he began *Sister Carrie*, which he published in 1900.

Although the novel was censored and cut before publication, it still disclosed a new sensibility—a literary realism that pictured Chicago in terms that forever corrected the prevailing fastidious view of the city. Unlike George Ade, Dreiser quite literally entered the rooms and private lives of the residents he observed. He detailed their immoralities, their desperate compromises, and their failures.

Dreiser confronted the city cultures represented at the World's Fair but from a remarkably different perspective.

Like many guidebooks and novels about the city, *Sister Carrie* began with a train trip into the city. Like Moody's prodigal son, Carrie abandons her small town for the perilous metropolis. For her the city presents two forms of life. One compelled hard work and placed Carrie outside the luxurious department stores and consumer culture represented in theaters, hotels, and fashionable resorts—a world where she would be forced to work hard merely to achieve a drab future. The other invited entry into the risky new moral and cultural life of that commercial culture. In this realm, everything was commercialized, even, finally, Carrie's own person.

Yet, in the end, she manages to achieve a form of success and social mobility. Exploiting her talent as an actress, she rises to the top of the new commercial world that had tempted her in her early days in Chicago. Taking advantage of the new mobility, she recreates herself, and with that leaves behind the past from which she emerged. Although Dreiser does not make this a painless accomplishment—indeed, it has tragic consequences for others—Carrie persists.

Dreiser's shocking presentation of social mobility in the world of Chicago's Midway culture was perhaps what the city's elite had always feared about the unregulated commercialism of this part of their city. Dreiser forced the city to look at this world, to see itself whole, and to include that significant portion of society that it had preferred to leave out of its plans for the future.[29]

After *Sister Carrie* there was for Chicago no looking back. The kaleidoscope had turned to change the pattern of perceptions forever. Shafts of realism illuminated new facets of the city. Dreiser's descent into poverty and desperation seemed to empower other writers. Upton Sinclair chose Chicago in 1904 to set his socialist study of the stockyards, and when he published his famous and shocking novel, *The Jungle*, in 1906, the whole nation shared his vision of the city. This work of immigrant life and working conditions in stockyards exposed another world—the exploitation of workers and, by extension, even consumers. Jack London later set his frightening picture of labor violence and repression, *The Iron Heel*, also in Chicago. Indeed, poet Carl Sandburg was probably making the best of it when he called forth contradictory characters of the city, "Hog butcher for the world . . . City of the Big Shoulders . . . wicked . . . brutal . . . Laughing.[30]

Even Chicagoan Frank L. Baum's children's novel, *The Wizard of Oz* (1900), reflected something of this new attitude to the city. Whisked into a fantasy world, Dorothy makes her way to the city— along a path taken by so many young men and women of the age. But once there she discovers the artifice of the place—as if Oz (the White City) wholly depended upon belief in a dream. In this insubstantial world of incomplete people—of characters without hearts or courage—her first wish is to be restored to her farm in Kansas. Perhaps this is what Baum felt constrained to say, giving momentary renewal to a traditional vision of rural social order. But in Baum's many sequels, Dorothy returns, dazzled by the vitality and adventure of glitter and magic. In this slight parody of the tale of the prodigal son, the moral lesson has collapsed entirely: commercial culture is far preferable to the onerous, small morality of rural America.

A different twist of imagination transformed the model city of 1893 from a visionary future into a kind of specimen of urban pathology for academic sociologists. There is an elegant irony in the words of the University of Chicago *Alma Mater* that testifies to this transition:

> The City White has fled the earth
> And where the azure waters lie
> Another city had its birth
> The City Gray that ne'er shall die.[31]

After the Fair burned in 1894, the new gray towers of the University of Chicago stood alone in the wrecked and lonely vista of the abandoned park. As part of its mission, the university dedicated itself, with sustained vigor, to exploring the reality of the city that grew to the north. In the new sociology department, a remarkable group of men developed a theory of the city that made it their laboratory for modern urbanism. In doing so, they helped to design a portrait of the city that helped replace the grand delusions of Pull-

Street in Cairo. Looking onto Cairo Street, it was impossible to miss the buildings of the new University of Chicago rising to the sides of the Midway. (Chicago Historical Society)

man, Moody, and Burnham with a more tangible if modest divination of its future.

In part, the sociology department built upon the work begun by Hull-House surveys and reform agitation. In the first two decades of the twentieth century, Robert Park, W. I. Thomas, Albian Small, and Charles Zueblin, together with John Dewey, Edith Abbott, and Jane Addams developed the exploratory function of urban sociology. The sociologist Frank Tolman described this when he wrote in 1902, "[T]he city of Chicago is one of the most complete social laboratories in the world."[32] In his assessment of contemporary sociology throughout the United States, Tolman explained this in words that almost mocked the boosterism of Chicago guidebooks:

> While elements of sociology may be studied in smaller communities . . . the most serious problems of modern society are presented by the great cities and must be studied as they are encountered in concrete form in large populations. No city in the world presents a wider variety of typical social problems than Chicago.[33]

The origins of this new sociological view of the city lay partly in the reform journalism of the turn of the century. Robert Park, for example, was first a newspaperman interested in the sort of city exposés written by Lincoln Steffens in this period.[34] Typical, too, was the background of Charles R. Henderson, a Protestant minister committed to social reforms. In fact, the sociology department of the University of Chicago became the center of a very large group of social reformers and businessmen and club women dedicated to changing the city.[35]

Eventually, this remarkable collection of sociologists and reformers developed a definition of the urban experience that emphasized the disorienting experience of city life—a distant counterpart to the earlier view. For those who came to the city to live, they wrote, the most important influence upon them was the power of the new culture to destroy what they carried with them. Inevitably, social disorganization became a constant danger in urban growth.[36] If the conclusion of much of this work led to the notion that movement out of the city through concentric rings of culture represented a positive adjustment to American life, then it should come as no surprise. The middle class, which represented its ideal, had, by that time, abandoned the city for its suburbs.[37]

These new conclusions completed a reorientation of the image of Chicago, from the proud harbinger of the future greatness of America's urban experiment in 1893, to the much less optimistic notion that the city might actually stand for all the problems of twentieth-century life. But in a curious way, that very Victorian moment of 1893, that prideful taking stock, that time of experimental "cities" in which the perplexing problem of bringing Chicago's complicated cultures together became something of a model for the rest of the century. The accomplishments of 1893 were modest and swept away by enormous changes, but the problems as posed were neither forgotten nor inconsequential. The twentieth century has continued to experience the same unresolved tensions of cultural struggle between groups in American society. The American middle class, beleaguered by excessive choice, is still unsure of its identity and location between versions of elite culture like the White City and the raw commerce and cultural mobility of the Midway. Again and again, as American subcultures changed and grew and as cultural opportunities expanded and flourished, middle-class and elite groups would unite to thwart the spread of cultural influences from the bottom of society. Time and again, those solutions proposed in 1893 would be revived as ways to deal with, even to conquer the problems of American diversity. But ironically, in the process of failing to stem this cultural turmoil, they would reproduce the complex cultural integration and separation seen so strikingly in Chicago during the year of the Fair.

Notes

PREFACE

1. See Edward Hungerford, script for "Wheels A'Rolling," September 27, 1948, Chicago Historical Society.

CHAPTER ONE

1. Mary P. Ryan, *Cradle of the Middle Class: The Family in Oneida County, 1790–1865* (Cambridge: Cambridge University Press, 1981). It is fascinating that this excellent work describes the region and class from which sprang a good many of Chicago's business and cultural leaders, particularly those discussed in this book.

2. Paul Johnson, *Shopkeepers' Millennium: Society and Revivals in Rochester, New York, 1815–1837* (New York: Hill & Wang, 1978). Johnson argues that the Burned-Over District revivals were crucial in making the middle class and imbuing it with a sense of its place and its responsibilities. He further declares that religion and not class was the principal division in the period that followed. See also John S. Gilkeson, Jr., *Middle Class Providence, 1820–1940* (Princeton: Princeton University Press, 1986).

3. Robert Wiebe, *The Search for Order, 1877–1920* (New York: Hill & Wang, 1967).

4. Burton J. Bledstein, *The Culture of Professionalism: The Middle Class and the Development of Higher Education in America* (New York: W. W. Norton, 1976).

5. Cindy Sondik Aron, *Ladies and Gentlemen of the Civil Service: Middle-Class Workers in Victorian America* (New York: Oxford University Press, 1987).

6. Stuart Blumin, "Black Coats to White Collars: Economic Change, Nonmanual Work, and the Social Structure of Industrializing America," in Stuart W. Bruchey, ed., *Small Business in American Life* (New York: Columbia University Press, 1980), pp. 100–121; Stuart

Blumin, "The Hypothesis of Middle Class Formation in Nineteenth-Century America: A Critique and Some Proposals," *American Historical Review* 90 (April 1985): 299–338.

7. Peter Gay describes America as having the purest bourgeoisie. For my purposes, the term *bourgeoisie* is too inclusive, rising too high in the social scale to include the elites that dominate society—especially at a time when the distinctions between middle class and such elites were becoming important politically. This is not to deny, however, a shared culture, even if it, too, is in the throes of differentiation and segmentation. Peter Gay, *The Bourgeois Experience: Victoria to Freud*, vol. 1, *The Education of the Senses* (New York: Oxford University Press, 1984).

8. An interesting variation on this theme is by William Toll, *The Making of an Ethnic Middle Class* (Albany: State University of New York Press, 1982). In this community study, Toll emphasizes the ethnically diverse middle class in America and the difference that makes in its measurement and history. Stuart Blumin, *The Emergence of the Middle Class: Social Experience in the American City, 1760–1900* (New York: Cambridge University Press, 1989).

9. Dreiser, *Jennie Gerhardt* (New York: Schocken, 1938), pp. 136–137. The novel itself is a marvelous exploration of the confrontation of two cultures in the city: evangelical and commercial.

10. Karen Halttunen, *Confidence Men and Painted Women: A Study of Middle-Class Culture in America, 1830–1870* (New Haven: Yale University Press, 1982).

11. U.S. Bureau of the Census, *Occupations at the 12th Census: Special Reports* (Washington, D.C.: Government Printing Office, 1904), pp. l–liii.

12. This table was constructed using figures assembled by the twelfth census and published in ibid., pp. l–lii. I do not mean to imply that all salespeople had wages significant enough to place them in the middle class. But many aspired to this position, and such hopes helped sharpen social distinctions between white- and blue-collar, manual and nonmanual workers.

13. These conclusions are based upon a comparative analysis of census figures for occupations in the United States, Illinois, and Chicago, for the year 1900. For example, native-born male workers made up more than 90 percent of the U.S. lawyers, telephone and telegraph workers, agricultural laborers, teachers and professors, stenographers and typewriters, and dentists, while the foreign-born dominated tailors, brewers, launderers, hucksters and peddlers, cabinetmakers, bakers, bleachers and cap and hat makers. See *Occupations at the 12th Census*, pp. cxl, cxxii–cxxiii.

14. Ibid., pp. 516 ff.

15. Washington Gladden, *Applied Christianity: Moral Aspects of Social Questions* (Boston: Houghton, Mifflin, 1886), p. 266. In his fascinating new book, Lawrence Levine argues that the 1890s was a time during which the old, universal public culture of the nineteenth century began to give way to class distinctions that could be characterized as "highbrow" and "lowbrow." Based upon the segmentation of society, this new differentiation was, in some respects, the result of an effort by elites to preserve "culture" from corruption by the masses. See Lawrence W. Levine, *Highbrow/Lowbrow: The Emergence of Cultural Hierarchy in America* (Cambridge, Mass.: Harvard University Press, 1988), passim.

16. See Roy Rosenzweig, *Eight Hours for What We Will: Workers and Leisure in an Industrial City, 1870–1920* (Cambridge: Cambridge University Press, 1983); John F. Kasson, *Amusing the Million: Coney Island at the Turn of the Century* (New York: Hill & Wang, 1978); Kathy Peiss, *Cheap Amusements: Working Women and Leisure in Turn-of-the-Century New York* (Philadelphia: Temple University Press, 1986); Elizabeth Ewen, *Immigrant Women in the Land of Dollars: Life and Culture on the Lower East Side, 1890–1925* (New York: Monthly Review Press, 1985). There are two important aspects to the point made by these authors. One is that new cultural tendencies responded to the special conditions of life in the American city among immigrants and lower-class Americans. The second, less stressed than it might be, is the enormous influence that these new cultural elements exercised on the rest of society even as they were absorbed and distorted by commercialization and mainstreaming.

17. Paul S. Boyer, *Urban Masses and Moral Order in America, 1820–1920* (Cambridge, Mass.: Harvard University Press, 1978), pp. 221, 1–7; see especially his comments on Chicago.

18. Jean-Christophe Agnew, *Worlds Apart: The Market and the Theater in Anglo-American Thought, 1550–1750* (Cambridge: Cambridge University Press, 1986), pp. x ff. See also Roger Abrahams, "The Discovery of Marketplace Culture," *Intellectual History Newsletter* 10 (April 1988): 28–29.

19. Michail Bakhtin, *Rabelais and His World*, trans. Helen Iswolsky (Bloomington: Indiana University Press, 1984), pp. 7 ff, 33, 153, 181–188. See also Katerina Clark and Michael Holquist, *Mikhail Bakhtin* (Cambridge, Mass.: Harvard University Press, 1984), pp. 301–320.

20. See Fredric Jameson, "Postmodernism & Consumer Society," in Hal Foster, *The Anti-Aesthetic: Essays on Postmodern Culture* (Port Townsend, Wash: Bay Press, 1983), pp. 111–125.

21. There are some interesting parallels between the growth of Chicago and Berlin. Like Berlin, Chicago was a center of immigration from

Central Europe, for example. See John Henry Zammito, "Art and Avant-Garde in the Metropolis: The Berlin Avant-Garde, 1900–1930" (Ph.D. diss., University of California, Berkeley, 1978), p. 42 ff.

22. Alan Trachtenberg, "Image and Ideology: New York in the Photographer's Eye," *Journal of Urban History* 10 (August 1984): 455. He continues that the effort to "locate" the city helped inspire efforts to explore and proclaim the aesthetics of cities.

23. Halttunen, *Confidence Men*.

24. Louis Wirth, "Urbanism as a Way of Life," *American Journal of Sociology* 44 (July 1938): 15–20. This is an early article but one that I find very useful. Alan Marcus writes that the early nineteenth-century city was predicated upon the notion of homogeneity. But rapid social and economic change added diversity to this original base until in the 1890s contemporary observers identified the city in terms of its discrete social systems and hierarchical parts. See Alan I. Marcus, "Back to the Present: Historians' Treatment of the City as a Social System during the Reign of the Idea of Community," in Howard Gillette, Jr., and Zane L. Miller, *American Urbanism: A Historiographical Review* (New York: Greenwood Press, 1987), pp. 9–17.

25. Gunther P. Barth, *City People: The Rise of Modern City Culture in Nineteenth-Century America* (New York: Oxford University Press, 1980), p. 232. Barth argues that this organization of the city declines with the coming of the automobile. It seems to me that Barth has romanticized the early period a bit, in which case his contrast to the present is not entirely valid.

26. Peter Hales, *Silver Cities: The Photography of American Urbanization, 1839–1915* (Philadelphia: Temple University Press, 1984), pp. 69–76, 120. Hales is particularly persuasive in his discussion of early photography and the camera angle used to stress permanence and monumentality.

27. James Schmiechen, "Victorians, the Historians, and the Idea of Modernism," *American Historical Review* 93 (April 1988): 315.

28. See Michael Ebner, "Re-Reading Suburban America: Urban Population Deconcentration, 1810–1980," in Gillette and Miller, *American Urbanism*, pp. 229–231. See also Ebner's larger work, *Creating Chicago's North Shore: A Suburban History* (Chicago: University of Chicago Press, 1988), passim.

29. Kenneth T. Jackson, *Crabgrass Frontier: The Suburbanization of the United States* (New York: Oxford University Press, 1985); Robert Fishman, *Bourgeois Utopias: The Rise and Fall of Suburbia* (New York: Basic Books, 1987). Fishman places the 1890s in about the middle of the suburban development, beyond the first tentative suburbs but not like the post–World War II versions. This reflects a similar evolution of the city, from its early

form in the mid-nineteenth century to the decentralized cities like Los Angeles surrounded by its exurbs. Fishman also notes that the particular form of city/suburb relationship was not inevitable, citing very different arrangements in France.

30. Helen Rosenau, *The Ideal City: Its Architectural Evolution in Europe*, 3d ed. (London: Methuen & Co., 1983), pp. 2, 162–176.

31. Andrew Lees, "The Metropolis and the Intellectual," in Anthony Sutcliffe, ed., *Metropolis: 1890–1940* (Chicago: University of Chicago Press, 1984), pp. 68–73.

32. Halttunen, *Confidence Men*, introduction, pp. 2–30.

33. Daniel Boorstin, *The Image: A Guide to Pseudo-Events in America* (New York: Athenaeum, 1961), pp. 28–101; Paul Fussell, "Bourgeois Travel: Techniques and Artifacts," in J. G. Links, ed., *Bon Voyage: Designs for Travel* (New York: Cooper-Hewitt Museum, 1968), pp. 55–93.

34. Dean MacCannell, *The Tourist: A New Theory of the Leisure Class* (New York: Schocken Books, 1976), pp. 13, 55. Yi-Fu Tuan has very perceptively written that "[h]uman places become vividly real through dramatization." See his *Space and Place: The Perspective of Experience* (Minneapolis: University of Minnesota Press, 1977), p. 178.

CHAPTER TWO

1. Everett Chamberlin, *Chicago and Its Suburbs* (New York: Arno Press [1874], 1974), passim. This remarkable book, bubbling with boosterism after the Chicago Fire, lists a great variety of suburban areas with several sorts of origins. Some grew up alongside railroad lines. Some were organized by land companies. Some were purchased by religious groups. Some were little satellite cities reproducing Chicago's variety itself. Others were refuges from the city, tending toward homogeneity of origin and income.

2. Asa Briggs, *Victorian Cities*, rev. ed. (Harmondsworth: Penguin Books, 1968), p. 56. See also Eric Lampard's essay on the general changes in late Victorian cities of which Chicago was exemplary: "The Urbanizing World," in H. J. Dyos and Michael Wolff, eds., *The Victorian City: Images and Realities*, 2 vols. (London: Routledge & Kegan Paul, 1973), pp. 3–57.

3. Michael H. Ebner and Eugene M. Tobin, "Introduction," *The Age of Urban Reform: New Perspectives on the Progressive Era* (Port Washington, N.Y.: Kennikat Press, 1977), pp. 44–48.

4. Ibid., pp. 44–45, 51–53. Of course, suburban areas had long tried to distinguish themselves from Chicago. Morgan Park and Beverly in Illinois are two contiguous areas that did so early on. See Harold M. Mayer and Richard C. Wade, *Chicago: Growth of a Metropolis* (Chicago: University of Chicago Press, 1969), pp. 160–170.

5. Louise Carroll Wade, *Chicago's Pride: The Stockyards, Packingtown, and Environs in the Nineteenth Century* (Urbana: University of Illinois Press, 1987), p. xiv. Over 1 million World's Fair visitors saw the stockyards in 1893.

6. Irving Cutler, *Chicago: Metropolis of the Mid Continent*, 3d ed. (Dubuque: Geographic Society of Chicago, 1982), p. 177.

7. U.S. Department of the Interior, Census Office, *Population by Color, Sex and General Nativity at the 11th Census*, June 1, 1890 (Washington, D.C.: Government Printing Office, 1893), pp. 8–9: this percent of foreign-born to native-born compares to that of New York, pp. 2–5. See Helen R. Jeter, *Trends in Population in the Region of Chicago* (Chicago: University of Chicago Press, 1927), pp. 33–34; Cutler, *Chicago*, p. 45.

8. Jeter, *Trends in Population*, pp. 31–32.

9. U.S. Department of the Interior, Census Office, *Compendium of the 11th Census, 1890, part I, Population* (Washington, D.C.: Government Printing Office, 1892), p. 544.

10. Ibid., p. 900.

11. U.S. Department of Interior, U. S. Census, *Compendium of the 11th Census, parts I–III* (Washington, D.C.: Government Printing Office, 1897), p. 965; U.S. Department of Interior, Census Office, *Report of the Social Statistics of Cities in the United States, 11th Census, 1890* (Washington, D.C.: Government Printing Office, 1895), pp. 133–134. Interest rates for mortgages were also slightly higher in Chicago generally than in Boston or Philadelphia.

12. Carroll Wright, *The Slums of Baltimore, Chicago, New York, and Philadelphia, Special Report of the Commissioner of Labor*, 53d Cong., 2d sess. (Washington, D.C.: Government Printing Office, 1894), pp. 12–30. U.S. Census, *Social Statistics*, p. 58.

13. U.S. Department of Interior, Census Office, *Abstract of the 11th Census, 1890* (Washington, D.C.: Government Printing Office, 1894), p. 137.

14. John W. Tebbel, *A History of Book Publishing in the United States*, vol. 2 (New York: R. R. Bowker, 1975), pp. 21–23, 170.

15. Wright, *The Slums of Baltimore, Chicago, New York, and Philadelphia*, p. 14.

16. U.S. Census, *Social Statistics*, pp. 41, 108; U.S. Census, *Occupations at the 12th Census*, pp. 516–518.

17. U.S. Census, *Occupations at the 12th Census*, p. cxc. Although this is generally a valid comparison of American-born and immigrant occupations, persons of German descent were slightly less likely to be working class and experienced greater mobility than some other groups. See Harmut

Keil, "Chicago's German Working Class in 1900," in Keil and John B. Jentz, *German Workers in Industrial Chicago: A Comparative Perspective* (DeKalb: Northern Illinois University Press, 1983), pp. 21–30.

18. U.S. Census, *Occupations at the 12th Census*, p. 516.

19. In domestic and manufacturing pursuits, the foreign-born tended to dominate such industries as baking, brickmaking, butchering, carpentry, iron and steel and machinists. Positions such as sales and clerking, however, were open to the foreign-born, and large percentages of them took advantage of these opportunities. U.S. Census, *Occupations at the 12th Census*, p. cxc.

20. U.S. Bureau of the Census, *Historical Statistics of the United States: Colonial Times to 1960*, pt. 1 (Washington, D.C.: Government Printing Office, 1975), pp. 167–168. In current, 1970 dollars. These are very approximate estimates, but they do show that farm laborers, school teachers, domestics, and, in general miners and manufacturing wage earners occupied the bottom of the employment wage pyramid with government employees, clerks, etc. in the middle, and postal, finance, real estate, and federal workers toward the top.

21. W. Lloyd Warner and James C. Abegglen, *Big Business Leaders in America* (New York: Harper & Bros., 1955), pp. 21–33, 178–79. Warner finds even in 1955 that the business elite came disproportionately from New England, mid-Atlantic, and Eastern North Central origins. See also F. W. Taussig and C. S. Joslyn, *American Business Leaders; A Study in Social Origins and Social Stratification* (New York: MacMillan Co., 1932), pp. 80 ff.

22. Richard Sennett, *Families against the City: Middle Class Homes of Industrial Chicago, 1872–1890* (Cambridge, Mass.: Harvard University Press, 1970), pp. 42, 54, 96. Eric Lampard suggests that a profound pessimism surrounded commentators on the city in the late Victorian period. Lampard, "Urbanizing World," pp. 27–29.

23. John V. Farwell, "Introduction," in John T. Dale, *The Secret of Success or Finger Posts on the Highway of Life* (Chicago: Fleming H. Revell, 1889), p. vii. Significantly, Farwell sets his moral cautionary tale on a train going to the city from the countryside, and he half-consciously refers to the tale of the Prodigal Son in describing the temptations of the young boy who has just left his mother's side.

24. Witten McDonald of First National Bank of Kansas City, to Turlington W. Harvey, May 19, 1887, Turlington Harvey papers, Harvey, Ill. (hereafter cited as Harvey MS).

25. Greg Singleton, "The Genesis of Suburbia: A Complex of Historical Trends," in Louis H. Masotti and Jeffrey K. Hadden, eds., *The Urbaniza-*

tion of the Suburbs (Beverly Hills, Calif.: Sage Publications, 1973), pp. 30–45; Robert Fishman, *Urban Utopias in the Twentieth Century: Ebenezer Howard, Frank Lloyd Wright and le Corbusier* (New York: Basic Books, 1977), pp. 109 ff. Humbert Nelli argues that Italians, unlike earlier Germans and Irish, were slower to move out of the urban core, thus helping to solidify the urban/suburban and intercity residential segregation. See Nelli, *Italians in Chicago: 1880–1930: A Study in Ethnic Mobility* (New York: Oxford University Press, 1970), pp. 27–28.

26. Everett Chamberlin, *Chicago and Its Suburbs*, p. 382.

27. Helen Lefkowitz Horowitz, *Culture and the City: Cultural Philanthropy in Chicago from the 1890s to 1917* (Lexington: University of Kentucky Press, 1976), p. 48.

28. There are a number of other institutions that accomplish the same end, but it seems to me to be no accident that the great movement to establish these institutions occurred in the 1890s.

29. Daniel Burnham and Edward A Bennett, *Plan of Chicago:* Prepared under the Direction of the Commercial Club, during the years 1906, 1907, 1908, ed. Charles Moore, (Chicago: Commercial Club, 1909), pp. 8, 99 ff.

30. Christiane Harzig, "Chicago's German North Side, 1880–1900: The Structure of a Gilded Age Ethnic Neighborhood," in Keil and Jentz, *German Workers in Industrial Chicago*, p. 129.

31. Bernard Duffey, *The Chicago Renaissance in American Letters: A Critical History* (East Lansing: Michigan State Press, 1954), pp. 134 ff. Duffey argues that by the mid-1920s the Chicago Renaissance had died.

32. Lewis Erenberg, "Ain't We Got Fun," *Chicago History* 14 (Winter 1985–1986): 4–10; Perry Duis, "Whose City? Public and Private Places in Nineteenth-Century Chicago," pts. 1 and 2, *Chicago History* 12 (Spring and Summer 1983): 4–27 and 3–23. In his second article, Duis notes four strategies to control this new culture: social and moral solutions, technological solutions, and the creation of the semipublic institution designed to screen out undesirables and therefore regulate behavior inside. An example might be a theater or baseball park that charged admission.

33. Ray Ginger gives a particularly dramatic picture of this struggle in *Altgeld's America: The Lincoln Ideal versus Changing Realities* (Chicago: Funk & Wagnells Co., 1958), passim.

34. Burnham and Bennett, *Plan of Chicago*, p. 51.

35. Kathleen D. McCarthy, *Noblesse Oblige: Charity and Cultural Philanthropy in Chicago, 1849–1929* (Chicago: University of Chicago Press, 1982), pp. 57 ff. McCarthy discusses the difference between two genera-

tions of businessmen-philanthropists. The second group, she argues, had stronger class feelings and a belief in "self-culture."

36. When I was assembling the information in this table about the backgrounds of key figures, I was impressed with the uniformity of their early religious experience and its geographic unity—except in the important instance of Harlow Higinbotham. He hailed from Illinois, and his parents were Dutch immigrants. I discovered, however, that in making their way to Joliet the parents had stopped in Oneida, New York, where they converted to Methodism. Thus, the exception appears to confirm the rule.

37. Joseph Kirkland, *The Story of Chicago*, 2 vols. (Chicago: Dibble Publishing Co., 1892), 1:335. See Helen Lefkowitz Horowitz, "The Art Institute of Chicago: The First Forty Years," *Chicago History* 8 (Spring 1979): 5, for discussion of the leadership and intentions of the board of directors of the Chicago Art Institute.

38. Whitney R. Cross, *The Burned-over District: The Social and Intellectual History of Enthusiastic Religion in Western New York, 1800–1850* (New York: Harper & Row, 1950), pp. 3–13.

39. Keith Hardman, *Charles Grandeson Finney 1792–1875: Revivalist and Reformer* (Syracuse: Syracuse University Press, 1987), pp. 176–177.

40. Hardman, *Charles Finney*, pp. 280, 343.

41. Michael Barkun, *Crucible of the Millennium: The Burned-over District of New York in the 1840s* (Syracuse: Syracuse University Press, 1986), pp. 31–82, 104. Barkun argues that two waves of unsettling economic change were crucial in driving these religious movements: first, the enormous explosion of population movement into the fertile valleys of the area; and then the economic calamity of 1837 to 1840.

42. Ibid., p. 151.

43. Harlow N. Higinbotham, "The Making of a Merchant," *Saturday Evening Post* pamphlet (Philadelphia: Curtis Publishing, 1900), pp. 3–5, 7–10.

44. Ibid., p. 11.

45. Oliver McKee, Jr., "Super-Salesman of Patriotism: A Portrait of Sol Bloom, Promoter of Washington's Bicentennial," *Outlook* 160, 3 February 1932, p. 139.

46. "Sol Bloom," *Current Biography* (New York: T. W. Wilson Co., 1943), pp. 55–56. During the early 1930s, Bloom was appointed co-commissioner of the federal commission to celebrate the bicentennial of the birth of George Washington. His appointment caused considerable comment, because of his reputation as a showman and, perhaps, because he was Jewish and came from immigrant stock. Those who reacted to the appointment of

a popular culture entrepreneur to celebrate the birth of America's Founding Father undoubtedly objected to the transformation of history into a salable commodity. Bloom made no pretense that this was not his purpose. As he said, "What we must do is to sell George Washington to the country. We must teach the biggest lesson in history ever given. We must create a demand for our product." To make sure of success, he hired historian Albert Bushnell Hart to check the facts in all the commission's publications, and George M. Cohan to write a theme song: "Father of the Land We Love." See Oliver McKee, Jr., "Super-Salesman of Patriotism," pp. 140, 146.

47. Sol Bloom, *The Autobiography of Sol Bloom* (New York: G. P. Putnam's, 1948), passim.

CHAPTER THREE

1. Lewis Mumford, *The Culture of Cities* (New York: Harcourt Brace Jovanovich [1938], 1981), p. 265.

2. Harry Carr, *Los Angeles: City of Dreams* (New York: D. Appleton-Century, 1935), p. 233; see also John A. Jakle, *The Tourist: Travel in Twentieth-Century North America* (Lincoln: University of Nebraska Press, 1985), p. 264, for an almost identical description of Los Angeles.

3. Asa Briggs, *Victorian Cities*, p. 27. Briggs says that Manchester, England; Chicago; and Los Angeles were each the shock cities of their day. Hugh Duncan, in his marvelous book *Culture and Democracy* published in 1965 looks at Chicago through the eyes of Louis Sullivan and modernism. He describes the coming together of a comprehensive and brilliant social analysis in the works of Dewey, Addams, Mead, Sullivan, Wright, Dreiser, and Veblen, in which the notion of form and function, subtly defined, becomes a decisive measure of art, philosophy, social policy, and architecture. The Chicago I am describing existed alongside this sophisticated modernism, participated, in some respects, in it but is, nonetheless different. See Hugh Dalziel Duncan, *Culture and Democracy: The Struggle for Form in Society and Architecture in Chicago and the Middle West during the Life and Times of Louis H. Sullivan* (New York: Bedminster Press, 1965), passim.

4. Knight, Leonard & Co., *Guide to the Columbian World's Fair*, rev. ed. (Chicago: Knight, Leonard & Co., 1892), p. 2.

5. Robert Herrick, *The Gospel of Freedom* (New York: MacMillan Co., 1898), pp. 102 ff. Herrick's description builds to an energetic climax of activity.

6. Daniel H. Burnham and Edward H. Bennett, *Plan of Chicago*, p. 124. Burnham made statements like this for several years.

7. Henry Justin Smith, *Chicago's Great Century, 1833–1933* (Chicago: Consolidated Publishers, 1933), p. 114.

8. Louise Wade notes that over 1 million tourists visited the Chicago Stockyards in 1893. See Louise Carroll Wade, *Chicago's Pride*, p. xiv.

9. In 1892, Florence Pullman wrote to her sister, Hattie, of a recent society bazaar in Chicago: "Of course you [have?] the Chicago papers this week, and if you have read them thoroughly you have a much better idea of the Bazar [*sic*] than I could attempt to write you." Florence Pullman to Hattie Pullman, Chicago, [?] 1892, Papers of Harriet Sanger Pullman, 1883–1943, Box 8, Chicago Historical Society (hereafter cited as Harriet Pullman MS). If this recounting of society's comings and goings was one purpose of major newspapers, so were the very different slice-of-life articles of writers like George Ade. Thus, even in journalism, Chicago's social classes vied for the same space.

10. Ade called his book of stories published in 1903 *In Babel: Stories of Chicago* (New York: McClure, Phillips, 1903).

11. George Ade, *Artie: A Story of the Streets and Town* (Chicago: Herbert Stone & Co., 1896), p. 39.

12. George Ade, "From the Office Window," *Stories of the Streets and of the Town from the Chicago Record, 1893–1900*, ed. Franklin J. Meine (Chicago: Carleton Club, 1941), pp. 167–171; George Ade, "The Advantage of Being Middle Class," *Chicago Stories* (Chicago: Henry Regnery Co., 1963), pp. 75–79. In another sketch, "An Experiment in Philanthropy," Ade uses the humorous entanglement of his narrator in the affairs of the object of his charity, to suggest placing charity on a cash basis in order to maintain an appropriate distance.

13. Dreiser did not just break with the sentimental realism of Ade in his writings. Dreiser's brother, Paul Dresser, represented another sort of sentimental/realist urban perspective that Dreiser rejected. A Broadway blade and portly roué, a frequenter of the seamier side of Broadway's Victorian counterculture, Dresser was also the author of several sentimental ballads celebrating motherhood and rural nostalgia including "My Gal Sal" and "The Banks of the Wabash."

14. Barbara C. Schaaf, *Mr. Dooley's Chicago* (New York: Doubleday, 1977), pp. 20–38.

15. These are the top five of the most widely borrowed library novels from a list compiled in 1893 by Hamilton W. Mabie. It is possible that the *Scarlet Letter* was read as a sentimental novel. See Hamilton W. Mabie, "The Most Popular Novels in America," *Forum* 14 (December 1893): 508–516.

16. Irving Cutler, *Chicago: Metropolis of the Mid Continent*, p. 45.

17. Henry Fuller, *The Cliff Dwellers* (Ridgewood, N.J.: Gregg Press [1893], 1968), pp. 53–54.

18. Hamlin Garland, *Crumbling Idols*, ed. Jane Johnson (Cambridge, Mass: Harvard University Press [1894], 1960), pp. 117–119.

19. Julian Ralph, *Harper's Chicago and the World's Fair* (New York: Harper & Brothers, 1893), p. 82.

20. Philip Forstall to author, 8 August 1988. Mr. Forstall, of the Rand McNally company, suggests that about 100,000 sales of guidebooks by the company in 1893 is a safe estimate.

21. There is no sure way to estimate how many Chicago visitors bought or consulted guidebooks to the city and to the Fair. Nonetheless, given the huge number of published guides and the known figures (probably 100,000 for Rand McNally and perhaps as many as 300,000 for Conkey's official guides), the number is undoubtedly quite significant.

22. Karen Halttunen, *Confidence Men*, introduction and pp. 2–30. Halttunen uses the concept of "liminality" to describe the transitional state she finds in the behavior of urban middle classes.

23. Alan K. Henrikson, "The Geographical 'Mental Maps' of American Foreign Policy Makers," *International Political Science Review* 1 (October 1980): 498.

24. Kevin Lynch, *The Image of the City* (Cambridge, Mass.: M.I.T. Press, 1960). Lynch calls this quality "legibility," pp. 3–4, passim. Michel de Certeau suggests the possibility that art, literature, and other symbolic forms can create compelling visions of the city that order experience, yet exist "in a perspective that no eye had yet enjoyed." See Michel de Certeau, *The Practice of Everyday Life* (Berkeley: University of California Press, 1984), pp. 92–95.

25. Quoted in Bernard Duffy, *The Chicago Renaissance in American Letters*, p. 43.

26. Carroll Ryan, *Chicago, the Magnificent* (New York: J. P. Williams, 1893), p. 43.

27. James S. Duncan has perceptively argued that the tourist's experience is generally colored by interaction with such intermediaries as guides and tour books. These translate experience either into "familiar terms" or "unique and quaint"—in both cases isolating an impression from the everyday experience of the traveler. I would add that such intermediaries probably do both, to extend the familiar into the unique, the quaint, and, in this particular case, the futuristic. See Duncan, "The Social Construction of Unreality: An Interactionist Approach to the Tourist's Cognition of Envi-

ronment," in David Ley and Marilyn S. Samuels, eds., *Humanistic Geography: Prospects and Problems* (Chicago: Maurouta Press, 1978), pp. 274–276.

28. Quoted from Lennox Bouton Grey, "Chicago and 'The Great American Novel': A Critical Approach to the American Epic" (Ph.D. diss., University of Chicago, 1935), p. 405.

29. This chapter is based upon a reading of about thirty-five such guidebooks and related histories published primarily in 1892 and 1893, with a few exceptions included to provide perspective on the changing format of the genre. One of the most remarkable aspects of these publications is the uniformity of style, purpose, information, and presentation. Their authors tended to be journalists, small publishers, and, of course, writers commissioned by larger publishers such as Rand McNally.

30. Trumbell White and William Igleheart, *The World's Columbian Exposition* (Philadelphia: P. W. Ziegler, 1893), p. 11.

31. Ralph, *Harper's Chicago*, p. 30.

32. Ralph, *Harper's Chicago*, p. 82. A great many of the guidebooks reproduced the same population chart showing representative numbers of each nationality.

33. Irving Cutler, *Chicago: Metropolis of the Mid Continent*, p. 277. See also Homer Hoyt, *One Hundred Years of Land Values in Chicago* (New York: Arno Press [1933], 1970), pp. 142–155.

34. A. T. Burley, *The Stranger's Guide to the City of Chicago . . . Also a Complete and Reliable Directory to the Business Houses and Streets* (Chicago: Knight & Leonard, 1874); *A Guide to the City of Chicago: A Stranger's Hand-Book* (Chicago: T. Ellwood Zell, 1868); Frank Glossop, *A Guide to the Hotels, Restaurants and Amusements of Chicago* (Chicago: Glossop & Edwards, 1880–1881); Albert N. Marquis, *Marquis' Hand-Book of Chicago* (Chicago: A. N. Marquis, 1885). This older sort of handbook persisted. In 1896, Rand McNally published *Unrivaled Chicago* which also included a weighty center section on businesses and businessmen. Marquis wrote another guidebook in 1893.

35. Harold Vynne, *Chicago by Day and Night: The Pleasure Seeker's Guide to the Paris of America* (Chicago: Thomas & Zimmermann, 1892). See also Dan Czitrom, "The Tabloid Tradition in Commercial Culture" (unpublished paper presented to the American Studies Association meeting of 24 November 1987).

36. Albert N. Marquis, *Ready Reference Guide to Chicago and the World's Columbian Exposition* (Chicago: A. N. Marquis, 1893), p. 201.

37. Minnie Gardiner, "Enquire Within" (Chicago: Minnie Gardiner, 1892). Authors include male and female journalists, publishers, and writers.

38. Martha J. Parker, "How to See the World's Fair with Little Money" (Chicago, 1893), pp. 6–10. See also Thomas E. Hill, *Hill's Souvenir Guide to Chicago and the World's Fair* (Chicago: Laird & Lee, 1892), p. 68. Hill also gives various salaries in Chicago: a brakeman, $650 per year; bricklayer, $5 per day; teacher $450–$1,000 per year; day laborer, $2 per day. Comparable wages elsewhere would confirm the extreme difficulty of making the trip to Chicago for certain classes of Americans, p. 154.

39. Charles D. Powers, *Heart of Chicago: At a Glance, Free Guide* (Chicago: Advancement Association, 1891), p. 1. This curious publication was distributed free at some of Chicago's hotels. Its purpose was, clearly, to advertise for the Cosmopolitan Dispensary, a medical center. Nonetheless, its language is quite typical.

40. Robert Musket, *Chicago, Yesterday and To-day: A Guide to the Garden City and the Columbian Exposition* (Chicago: Donohue & Henneberry, 1893), pp. 18 ff.

41. Author unknown, *Godey's Illustrated Souvenir Guide to the Chicago World's Fair and New York* (New York: E. Lockwood & Co., 1893), passim.

42. Even when the opening chosen by a writer employed a different tactic, most guidebooks introduced the themes of cultural and ethnic multiplicity at some point in their work. For everyone, it was a defining attribute of the city.

43. Rand McNally, *Handy Guide to Chicago and the World's Columbian Exposition* (Chicago: Rand McNally & Co., 1893), pp. 31 ff.

44. Hill, *Souvenir Guide to Chicago*, pp. 68 ff.

45. John J. Flinn, *Chicago: The Marvelous City of the West*, 2d ed. (Chicago: Standard Guide Co., 1892), frontispiece, pp. 17–18.

46. Hubert H. Bancroft, *Book of the Fair*, 2 vols. (Chicago: Bancroft Co., 1895), 1:35; Robert Mushet, *Chicago, Yesterday and To-day*, pp. 4–8.

47. Ryan, *Chicago, the Magnificent*, pp. 3, 11.

48. *A History of the City of Chicago: Its Men and Institutions* (Chicago: Inter Ocean, 1900), p. 18.

49. Yi-Fu Tuan, *Space and Place*, p. 65. I have reversed Tuan's fascinating formulation that "[t]he world feels spacious and friendly when it accommodates our desires, and cramped when it frustrates them." My paraphrase would be: when the world looks spacious and friendly, it seems to accommodate our desires and fantasies.

50. Moses P. Handy, *The Official Directory of the World Columbian Exposition* (Chicago: W. B. Conkey Co., 1893), p. 43.

51. Burnham and Bennett, *Plan of Chicago*, pp. 87, 117.

52. Rand McNally, *Handy Guide to Chicago*, passim.

53. Louis Schick, *Chicago and Its Environs* (Chicago: F. P. Kenkel, 1893), passim, p. 100.

54. David Lowenthal, *The Past as a Foreign Country* (Cambridge: Cambridge University Press, 1985), pp. 93–121, 215. Lowenthal notes that the Haymarket affair was particularly important in touching off nostalgia for the past.

55. For example, see Ernest Ingersoll, *A Week in New York* (New York: Rand McNally, 1892). This guide is particularly comprehensive. See also Taintor Brothers, *The City of New York: A Complete Guide* (New York: Taintor Bros., 1895); and Cornwell Childe, *New York: A Guide in Comprehensive Chapters* (Brooklyn: Brooklyn Eagle, 1903). The writer was editor of [New York's] "Trolley Exploring." The *New York Sun* Guidebook in particular stressed the city's culture. See H. Swingstone, *The Sun's Guide to New York: Replies to Questions Asked Every Day by the Guests of Citizens of the American Metropolis* (Jersey City: R. Wayne Wilson, 1892).

CHAPTER FOUR

1. State of Wisconsin, "Visitor's Register, World's Columbian Exposition, 1893," July–September 1893. World's Fair Documents, vol. 54, Chicago Historical Society.

2. George Ade et al., *The Chicago Record's History of the World's Fair*, (Chicago: Chicago Daily News Co., 1893), p. 55.

3. Theodore Dreiser, "Third Day at the Fair," *The Republic*, 20 July 1893, p. 5.

4. Theodore Dreiser, *A History of Myself: Newspaper Days* (New York: Horace Liveright, 1931), p. 252. On 4 June 1893, the *Chicago Sunday Post*, in a short piece, "M'Neery at the Fair," describes a visit by two Irishmen who insist upon going to the Irish Exhibit.

5. Frances M. Glessner Journal, transcript for 16 April 1893, p. 63. Frances M. Glessner Manuscripts, Chicago Historical Society (hereafter cited as Glessner MS).

6. Glessner Journal, 18 June 1893, p. 97, Glessner MS.

7. James S. Duncan, "The Social Construction of Unreality: An Interactionist Approach to the Tourist's Cognition of Environment," in David Ley and Marilyn S. Samuels, *Humanistic Geography*, p. 277.

8. See Robert W. Rydell, *All the World's a Fair: Visions of Empire at American International Expositions, 1876–1916* (Chicago: University of Chicago Press, 1985); and Alan Trachtenberg, *The Incorporation of America: Culture and Society in the Gilded Age* (New York: Hill & Wang, 1982); Ernest Poole, *Giants Gone: Men Who Made Chicago* (New York: McGraw-Hill, 1943), p. 184.

9. Louis Sullivan, *The Autobiography of an Idea* (New York: Dover, 1956), p. 325. Sullivan's words quite possibly relate to the infection of syphilis, widely known by this time to cause brain lesions. See Terra Ziporyn, *Disease in the Popular American Press* (New York: Greenwood, 1988), pp. 114 ff.

10. See in particular Hugh Dalziel Duncan, *Culture and Democracy*. Other historians echo Sullivan's judgments. See, for example, Elliott Gorn, *The Manly Art: Bare-Knuckle Prize Fighting in America* (Ithaca: Cornell University Press, 1986), p. 247. See also Harold M. Mayer and Richard C. Wade, *Chicago*, p. 196.

11. Dimitri Tselos, "The Chicago Fair and the Myth of the 'Lost Cause,'" *Journal of the Society of Architectural Historians* 26 (December 1967): 259–268; and Robert Knutson, "The White City: The World's Columbian Exposition of 1893" (Ph.D. diss., Columbia University, 1956), esp. pp. 98–116.

12. Trachtenberg, *Incorporation of America*, pp. 209–225.

13. Rydell, *All the World's a Fair*, p. 236. There may be a general "evolutionary" movement in the arrangement of concessions on the Midway, but there are so many exceptions that it is hardly apparent. See also Hales, *Silver Cities*, pp. 69–71. Hales argues that the photographic work on the Fair tended to stress monumentality and privilege.

14. John F. Kasson, *Amusing the Million*, pp. 23–26. This short book is very rich in ideas and assessments of the Fair.

15. Russell Lewis, "Everything under One Roof: World's Fairs and Department Stores in Paris and Chicago," *Chicago Historical Review* 12 (Fall 1983): 29–43. Russell summarizes by saying that the Fair was "the idea of the department store applied to a city scale." Neil Harris uses the World's Fair as an incident in the evolution of various forms of public spaces such as museums and department stores. This marvelous article demonstrates the interchangeability and distinctions between these formats of public presentation of objects. See Harris, "Museums, Merchandising, and Popular Taste: The Struggle for Influence," in Ian M. G. Quimby, *Material Culture and the Study of American Life* (New York: W. W. Norton, 1978), pp. 140–174.

16. Lewis Mumford, *The Culture of Cities*, p. 265. In many respects, Mumford's theory is close to that of Mikhail Bakhtin. See Mikhail Bakhtin, *Rabelais and His World*, 1984.

17. David Burg, *Chicago's White City of 1893* (Lexington: University Press of Kentucky, 1976), p. 101. There is some dispute about Burnham's actual power in making decisions and, therefore, his role in nationalizing the architecture of the Fair. See Titus M. Karlowicz, "D. H. Burnham's

Role in the Selection of Architects for the World's Columbian Exposition," *Journal of the Society of Architectural Historians* 29 (October 1970): 247–254.

18. Ben C. Truman et al., *History of the World's Fair* (Philadelphia: H. W. Kelley, 1893), p. 31; Kasson, *Amusing the Million*, p. 17; Burg, *White City*, pp. 101–105; and Reid Badger, *The Great American Fair: The World's Columbian Exposition and American Culture* (Chicago: Nelson Hall, 1979), p. 56.

19. The gist of the attack is that Burnham, in opening the central core of the White City to conservative New York architects, betrayed the dynamism and virtue of Chicago architecture. See Rober Knutson, "The White City," p. 64.

20. E. C. Shankland, "The Construction of Buildings, Bridges, etc. at the World's Columbian Exposition," *Inland Architect and News Record* 22 (August 1893): 8–9.

21. F. D. Millet, "The Designers of the Fair," *Harper's* 85 (November 1892): 878. Millet concluded by saying that the architects could perfect ancient architecture in a way that no autocrat or government ever could. In another article, Millet wrote that the interior structures satisfied the spirit of form following function, although he did not use this term. "I refer to the wonderfully beautiful iron-work of these buildings, which satisfies to an eminent degree both the utilitarian and aesthetic requirements." See Millet, "The Decoration of the Exposition," in *Some Artists at the Fair* (New York: Charles Scribner's Sons, 1893), p. 10.

22. Bloom, *The Autobiography of Sol Bloom*, pp. 106, 199–215. This work seems very forthright, but it should be read with some caution. Bloom promoted himself as skillfully as he promoted his acts.

23. Daniel Burnham, "Design of the Fair," in James William Ellsworth Papers of the World's Columbian Exposition, 1888–1906, Box 9, Chicago Public Library (hereafter cited as Ellsworth MS).

24. Hines, *Burnham of Chicago*, p. 96.

25. Millet, "Designers of the Fair," p. 883.

26. Daniel Burnham, "Design of the Fair," describing a trip to the grounds 10 January 1891, Ellsworth MS.

27. Quoted in Clara Marburg Kirk, *W. D. Howells: Traveler from Altruria, 1889–1894* (New Brunswick: Rutgers University Press, 1962), p. 101.

28. Daniel Burnham and Francis D. Millet, *The Book of the Builders: Being a Chronicle of the Origin and Plan of the World's Fair . . .* (Chicago: Columbian Memorial Society, 1893), p. 21.

29. Kirk, *Howells*, p. 106.

30. George Ferris to L. V. Rice, 14 June 1893, George Washington Ferris Manuscripts, Chicago Historical Society.

31. Daniel Burnham and Edward H. Bennett, *Plan of Chicago*, pp. 99 ff.

32. Ibid., p. 8.

33. Frederick Law Olmsted, "The Landscape Architecture of the World's Fair," *Inland Architect and News Record* 22 (September 1893): 19.

34. Ibid., p. 20.

35. Henry Adams, *The Education of Henry Adams* (Boston: Houghton, Mifflin, 1974), p. 340.

36. William Dean Howells to Elinor M. Howells, 20 September 1893, in William Dean Howells, *Selected Letters*, 1892–1901, ed. Thomas Wortham et al. (Boston: Twayne Publishers, 1981), 4:50.

37. William Dean Howells, *A Traveler from Altruria*, p. 188. See also Kirk, *Howells*, pp. 4–10.

38. Harlow Higinbotham, *Report of the President to the Board of Directors of the World's Columbian Exhibition* (Chicago: Rand McNally, 1898), pp. 469–470.

39. Ibid., pp. 84–86.

40. Randolph Bourne, "Trans-National America," in Carl Resek, ed., *War and the Intellectuals* (New York: Harper, 1964), p. 115.

41. Council of Administration Minutes, 25 August–23 December 1892, World's Columbian Exhibition Papers, vol. 45, p. 25, Chicago Historical Society (hereafter cited as World's Columbian MS, CHS).

42. Ibid., 23 December 1892.

43. "Egypt-Chicago Exposition Company Agreement," in *Concession Agreements*, 1:3; "World's Fair and Elia-Souharin Sadullah and Co. of Constantinople Agreement," in *Concession Agreements*, 1:1–4. Both of these contracts are in the Chicago Historical Society holdings.

44. Higinbotham, *Report of the President*, p. 82.

45. Entry, 20 July 1893, Minutes of the Council of Administration, vol. 49, p. 15, World's Columbian MS, CHS.

46. Entry, 25 August 1893, Minutes, vol. 49, p. 3, World's Columbian MS, CHS.

47. C. D. Arnold and H. D. Higinbotham, *Official Views of the World's Columbian Exposition* (Chicago: Chicago Photo-Gravure, 1893). Peter Hales makes the very interesting argument that this monumental perspective related to a larger myth of the urban endeavor as a conscious creation of American civilization. Therefore, the function of the photographer was to record this. See Hales, *Silver Cities*, pp. 136–153, 186–187.

48. Moses P. Handy, *The Official Directory of the World Columbian Exposition.*

49. Executive Committee Minutes, passim, vol. 35, World's Columbian MS, CHS. See also "Appendix E," in World's Columbian Exhibit, Higinbotham, *Report of the President*, p. 483. There was, apparently, considerable comment and opposition to Conkey's monopoly. See Executive Committee Minutes, 14 December 1892 and 18 January 1893, vol. 35, pp. 546 ff. and 599, World's Columbian MS, CHS. Conkey's *Condensed Catalogue* was oddly organized, without an itinerary and with exhibits listed in alphabetical order. The guide called the Midway "Isolated Exhibits," in effect paying scant attention to it. See W. B. Conkey, *Condensed Catalogue of Interesting Exhibits with Their Locations in the World's Columbian Exposition* (Chicago: W. B. Conkey Co., 1893).

50. The central importance of the Manufactures Building is made clear in the officially sanctioned exhibit guide. See *Conkey's Complete Guide to the World's Columbian Exposition* (Chicago: W. B. Conkey, 1893).

51. Mildred Howells, ed., *Life in Letters of William Dean Howells*, 2 vols. (New York: Russell & Russell [1928], 1955), 1:40.

52. Trumbell White and William Igleheart, *World's Columbian Exposition*, pp. 102–103.

53. Ibid., p. 314.

54. John Romer, "Advertising lessons at the Fair Grounds," *Printer's Ink* 9, 6 September 1893, pp. 256–257.

55. W. W. Brett, "World's Fair Advertising," in *Printer's Ink* 9, 30 August 1893, p. 233.

56. Jeanne Madeline Weimann, "A Temple to Women's Genius: The Women's Building of 1893," *Chicago History* 6 (Spring 1977): 23.

57. Bertha Honore Palmer, "Introduction to Woman's Department," in White and Ingleheart, *World's Columbian Exposition*, p. 440.

58. Maud Howe Elliott, *Art and Handicraft in the Woman's Building of the World's Columbian Exposition, Chicago, 1893* (New York: Goupil & Co., 1893), passim.

59. Weimann, "A Temple to Women's Genius," p. 27. See also Rossiter Johnson, *A History of the World's Columbian Exposition* (authorized by the board of directors), 4 vols. (New York: D. Appleton Co., 1897), 3:451.

60. William C. Cameron, *History of the World's Columbian Exposition*, 2d ed. (Chicago: Columbian History Co., 1893), p. 313.

61. Hines, *Burnham of Chicago*, p. 96.

62. *Catalogue of the Exhibits of the State of Pennsylvania and of Pennsylvania at the World's Columbian Exposition* (State Printers, 1893), p. 14.

63. J. H. Vaill, *Connecticut at the World's Fair*, Report of the Commissioners from Connecticut of the Columbian Exhibition of 1893 at Chicago (Hartford: Case, Lockwood, & Brainard, 1898), p. 153. The report noted that 3.4 percent of the state's population visited the fair as opposed to 7.4 percent who went to (nearby) Philadelphia in 1876.

64. *Report of the Board of General Managers of the Exhibit of the State of New York at the World's Columbian Exposition* (Albany: James B. Lyon, 1894), p. 47.

65. Knight, Leonard & Co., *Guide to the Columbian World's Fair*, p. 59. It is instructive that Duane Doty, describing the great water tower at Pullman in 1890, referred to it as a "Tower of Babel": "Pullman, the Water Tower," *Pullman Review*, 6 December 1890, at Pullman Historical Society, Hotel Florence, Pullman, Illinois (hereafter cited as Pullman MS, PHS). "For an Eiffel Tower in Chicago," *Scientific American*, 31 October 1891, p. 273; and "A Proposed World's Fair Tower," *Scientific American*, 2 July 1892, p. 4. This latter article describes something close to that depicted in Knight, Leonard's *Guidebook*.

66. Werner Plum, *World Exhibitions in the Nineteenth Century: Pageants of Social and Cultural Change* (Bonn: Friedrich-Ebert-Stiftung, 1977), pp. 19–22.

67. Ben C. Truman et al., *History of the World's Fair*, p. 14.

68. Reid Badger, *The Great American Fair*, pp. 80, 107.

69. Rossiter Johnson, ed., *A History of the World's Columbian Exposition*, 4 vols. (New York: Appleton & Co., 1898), 1:75.

70. F. W. Putnam, *Oriental and Occidental Northern and Southern Portrait Types of the Midway Plaisance* (St. Louis: N. D. Thompson, 1894), passim.

71. B. J. L. Kaine, "Best Things to See and How to Find Them" (Chicago: White Publishing, 1893), p. 107. See also John J. Flinn, *The Best Things to Be Seen at the World's Fair* (Chicago: Columbian Guide Co., 1893), p. 69.

72. Putnam, *Portrait Types*, p. 2. Robert Rydell makes Putnam the center of an important didactic purpose which he sees in the entire Fair, that is, to preach the racial superiority of Europeans and the cultural superiority of American civilization. See Rydell, *All the World's a Fair*, passim. Perhaps some of this is true, but I think Rydell misses the complexity of the Fair.

73. For paintings, see Dwight Miller, *Street Criers and Itinerant Tradesmen in European Prints* (Stanford, Calif., 1970). For photographs, see Sigmund Krausz, *Street Types of Chicago: Character Studies* (Chicago: M. Stern & Co., 1892); and Krausz, *Street Types of Great American Cities* (Chicago: Werner Co., 1896).

74. *World's Fair Puck*, 1 May–30 October 1893 (Chicago, 1893). This weekly journal was published and sold at the Fair.

75. The history of "anthropological" exhibits before the Midway was ambiguous in origin and purpose. The 1889 Paris Exposition displayed anthropological exhibits from French colonial possessions. But in 1884, P. T. Barnum had included an ethnological exhibit entitled "The Grand Congress of Nations" as part of his circus.

76. Ben Holt, *Good Style, Small Expense, or We'll Never Go There Anymore* (New York: Published for the Trade, 1894), p. 179.

77. Higinbotham, *Report of the President*, pp. 482–491.

78. Jean-Jacques Bloch et Marianne Delort, *Quand Paris allait a l'Expo* (Paris: Fayard, 1980), p. 94.

79. John J. Flinn, *Official Guide to Midway Plaisance, Otherwise Known as the Highway through the Nations* (Chicago: Columbian Guide Co., 1893), p. 20; and Rand McNally & Co., *Handy Guide to Chicago and World's Columbian Exposition*, p. 206.

80. *The Moorish Palace*, souvenir book (Chicago, 1893), in Newberry Library Collection, Chicago, Illinois.

81. Burg, *White City*, p. 224. See also Norman D. Anderson and Walter R. Brown, *Ferris Wheels* (New York: Pantheon, 1983), pp. 13–18.

82. If Louis Sullivan had wished, he might have found in the Ferris Wheel precisely the sense of form and function he found so lacking in the architecture of the Fair. Certainly there was no more beautiful structure by the standards of form and function at Jackson Park.

83. Flinn, *Official Guide to the Midway*, p. 30.

84. White and Ingleheart, *World's Columbian Exhibit*, p. 583.

85. Mrs. Mark Stevens, *Six Months at the Fair* (Detroit: Detroit Free Press, 1895), p. 322.

86. *Exhibits of New York State at the World's Columbian Exposition, Chicago, 1893* (Chicago: A. C. McClurg, 1893), passim.

87. M. P. Handy, *Official Catalogue*, p. 11.

88. Julian Hawthorne, *Humors of the Fair* (Chicago: E. A. Weeks & Co., 1893), pp. 104–105.

89. Mary Catherine Crowley, *The City of Wonders: A Souvenir of the World's Fair* (Detroit: William Graham, 1894), pp. 9 ff; Stuart C. Wade and Walter S. Wrenn, *The NutShell* (Chicago: Merchant's World's Fair Bureau of Information Company, 1893), p. 38; James B. Campbell, *Campbell's Illustrated History of the World's Columbian Exposition* (Chicago: N. Juul, 1894), 2:628.

90. David Glassberg, "History and the Public: Legacies of the Progressive Era," *Journal of American History* 73 (March 1987): pp. 964–965. The

much-quoted account of the Fair, *The Adventures of Uncle Jeremiah at the Fair*, by Quondam (Chicago: Laird & Lee, 1893), p. 209, notes: "When Mr. Moody preaches to the Midway Plaisance, surely the scripture will be fulfilled as to preaching the gospel to all the nations of the earth."

91. White and Ingleheart, *World's Columbian Exhibit*, p. 595.

92. Anne Sergal, "The Midway: A Burlesque Entertainment" (Chicago: Dramatic Publishing Co., 1894), passim, 17.

93. Albert W. Fulton, "What Will It Cost Me to See the World's Fair?" (Chicago: Donohue & Henneberry, 1893), pp. 6–14.

94. "Salem at the World's Columbian Exposition," Report of the Essex Institute Committee (Salem: Essex Institute, 1893), passim; World's Fair Accommodation Association, *The World's Fair Tourist* (Chicago: D. C. Boley, 1892), pp. 3–10; International Exhibition Information Co., *Columbian Exposition* (Chicago: 1893).

95. Higinbotham, *Report of the President*, pp. 482–491. Most of the Midway's exhibitions charged a twenty-five-cent entry fee, although there were sometimes additional events that cost ten cents to enter. Taking the German revenues at $622,000, this would approximate 2 million entries with additional expenditures. With the enormous crowds of Chicago Day on 9 October Horace Tucker, superintendent of admissions, noted that Buffalo Bill's admissions were 70,000. See Horace Tucker to James William Ellsworth, 12 October 1893, Ellsworth MS.

96. Chicago Tribune, *Glimpses of the World's Fair through a Camera* (Chicago: Laird & Lee, 1893), passim.

97. George Ade et al., *The Chicago Record's History of the World's Fair*, pp. 169–170. This essay is not signed but appears to be by Ade. See also Ripley Hitchcock, ed., *The Art of the World's Fair* (New York: D. Appleton & Co., 1894), 1:passim. John Farwell's introduction to John Dale's success book in 1889 almost literally described the next scene in this moral tableau. Sitting on the train racing to the city is a young man: "A few short hours ago he opened the door of the old farmhouse where he had been carefully reared, and started out to achieve a career. His mother followed him to the gate, imprinted her farewell kiss upon his lips and with tearful eyes bade him read good books, associate with good companions, and allow himself only pure amusements." See Farwell, "Introduction," in John T. Dale, *The Secret of Success*, p. ix.

98. William G. McLoughlin, *The Meaning of Henry Ward Beecher* (New York: Alfred A. Knopf, 1970), p. 88.

99. Hezekiah Butterworth, *Zig Zag Journeys in the White City with Visits to the Neighboring Metropolis* (Boston: Estes & Lauriat, 1894), p. 126.

100. For an example of how this city culture could be negotiated, see Rand McNally, *Handy Guide to Chicago,* passim; and the very different *Chicago by Day and Night: The Pleasure Seekers' Guide to the Paris of America* (Chicago: Thompson & Zimmerman, 1892).

101. Quote in J. F. Martin, *Martin's World's Fair Album, Atlas and Family Souvenir* (Chicago: C. Ropp & Sons, 1892), n.p.

102. Mable L. Treseder, "A Visitor's Trip to Chicago in 1893," ed. Sheldon T. Gardner (typescript at Chicago Historical Society), p. 30.

103. Joseph Kirkland, *The Story of Chicago,* 2:69, 84.

104. Lucinda H. Stone, "Higher Lessons of the World's Fair," in Mary Eagle, *The Congress of Women,* 2 vols. (Chicago: W. B. Conkey Co., 1894), 2:447.

105. Johnson, ed., *History of the World's Columbian Exposition,* 4:332–335.

106. The Fair's Joint Committee on Ceremonies on 31 May 1893 passed a resolution requesting the Council of Administration to invite Dwight Moody to preach at the Fair next Sunday (the first Sunday of June). Moody did not agree. Minutes of a meeting, 1 June 1893, Council of Administration, vol. 48, p. 137, World's Columbian MS, CHS.

107. *Illustrated World's Fair* 1 (December 1891), p. 17. *World's Fair Puck,* 24 July 1893, p. 134.

108. Lloyd Lewis, *Chicago: The History of Its Reputation* (New York: Harcourt, Brace & Co., 1929), pp. 209–210; *Chicago Inter Ocean,* 9 October 1893, p. 3.

109. Truman et al., *History of the World's Fair,* p. 88.

110. "Official Souvenir Program of Chicago Day at the World's Fair" (Chicago: Thomas Knapp Publishing, 1893), n.p.

111. This appears to be one of the essential characteristics of mass culture. As Walter Benjamin has written, "Even the most perfect reproduction of a work of art is lacking in one element: its presence in time and space, its unique existence at the place where it happens to be." That is also the characteristic of the White City and the Midway. See Walter Benjamin, "The Work of Art in the Age of Mechanical Reproduction," in *Illuminations* (New York: Harcourt, Brace & World, 1955), p. 222.

CHAPTER FIVE

1. "The Pride of Pullman," *Inter Ocean,* 10 January 1863, Miscellaneous Pamphlets, Chicago Historical Society. See also invitation to the gala affair.

2. Ibid., p. 3.

3. Richard Ely, "Pullman: A Social Study," *Harper's New Monthly Magazine* 70 (February 1885): 456. Much of this article is sharply critical of Pullman's paternalism.

4. See John R. Stilgoe, *Metropolitan Corridor: Railroads and the American Scene* (New Haven: Yale University Press, 1983), p. 252, for an interesting comment on the importance of seeing Pullman from the train.

5. Duane Doty, "Pullman, the Great Corliss Engine," in Box 2, Pullman Papers, Pullman Historical Society, Pullman, Illinois. (hereafter cited as Pullman MS, PHS). Doty was a publicist for the town.

6. Mr. Fritsch to George M. Pullman, 21 June, 5 July, 6 July, and 6 September 1893, Box 2, George M. Pullman Papers, Chicago Historical Society (hereafter cited as G. Pullman MS, CHS).

7. Ernest Poole, *Giants Gone*, pp. 196–200.

8. Stanley Buder, *Pullman: An Experiment in Industrial Order and Community Planning, 1880–1930* (New York: Oxford University Press, 1967), p. 147.

9. Miscellaneous genealogical material, Box 3, Harriet Sanger Pullman Papers and Diaries, Chicago Historical Society (hereafter cited as H. Pullman MS, CHS). These documents are stored temporarily at the society and their arrangement is not stable. See also George M. Pullman Obituary News Clipping collection, 1897–1898, Chicago Historical Society (hereafter cited as Pullman Obits, CHS); Nancy Miller and Fred Levitt, *Pullman: Portrait of a Landmark Community* (Chicago: Historic Pullman Foundation, 1981), p. 8; Buder, *Pullman*, pp. 3–4.

10. "Pullman," *The Graphic* 3, 10 June 1893, p. 403.

11. George Pullman to his mother, 2 July 1860, Denver, Box 2, G. Pullman MS, CHS.

12. Miller and Leavitt, *Pullman*, p. 8; John Moses and Major Joseph Kirkland, *History of Chicago, Illinois: Aboriginal to Metropolitan*, 2 vols. (Chicago: Munsell, 1895), 2:719.

13. Buder, *Pullman*, pp. 32–33.

14. *Chicago Tribune*, 19 December 1882, in Harriet Pullman Scrapbooks, vol. 1, Chicago Historical Society (hereafter cited as H. Pullman Scrapbooks, CHS).

15. "The New Pullman Office and Apartment Building," *Western Manufacturer* 12, 31 March 1884, p. 1.

16. Miller and Leavitt, *Pullman*, p. 9. See also Mrs. Spencer Beman, "A Paper on the Creation of the Model Town of Pullman by George M. Pullman in Collaboration with S. S. Beman, Architect, 1879–1882," in Solon Spencer Beman Papers, Chicago Historical Society. Beman also designed Ivorydale for Proctor and Gamble near Cincinnati.

17. See Diaries of H. Pullman, passim, H. Pullman MS, CHS.

18. Article in H. Pullman Scrapbook, vol. 2, CHS.

19. Florence Lowden Miller, "The Pullmans of Prairie Avenue: A Domestic Portrait from Letters and Diaries," *Chicago History* 1, n.s. (Spring 1971): pp. 148 ff.

20. Harriet Sanger Pullman to George Pullman, 25 February 1894, Dansville, N.Y., from Box 6: George M. Pullman Family Correspondence; Correspondence with his Wife, H. Pullman MS, CHS.

21. George Pullman to Hattie Pullman, Chicago, 25 February 1894. Although Harriet's diary is incomplete, it by no means confirms the constant health complaints that she made to George in letters. In a letter of 27 January 1888, Hattie refers to a serious disagreement with George but gives no indication why. See Hattie to George Pullman, 27 January 1888, Box 5: George M. Pullman, Family Correspondence, H. Pullman MS, CHS.

22. Harriet Pullman diaries, passim, H. Pullman MS, CHS.

23. "Pullman on the Christening of His Grandson," p. 1, in Pullman Miscellaneous Memorabilia file in H. Pullman MS, CHS.

24. Almont Lindsey, *The Pullman Strike: The Story of a Unique Experiment and of a Great Labor Upheaval* (Chicago: University of Chicago Press, 1942), p. 25.

25. Duane Doty, *The Story of Pullman* (Pullman, Ill., 1893), p. 5. This is the souvenir book distributed at the World's Fair.

26. Duane Doty, clipping, 1 June 1887, Scrapbook, Pullman MS, PHS.

27. Mrs. Duane Doty, *The Town of Pullman: Its Growth with Brief Accounts of Its Industries* (Pullman, Ill.: T. P. Struhsacker, 1893), p. 16. It is interesting that one of Pullman's severest later critics, Carroll Wright, signed this favorable report published in 1885.

28. Paul de Rousiers, "The Rise of a Modern City," in Bessie Louise Pierce and Joe L. Norris, *As Others See Chicago: Impressions of Visitors, 1673–1933*, (Chicago: University of Chicago Press, 1933), p. 271. Richard Ely in his article on Pullman noted that there were important distinctions in living conditions in the town according to wage and position in the factory. See Ely, "Pullman," p. 463.

29. Ray Ginger, *Altgeld's America*, p. 145. Ginger indicates that Pullman paid informers to report on family activities in the town. Pullman also hoped to attract the best sort of workers to the town, from the point of view of skills and reliability. See Ira J. Bach, "Pullman: A Town Reborn," *Chicago History* 4 (Spring 1975): 45.

30. Gwendolyn Wright, *Moralism and the Modern Home: Domestic Architecture and Cultural Conflict in Chicago, 1873–1913* (Chicago:

University of Chicago Press, 1980), pp. 4–5, 74–75. Stephen George Cobb rightly sees the Pullman experiment in the context of late nineteenth-century paternalism represented best by Andrew Carnegie. See Cobb, "William Carwardine and the Pullman Strike" (Ph.D. diss., Northwestern University, 1970), pp. 14 ff. See also Thomas J. Schleredth, "Solon Spencer Beman, Pullman and the European Influence in His Chicago Architecture," in John Zukowsky ed., *Chicago Architecture, 1872–1922* (Munich: Prestel-Verlag, 1988), pp. 174–176. Beman designed several other housing projects although none quite on the scale of Pullman.

31. Mrs. Doty, "Town of Pullman," p. 4.

32. *The Graphic* in its description of Pullman in 1893 captured this vision from the rail station perfectly. See "Pullman," *The Graphic*, p. 399.

33. Henry R. Koopman, *Pullman: The City of Brick* (Roseland, Ill.: H. R. Koopman, 1893), p. 1. This publication was probably intended for World's Fair visitors.

34. Mrs. Doty, "Town of Pullman." p. 107.

35. Kirkland, *The Story of Chicago*, 1:392.

36. Jane Addams called saloons, cheap theaters, and dance halls "vicious amusements." Quoted in Thomas Lee Philpott, *The Slum and the Ghetto: Neighborhood Deterioration and Middle-Class Reform, Chicago, 1880–1930* (New York: Oxford University Press, 1978), p. 73. Although Addams was later very disapproving of Pullman's activities during the strike of 1894, she did agree, in general, with his cultural attitudes and, in some very direct ways, paralleled his efforts to teach middle-class culture to working-class Chicagoans.

37. "Photos of Pullman," souvenir book published about 1888, in Scrapbook, Pullman MS, PHS.

38. Buder, *Pullman*, p. 61. Throughout the existence of the suburb, Pullman was heavily populated by the foreign-born, with estimates of over 70 percent in 1892. See Ray Ginger, *Altgeld's America*, p. 148.

39. Charles H. Eaton, "Pullman, a Social Experiment," *Today* 2 (January 1895): p. 6.

40. Buder, *Pullman*, p. 67.

41. Mrs. Doty, "Town of Pullman," p. 9.

42. Quoted by C. W. Tyler in "Appendix," Mrs. Doty, "Town of Pullman," p. 23.

43. Dr. De Wolf, in Massachusetts Bureau of Statistics of Labor, *Sixteenth Annual Report to the Massachusetts Department of Labor and Industries, Division of Statistics*, pt. 1, "Pullman" (Boston: Wright & Potter, 1885), p. 17.

44. "The Boycotting of Booth," from *Chicago News Setter* (1886[?]), collected in Mrs. Harriet S. Pullman Scrapbooks, vol. 1, H. Pullman Scrapbooks, CHS.

45. Diary entry, 28 January 1878, Box 1, H. Pullman MS, CHS. Given the phrasing of this entry, it is possible that the "we" does not include George. It is unlikely, however, that it would mean just Hattie and her children who were at that time probably too young for such an activity.

46. Ibid., Diary entry, 7 August 1871.

47. Clipping from unidentified paper, 1904[?], vol. 2, H. Pullman Scrapbooks, CHS. See *St. Louis Post Dispatch*, 24 January 1885, in vol. 1, Scrapbooks.

48. Unidentified article, vol. 1, H. Pullman Scrapbooks, CHS. In 1885, the Dramatic Society put on at least two plays, "A Rough Diamond," and "A Quiet Family." Scrapbook, Pullman MS, PHS.

49. Massachusetts Bureau, "Pullman," p. 10.

50. Diary entry Friday, 27 June 1883, H. Pullman MS, CHS.

51. Program for performance in vol. 1, H. Pullman Scrapbooks, CHS.

52. See Richard Ely's critique of the town, "Pullman," *Harper's*, pp. 452–466.

53. Lindsey, *Pullman Strike*, p. 70.

54. "Testimony of George M. Pullman," in U.S. Strike Commission, *Report on the Chicago Strike of June–July, 1894* (Washington, D.C.: Government Printing Office, 1895), p. 529.

55. See L. A. Draper to A. M. Walter of Pullman Company, 9 January 1955, p. 2, Box 1, File 4 in the G. Pullman MS, CHS. In this letter, Draper reminisces about life in Pullman.

56. The corrupting potential of this power is clear from a letter of a cousin of Harriet Pullman, Edward W. Henricke, in 1882. Worrying about retaining his position in the company, he asked Mrs. Pullman to intercede in his behalf. He also proposed to run for clerk of Hyde Park in order to put himself "in the best possible position to guard his [Mr. Pullman's] interests in case they were threatened." See Henricke to Mrs. Harriet Sanger, 12 March 1882, Box 1, Miscellaneous Letters Received by his Wife, H. Pullman MS, CHS.

57. Florence Lowden Miller, "The Pullmans," p. 148.

58. H. H. Higinbotham to Mrs. Pullman, 24 October 1893, Box 2: Personal letters received by his wife, H. Pullman MS, CHS. See also undated expense memo entitled, "A Costly Walk through Midway Plaisance," from the Fritsch letters in G. Pullman MS, CHS.

59. Diary entry, 30 May 1893, H. Pullman MS, CHS.

60. Buder, *Pullman*, pp. 149 ff. See also Lindsey, *Pullman Strike*, pp. 91 ff.

61. U.S. Strike Commission, *Report*, p. xxxv.

62. Mrs. Potter Palmer, Bar Harbor, 11 August 1894, to Ralph Easley, Chicago World's Columbian Exposition, President's Letters, Board of Lady Managers, File: 14 February 1894–8 November 1895, vol. 17a, World's Columbian MS, CHS.

63. George C. Sikes to Madeleine Wallace Sikes, 24 July 1894, p. 5 (verso), in Madeleine W. Sikes Papers, 1894–1911, Chicago Historical Society.

64. Thomas Burke Grant, "Pullman and Its Lessons," *American Journal of Politics* 5 (August 1894): 194.

65. On the strike see Buder, *Pullman*; Lindsey, *Pullman Strike*; and Nick Salvatore, *Eugene V. Debs: Citizen and Socialist* (Urbana: University of Illinois, 1982).

66. George Pullman to Hattie Pullman, Chicago, 25 March 1894, Box 6; and Hattie Sanger Pullman to George M. Pullman, Aix Les Bains, 31 August 1894, p. 4, Box 6, H. Pullman MS, CHS.

67. George Pullman to Hattie Pullman, 2 September 1894, Box 6, H. Pullman MS, CHS.

68. Diary entry, 8 July 1894, Frances Glessner Journal, File, 16 June 1894–21 April 1895, Glessner MS. The U.S. Strike Commission reported that those who rioted after July 3 and attacked property were by "general concurrence in the testimony, composed generally of hoodlums, women, a low class of foreigners, and recruits from the criminal classes"—in other words, not Pullman strikers. See U.S. Strike Commission, *Report*, pp. xlv–xlvi.

69. Hattie Pullman to George Pullman, St. Augustine, Fla., 28 March 1897, Box 6, H. Pullman MS, CHS.

70. Diary entry, 13 June 1897, H. Pullman MS, CHS; Pullman Obits, CHS.

71. Kathryn Allamong Jacob, "High Society in Washington during the Gilded Age" (Ph.D. diss., Johns Hopkins University, 1986), pp. 253–254.

72. Dr. N. D. Hillis, "Eulogy, Pullman Obits, CHS."

73. Miller and Levitt, *Pullman*, pp. 12–13.

CHAPTER SIX

1. Material for this sketch is based in part upon listening to recordings of Moody and Sankey.

2. This scene is a composite of a number of accounts of Moody preaching. The sermon is reproduced in Box 13, File 68 of the D. L. Moody Ser-

mon Series at the Yale Divinity School Library (hereafter cited as Moody MS).

3. Untitled article, 7 July 1893, from Moody Scrapbook, vol. 1, Moody MS.

4. Bernard Weisberger discusses this borrowing in his book, *They Gathered at the River: The Story of the Great Revivalists and Their Impact upon Religion in America* (New York: Farrar, Straus, & Giroux, 1979), pp. 230–237.

5. H. M. Wharton, *A Month with Moody in Chicago: His Work and Workers* (Baltimore, 1894), p. 30.

6. H. B. Hartzler, *Moody in Chicago or the World's Fair Gospel Campaign* (New York, 1894), p. 201. Hartzler was one of several ministers called especially to Chicago to help Moody in the campaign.

7. Anecdotes of Moody's Life, Box 8, Moody MS.

8. James F. Findlay, Jr., *Dwight L. Moody: American Evangelist, 1837–1899* (Chicago, 1969), pp. 30 ff; George Marsden, *Fundamentalism and American Culture: The Shaping of Twentieth-Century Evangelicalism, 1870–1925* (New York, 1980), p. 36.

9. Scrapbook, vol. 2, Moody Ms.

10. Findlay, Jr., *Moody*, 183; John Charles Pollock, *Moody: A Biographical Portrait of the Pacesetter in Modern Mass Evangelism* (New York, 1963), p. 292; and Marsden, *Fundamentalism*, p. 35.

11. Whitney R. Cross, *The Burned-over District: The Social and Intellectual History of Enthusiastic Religion in Western New York, 1800–1850* (New York: Harper & Row, 1950), pp. 151 ff., 174 ff; Michael Barkun, *Crucible of the Millennium: The Burned-over District of New York in the 1840s* (Syracuse: Syracuse University Press, 1986), pp. 104–118; Keith J. Hardman, *Charles Grandison Finney, 1792–1875: Revivalist and Reformer* (Syracuse: Syracuse University Press, 1987), esp. pp. 176–177.

12. Keith J. Hardman, *The Spiritual Awakeners: American Revivalists from Solomon Stoddard to D. L. Moody* (Chicago: Moody Press, 1983), pp. 189 ff.

13. Author unknown, "A Revival in Frogtown," *Catholic World* 22 (1876): pp. 700–706.

14. Quoted in Wharton, *A Month with Moody*, pp. 257–258.

15. Gene A. Getz, *MBI: The Story of the Moody Bible Institute*, rev. James M. Vincent (Chicago: Moody Press [1969], 1986), pp. 18–23; Emmett Dedmon, *Great Enterprises: 100 Years of the YMCA of Metropolitan Chicago* (New York: Rand McNally, 1957), pp. 42 ff.

16. Moody had a special relationship to the McCormick family, esp. Mrs. Nettie McCormick. Moody was a frequent visitor to the McCormick

household, and between Cyrus McCormick and Moody "there was a very strong sympathy between these two men of indomitable will." Furthermore, the McCormicks were major contributors to Moody's many projects. See "Editorial Topics: Recollections of Mrs. McCormick," *The Interior,* 4 January 1900, in File 4, Box 15, Moody MS.

17. Dennis E. Graf, "Dwight L. Moody and the 1893 Chicago World's Fair Campaign" (M.A. thesis, Wheaton College, 1965), p. 90. See also Sandra S. Sizer, *Gospel Hymns and Social Religion: The Rhetoric of Nineteenth-Century Revivalism* (Philadelphia, 1978), p. 142. Sizer relates revivals to political crises and sees them, in part, as "strategies of pacification."

18. Turlington W. Harvey, "Letter to a Friend," 17 November 1888, from Harvey File, Moody Bible Institute Library, Chicago, Ill. (hereafter cited as Harvey MS, MBI). Reacting to strikes at Pullman in 1884 and in 1885 at his benefactor Cyrus McCormick's plant (culminating in the 1886 Haymarket Riot), Moody warned: "Either these people are to be evangelized or the leaven of communism and infidelity will assume such enormous proportions that it will break out in a reign of terror such as this country has never known." See Findlay, *Moody,* p. 327.

19. There is evidence that businessmen were interested in Moody's role in dampening labor unrest. For example, in April, during the McCormick strike and just before the Haymarket Riot, Turlington Harvey organized a meeting with McCormick, Marshall Field, Armour, Moody, and himself to raise funds for Moody's Christian Workers' Training School. See Turlington W. Harvey to Cyrus McCormick, April 1886, in Harvey MS, MBI.

20. Hartzler, *Moody in Chicago,* p. 15.

21. Ibid., p. 17; Graf, "Dwight L. Moody," p. 46.

22. Hartzler, *Moody in Chicago,* pp. 229–230.

23. For an excellent treatment of Chicago's lay Protestant institutions during this period, see L. David Lewis, "The Efficient Crusade: Lay Protestantism in Chicago, 1874–1925" (Ph.D. diss., University of Chicago Divinity School, 1979). Writing in *The Pit,* Chicago novelist Frank Norris obviously understood the links between Moody and the business community. He has his character Jadwin comment that, were D. L. Moody alive, he would approve of his efforts to take over "a half dozen broken-down, bankrupt Sunday-school concerns" and apply business principles to them. See Frank Norris, *The Pit: The Epic of Wheat, a Story of Chicago* (New York, 1902), p. 123.

24. There is an interesting parallel between Moody's rural homestead and Pullman's construction of a retreat at the Thousand Islands.

25. "A Modern Eden," *Springfield Daily Union*, 2 June 1988.

26. Wharton, *Month with Moody*, pp. 12–13.

27. Hartzler, *Moody in Chicago*, p. 20.

28. Lewis, "Efficient Crusade," pp. 116–117. Lewis credits Moody with a compromising view toward many of the issues then beginning to divide secular and religious Protestants. Part of the impetus to close the Fair came from the same groups determined to shut down immigrant recreational spots on Sundays, particularly saloons.

29. Minutes of the Council of Administration, 1 June 1893, vol. 48, p. 137, in World's Columbian MS, CHS.

30. Paul Carus, "The Dawn of a New Religious Era," *Forum* 16 (November 1893): 392.

31. Pollock, *Moody*, pp. 279–280. Moody himself offered a kind of ecumenism, since he adhered to no established church nor did he use the revival to sort Christians into one or another sect.

32. Graf, "Dwight L. Moody," pp. 33, 43, 75. Apparently there was occasional violence when ministers tried to move the crusade into tougher, immigrant parts of the city.

33. Hartzler, *Moody in Chicago*, p. 70. See also Pollock, *Moody*, p. 284.

34. "Expense of the World's Campaign 1893," in World's Fair file, n.p., Moody Papers, Moody Bible Institute, Chicago, Ill. (hereafter cited as Moody MS, MBI).

35. *Chicago Tribune*, 1 November 1893, p. 6.

36. Examples of some of the addresses includes: Milwaukee and Powell, Center Avenue and Orchard, Archer and Twenty-third Place, Paulina and Walnut, North Clark and North Avenue, West Fourteenth St. and Paulina, Roby and Iowa, Roby and Ohio, and West Chicago and Lincoln.

37. Perry Duis argues that Moody borrowed the idea of the tent from circuses. See *Chicago: Creating New Traditions* (Chicago, 1976), p. 59. Robert Bruce Huber in "Dwight L. Moody: Salesman of Salvation: A Case Study in Audience Psychology" (Ph.D. diss., University of Wisconsin, 1942), pp. 272 ff., itemizes many of the ploys that Moody and Sankey used to heighten the suspense and excitement surrounding their various campaigns.

38. *Chicago Tribune*, 12 June 1893, p. 1.

39. William Revell Moody, *The Life of Dwight L. Moody* (New York and Chicago: Fleming H. Revell Co., 1900), p. 415.

40. *Nation* 22, 9 March 1876, p. 157, quoted in Findlay, Jr., *Dwight Moody*, p. 210. See also Marian L. Bell, *Crusade in the City: Revivalism in Nineteenth Century Philadelphia* (Lewisburg, Pa., 1977), p. 208; Graf, "Dwight L. Moody," pp. 48–49. Robert Morss Lovett astutely noted in 1927

the role of popular music in Moody and Sankey hymns as well as much of the popular culture symbolism exploited by the evangelist. See Robert Morss Lovett, "Moody and Sankey," *New Republic* 53, 14 December 1927, pp. 94–96.

41. Quoted by the *Chicago Tribune*, 1 November 1893, p. 6.

42. Bills Paid, World's Fair File, Moody Bible Institute (hereafter cited as World's Fair MS, MBI).

43. *Chicago Herald*, 19 April 1894, from File, Harvey MS, MBI.

44. Biographical material from a letter by Henry S. Harvey, copy in Harvey Manuscripts, Harvey Public Library, Harvey, Ill. (hereafter cited as Harvey MS, HPL). See also Moses and Kirkland, *History of Chicago, Illinois*, pp. 696–698. See also T. W. Harvey to Jane Addams, 23 December 1893, Box 1, File 1, Civic Federation Papers of Chicago, Chicago Historical Society.

45. Moses and Kirkland, *History of Chicago*, p. 696.

46. Chicago Title and Trust Company as Trustee of Harvey Land Association, "Contract of Sale" (Chicago, 1893). Harvey Land Company Manuscripts, Thornton Township Historical Society (hereafter cited as Harvey Land Co. MS, THS).

47. Homer Hoyt demonstrates that the years 1890–1893 included the time of the wildest speculation in land in and around Chicago. It was the height of a boom that had begun in mid-century and would not reappear for thirty years. Morgan Park, also near Chicago, was a temperance town organized in 1869. It lasted as a dry village until 1914. See Hoyt, *One Hundred Years of Land Values in Chicago*, p. 417.

48. See Perry R. Duis, *The Saloon: Public Drinking in Chicago and Boston, 1880–1920* (Urbana, Ill., 1983), passim, for the importance of saloons in Chicago.

49. Harvey Land Association, *The Town of Harvey, Illinois: Manufacturing Suburb of Chicago: Aged Two Years* (Chicago, 1892), p. 14.

50. T. W. Harvey to J. P. Adams, 18 March 18[??], Letter Copy Book, Harvey Land Co., MS, THS. Even if Harvey encouraged other owners of new factories to move to his new town, he maintained his elegant Chicago residence.

51. Harvey Land Association, *The Town of Harvey, Illinois*, p. 14 and passim. See *Chicago Tribune*, 2 February 1890; see also Turlington Harvey papers, "Owners of Shares in Harvey Land Association, Liquidation File," Harvey Land Co. MS, THS. These papers are unorganized, and, therefore, volumes have no name. See Dwight Moody to Will Moody, 22 January 1890, Box 8, Moody MS.

52. Harvey Land Association, *Town of Harvey*, p. 32; John Beck recollections from Clipping File (Lucy Page Gaston) in Harvey Biographies File, Harvey Public Library, Harvey, Ill., n.p.; Peter Lamb to T. W. Harvey, 4 January 1892, pp. 1–2, Correspondence files, Harvey Land Co. MS, THS.

53. "As Seen by Others," *Harvey Tribune-Headlight*, 2 July 1892, p. 1, Thornton Township Historical Society.

54. Special Advertising Ledger on Harvey, 1892–1893, Harvey Land Co. MS, THS. The volume includes about 3,000 names. Entries list types of material sent and mention of place (if known) where correspondent heard of Harvey. There is also a corresponding letter file containing inquiry letters.

55. Freeman Manter to Harvey Land Association, 3 February 1894, in Correspondence File, Harvey Land Co. MS, THS.

56. Arthur Mills to Harvey Land Association, 18 April 1893, Harvey Land Co. MS, THS; *Harvey Tribune*, 3 June 1893. The two largest Harvey hotels that were planned for the Fair burned. Only the Harvey World's Fair Hotel was rebuilt. City of Harvey, "Golden Jubilee" (Harvey, Ill., 1941), p. 77.

57. Hoyt, *One Hundred Years of Land Values in Chicago*, p. 157.

58. William G. McLoughlin, *American Evangelicals, 1800–1900: An Anthology* (New York, 1968), pp. 255, 174.

59. Findlay, Jr., *Moody*, pp. 270, 281, 296 ff. Findlay argues that Moody created an "effective bridge for many people between the old and the new in American society." It might be better to state that Moody pushed old ideas into a new cultural context. Findlay's formulation makes it seem as if people abandoned the old in favor of the new. In addition, it is important to recognize that Moody was not exactly a Fundamentalist. Indeed, after his death the tensions between modernists and traditionalists in Protestant Chicago were greatly accentuated.

60. McLoughlin, *American Evangelicals*, p. 185; Findlay, Jr., *Moody*, pp. 245 ff; Martin Marty, *Modern American Religion*, vol. 1, *The Irony of It All, 1893–1919* (Chicago,: University of Chicago Press, 1986), pp. 210–212. Premillennialism is the belief that before the return of Christ there will be a long period of turmoil, strife, and sin.

61. On reconversion, see Findlay, Jr., *Moody*, p. 276.

62. William H. Leach, "The Profile of an Era," *Church Management* (January 1945): 13. Marty, *Modern American Religion*, 1:209.

63. Marsden, *Fundamentalism*, pp. 5 ff; Bell, *Crusade in the City*, p. 225. See also Lewis, "Efficient Crusade," p. 33, for discussion of the economic backgrounds of Chicago Protestants.

64. William R. Harper to Dwight L. Moody, Chicago, 22 September 1899, Folder 13, Box 1, Moody MS. Here, Harper suggests that he, not Moody, was the outsider.

65. Graf, "Dwight L. Moody," p. 33.

66. Bell, *Crusade in the City*, p. 229. Moody tried to enlist Wanamaker as a revivalist. Moody's use of Barnum's American Museum for a later New York revival illustrates a different sort of link to enterprise—in this case, popular culture.

67. Hartzler, *Moody in Chicago*, pp. 106, 211.

68. Figures on entries into concessions were arrived at by multiplying concession revenues by four. Most concessions charged an admission of twenty-five cents, although these figures may, also, include special admissions to theaters inside the concessions or souvenirs. See Chap. 4, "First City: Form and Fantasy."

69. "Record of Sunday Meetings Only, May 28–October 29, 1893," World's Fair MS, MBI.

70. *Hartford* (Conn.) *Times*, 28 December 1899. Copy in Moody MS, MBI. See also McLoughlin, *American Evangelicals*, pp. 184–185.

71. Wharton, *Month with Moody*, p. 13. It is almost unnecessary to indicate the similarity of Moody's campaign and techniques to contemporary popular evangelism. See Ben Armstrong, *The Electric Church* (Nashville, Tenn., 1979).

72. Ralph Connor [Charles William Gordon], *The Sky Pilot: A Tale of the Foothills* (Chicago: F. H. Revell Co., 1899); and Ralph Connor [Charles William Gordon], *Black Rock: A Tale of the Selkirks* (Chicago: F. H. Revell Co., 1900).

73. Greg Singleton argues that Fundamentalism in the country is often an expression of social cohesion while in the city it represents social breakdown. This would certainly explain Moody's success with such themes as the Prodigal Son which might appeal to both. See Greg Singleton, "Fundamentalism and Urbanization: A Quantitative Critique of Impressionistic Interpretations," in Leo F. Schnore, *The New Urban History: Quantitative Explorations by American Historians* (Princeton: Princeton University Press, 1975): pp. 205–227.

74. I define mass culture as those signs, symbols, language, institutions, and behavior by which one defines oneself and interacts with others that are translated through and communicated by the commercial media.

CHAPTER SEVEN

1. H. G. Wells, *The Future in America* (New York: Arno Press [1906] 1974), pp. 59–60.

2. Glessner Journal, 4 November 1893, p. 15, File, 1 October 1893–11 June 1894, Glessner MS.

3. Bancroft, *The Book of the Fair*, 2:961.

4. H. H. Van Meter, "The Vanishing Fair" (Chicago: Literary Art, 1894), p. 10.

5. Robert Herrick, *The Web of Life* (New York: MacMillan, 1900), p. 135.

6. Poole, *Giants Gone*, p. 190.

7. Ray Stannard Baker, *American Chronicle: The Autobiography of RSB* (New York: Charles Scribner's Sons, 1945), p. 2.

8. Buder, *Pullman*, pp. 149 ff; Salvatore, *Debs*, pp. 130 ff.

9. Buder, *Pullman*, p. 171. Pullman had certainly not supported the Democrats in the 1892 election, but before that time he had often been a guest at the White House.

10. Buder, *Pullman*, p. 188.

11. Kathryn Jacob, "High Society in Washington," pp. 241–253.

12. William Thomas Stead, *If Christ Came to Chicago* (New York: Clarion Press, 1964), p. 339.

13. Ibid., pp. 409 ff.

14. The Chicago Civic Federation is one of the results of the depression and Stead's prodding for Chicago leaders to take up the burden of reform.

15. Thomas Lee Philpott, *Slum and the Ghetto*, p. 22.

16. Ibid., pp. 74 ff.

17. Perry Duis, *Chicago: Creating New Traditions*, pp. 113 ff. See also Helen Lefkowitz Horowitz, "Hull House as Women's Space," *Chicago History* 12 (Winter 1983–1984): pp. 47–48.

18. Burg, *White City*, p. 35; Moses and Kirkland, *History of Chicago*, p. 498.

19. *Field Museum of Natural History Handbook* (Chicago: Field Museum, 1931), pp. 10–15. Preservation of the Arts Palace was possible because it was built of cement and brick—for insurance purposes. See Herman Kogan, *A Continuing Marvel: The Story of the Museum of Science and Industry* (New York: Doubleday, 1973), pp. 4, 46–47.

20. Walter D. Moody, "Teachers' Hand Book: Wacker's Manual of the Plan of Chicago: Municipal Economy" (Chicago: Walter D. Moody, 1911), pp. 56 ff.

21. Daniel H. Burnham and Edward H. Bennett, *Plan of Chicago*, passim.

22. Ira J. Bach, "A Reconsideration of the 1909 'Plan of Chicago,'" *Chicago History* 2 (Spring 1972): pp. 132–141.

23. "The White City," *The Midway* 1 (March 1905): 5. The name "White City" is obviously borrowed from the 1893 Fair, probably to lend respectability to what was, in effect, a reproduction of the Midway. Coney Island amusement centers also conflated the two segments of the Fair culture. See Kasson, *Amusing the Million*, passim.

24. "Among the Summer Parks," *Midway Magazine* 1 (December 1905): 9.

25. Louis Sullivan, *Testament of Stone*, ed. Maurice English (Evanston: Northwestern University Press, 1963), p. 146.

26. Hales, *Silver Cities*, pp. 158 ff. This is an interesting discussion of Riis and his impact on photography in general, and, Chicago specifically.

27. Robert Herrick, *The Web of Life*, p. 59.

28. Theodore Dreiser, *A History of Myself*, p. 20; Dorothy Dudley, *Dreiser and the Land of the Free* (New York: Beechhurst Press [1932], 1946), p. 55.

29. Theodore Dreiser, *Sister Carrie* (Philadelphia: University of Pennsylvania Press, 1981), passim; Richard Lingeman, *Theodore Dreiser: At the Gates of the City, 1871–1907* (New York: Putnam, 1986). See also Gwendolyn Wright, *Moralism and the Modern Home: Domestic Architecture and Cultural Conflict in Chicago, 1873–1913* (Chicago: University of Chicago Press, 1980), pp. 225 ff. Wright discusses realism in art and architecture after the Columbian Exhibition.

30. Carl Sandburg, "Chicago."

31. Tselos, "The Chicago Fair," p. 261.

32. Lester Kuntz, *Evaluating Chicago Sociology* (Chicago: University of Chicago Press, 1984), p. 60.

33. Frank Tolman, "The Study of Sociology in Institutions of Learning in the United States," *Journal of Sociology* 7 (May 1902): 116.

34. Ernest W. Burgess and Donald J. Bogue, *Contributions to Urban Sociology* (Chicago: University of Chicago Press, 1964), pp. 3–4.

35. Steven J. Diner, *A City and Its Universities: Public Policy in Chicago, 1892–1919* (Chapel Hill: University of North Carolina Press, 1980), pp. 56 ff.

36. Martin Bulmer, *The Chicago School of Sociology: Institutionalization, Diversity, and the Rise of Sociological Research* (Chicago: University of Chicago Press, 1984), p. 61.

37. Lester Kurtz, *Evaluating Chicago Sociology* (Chicago: University of Chicago Press, 1984), pp. 24 ff.

Note: Boldface numerals indicate pages where illustrations appear.